A Yeats Dictionary

 Sanford Sternlicht, *Series Editor*

Pencil drawing of William Butler Yeats by William Hoth
after a charcoal drawing by John Singer Sargent.
Courtesy of the artist.

A Yeats Dictionary

*Persons and Places
in the Poetry of
William Butler Yeats*

Lester I. Conner

 Syracuse University Press

First Paperback Edition 1999

99 00 01 02 03 04   6 5 4 3 2 1

The paper used in this publication meets the minimum requirements of American National Standard for Information Sciences—Permanence of Paper for Printed Library Materials, ANSI 39.48-1984. ∞™

Library of Congress Cataloging-in-Publication Data
Conner, Lester I.
    A Yeats dictionary : persons and places in the poetry of William
Butler Yeats / Lester I. Conner. — 1st ed.
       p. cm. — (Irish studies)
    Includes bibliographical references (p.   ).
    ISBN 0-8156-2769-6 (cloth : alk. paper).   0-8156-2770-X (pbk: alk. paper)
    1. Yeats, W. B. (William Butler), 1865–1939—Dictionaries.
2. Characters and characteristics in literature—Dictionaries.
3. Names, Geographical, in literature—Dictionaries. 4. Names,
Geographical—Ireland—Dictionaries. 5. Names, Personal—Ireland—
Dictionaries. 6. Ireland—In literature—Dictionaries. 7. Names,
Irish—Dictionaries. I. Title. II. Series: Irish studies
(Syracuse, N.Y.)
PR5906.A23 1998
821'.8—dc21   97-34458

Lester I. Conner has taught in a number of American colleges and universities, but perhaps his richest experience was provided by Trinity College, Dublin, where he was five times a visiting professor, and at the Yeats International Summer School in Sligo. His connection with the Yeats School began in 1967 and has continued during the years since, principally as associate director. Most recently, Professor Conner has been an adjunct professor in the Irish Studies Program at Villanova University.

Contents

Introduction   ix

A Yeats Dictionary   3

Genealogical Information   197

Books Consulted   201

Introduction

This dictionary of the names of persons and places in the poetry of William Butler Yeats has as its primary purpose the identification of those names; and its audience, first and foremost, is the student and general reader of Yeats's poetry. It also throws light upon the context in the poem where the name appears.

Many names that appear in this dictionary are well known and would not ordinarily need identification—names such as Michelangelo, Swift, Parnell; and there are many well-known names, historical and literary, from classical antiquity. But Yeats often uses such names in a very special, personal way, a way that can be known to the general reader of Yeats's poetry only by a study of Yeats's nonpoetic writings, or the vast library of writings Yeats is known to have drawn upon, or the writings of the principal interpreters of Yeats's works. This dictionary broadens and supplements mere identification to include these additional references where they touch significantly upon the names.

There is no intention here to explicate poems; that is for the writers of poetry criticism and, for Yeats's poetry, has been well-attended to. Certain inferences can be drawn, however, from the material given along with the identification of a name. Frequently, the information given might explain the imagery that surrounds the name in the context of the poem. For example, we can learn from many sources that Lady Kytler was a fourteenth-century sorceress in Ireland, but one might have to read an account of her trial, such as the account given by St. John D. Seymour in *Irish Witchcraft and Demonology,* to learn that her sacrifice to her incubus, Robert Artisson, consisted of "nine red cock's combs and nine peacock's eyes," very close to the words that Yeats actually uses in the poem in which her name appears, "Nineteen Hundred and Nineteen." All this information is contained in the entry for Lady Kyteler's name.

If many names that appear in the poetry are well known to the general reader, there are many more that are strange, requiring basic identification; many that are local and familial, requiring explanation of the poet's relationship to the name; and many that are of Gaelic, that is, Irish origin, requiring pronunciation assistance and, where useful, etymological information as well. Names such as Anashuya, Crazy Jane, Loïe Fuller, Mancini, or the Abbé Michel de Bourdeille may be strange or curious to most readers. Their identification or explanations will enhance the readability of the poems in which they appear. Names such as Armstrong, Middleton, Ormonde, or Pollexfen are names to which the poet claims a family relationship, the nature of which should be understood by readers of the poems. Sligo, Gort, Coole, Galway, Innisfree—these are local names of places to which the poet had a precise physical relationship that should also be clear to his readers. Pronunciation assistance, given phonetically, is surely needed by most people to handle such names as Caoilte [kweel'-tcha], Naoise [nee'sha], or Oisin [ush'een]. It may be of little importance for a reader to know that the Gort near Yeats's tower home in county Galway was in ancient times called Gort-innsi-Guaire, the field of the island of Guaire [gwar'a], after an Irish king who lived in that province. But increased interest comes with an insight into Yeats's own association of Gort and Guaire when he uses them in the same poem, "The Three Beggars."

Such identification can be very helpful to the ordinary reader of Yeats, but it may also be useful to scholars and critics who would wish to have such information before going on to other matters concerning poem or poet. I repeat, however, this compilation is aimed at the student and the general reader.

Yeats uses proper names in his poetry for several ends. In the poetic tradition of allusion, he uses names, particularly classical ones, as William York Tindall indicated in his *Literary Symbol,* as "importers of things from outside the work to enrich it . . . [uniting] times, places, and other cultures with our own" (191). His many references to Homer, Plato, and Aristotle and to the figures mortal and immortal of the *Iliad* and Greek mythology illustrate the point.

About 1902, Yeats's poetry lost many of the ephemeral qualities of his early escapist work and began to take on the harder, less dream-burdened, more controversial manner that marks his poetry thereafter. His experiences in the Irish theatre and on the Irish political scene share, as the next years go by, a good deal of the responsibility for this change. It is from this point, too, that he begins to work into the very texture of his poetry the names of his friends, of theatre people and artists, and of public figures with whom he was frequently associated or knew by reputation. He mentions Maud Gonne by name only once in his poetry, though she is virtually omnipresent; his wife, George, only once; and his dear friend Olivia Shakespeare not at all, which may indicate his unwillingness to share his most personal relationships. But these few excepted, the names of friends, political figures, and of artists abound; Lady Gregory, Robert Gregory, John Millington Synge, Sir Hugh Lane, Florence Farr Emery, Lionel Johnson, Ernest Dowson, Thomas MacDonagh, Con Markiewicz —the list goes on and on in rich and varied manner.

Yet, it is the use of Irish names in the poetry, the characters and places of his Irish themes, that is perhaps most significant. It is these names that give Yeats's poetry such a strong sense of place. Early on, he wrote in newspaper pieces for America, collected and edited by Horace Reynolds in *Letters to the New Island:*

> To the greater poets everything they say has its relation to the national life, and through that to the universal and divine; nothing is an isolated artistic moment; there is a unity everywhere; everything fulfills a purpose that is not its own; the hailstone is a journeyman of God; the grass blade carries the universe upon its point. But to this universalism, this unity everywhere, you can only attain through what is near you, your nation, or, if you be no traveller, your village and the cobwebs on your walls. You can no more have the greater poetry without a nation than religion without symbols. One can only reach out to the universe with a gloved hand—that glove is one's nation, the only thing one knows even a little of.
> (174)

A knowledge of Irish history, perhaps more in the heart than in the mind, was a prequisite for an Irish literature, as he also writes about in *Letters to the New Island:*

> The first thing needful if an Irish literature more elaborate and intense than our fine but primitive ballads and novels is to

come into being is that readers and writers alike should really know the imaginative periods of Irish ... history. It is not needful that they should understand them with scholars' accuracy, but they should know them with the heart. (107)

Yeats had no Gaelic; he said of Douglas Hyde and Hyde's book of Gaelic poems, "I hope he will take pity on us poor folk who have no Gaelic and translate it some day" (79), again in *Letters to the New Island,* where he also notes some of the books written in English that would help him to know Irish history and themes, particularly Standish O'Grady's *History of Ireland,* Lady Ferguson's *Story of the Irish Before the Conquest,* and Sophie Bryant's *Celtic Ireland.* But there were many more that he is known to have used: Sister Mary Ann Monica Egerer, C.S.C., in her 1962 dissertation for Radcliffe College, entitled "The Rogueries of William Butler Yeats," lists forty such books. Foremost would be those books of Lady Gregory, for which he wrote prefaces: *Cuchulain of Muirthemne* and *Gods and Fighting Men.*

Beyond books, there was his personal research into Irish folklore. He remembered the stories and places of his youthful years in Sligo. Later, often accompanied by Lady Gregory, he visited cottages in the west of Ireland and talked with the Irish peasantry to learn their stories and their superstitions at first hand. He collected them and edited them in his *Fairy and Folk Tales of the Irish Peasantry* and *The Celtic Twilight,* and the names and themes carry over into his poetry and plays. Sometimes, of course, he would appeal to his friend Douglas Hyde, a great folklorist and Gaelic scholar, for help with Gaelic matters; but often he simply took liberties, poetic license perhaps, and set down Gaelic names as best he could, but not always to the satisfaction of his critics. Thomas MacDonagh, shortly before his execution for his part in the Easter Rebellion of 1916, had published a critical work entitled *Literature in Ireland,* in which he wrote:

What then of Mr. W. B. Yeats who confesses that when he wrote the greater number of his poems, he had hardly considered seriously the question of the pronunciation of Irish words, who copied at times somebody's perhaps fanciful spelling, and at times the ancient spelling as he found it in some literal translation, pronouncing the words as they were spelt? That is, pronouncing the words as if they were English. Mr. Yeats, however, is quite honest in the matter. He would not, he says, have defended his system at any time. If he ever learns the old pronunciation of the proper names he has used he will revise the poems. He is content to affirm that he has not treated his Irish names as badly as the mediaeval writers of the stories of King Arthur treated their Welsh names. But Mr. Yeats is not living in the Middle Ages. Whether we regret it or not, we cannot ignore the knowledge of those to whom we communicate our works. (50)

Yeats, in early editions of his poetry, tried to use phonetic forms of the names—Usheen for Oisin—but he did make revisions in the spelling of Irish names, as successive editions of his poems demonstrate. Still, it is impossible to arrive at a consistent system of pronunciation. Even Irish speakers are not in agreement. The Irish name Emer was said by one expert to be pronounced Ee'ver, but Professor Helen Vendler pointed out that Yeats rhymes it with Schemer. For the purposes of this dictionary, to aid readers of the poetry, the pronunciations given are based on his early phonetics; his use of Lady Gregory's guides to pronunciation, on meter and rhyme where applicable, and, of course, on the pronunciation Yeats sometimes supplies in his writings.

Yeats's inaccuracies were not confined to things Irish. He sometimes takes liberty with quoted matter: the epigraph to "Crossways" is a misquotation of Blake. But Yeats was never too disturbed by his errors. A. H. Bullen, his publisher, was more upset, and perhaps a little condescending, when he wrote to Sir Sidney Cockerell, in a letter dated May 23, 1903, in which he said, "When I remonstrated with Yeats for being so inaccurate he affected to take a pride in his errors. He is a whimsical fellow but writes devilish well at times." That letter was pasted inside Sir Sidney's copy of Yeats's *Ideas of Good and Evil,* published that year by Bullen. The copy was inscribed to Sir Sidney by both Bullen and Yeats. This book, with letter intact, came into the possession of Clive Driver, to whom I am indebted for this reference.

To return to pronunciation factors again, I must point out that from the 1933 edition of his poems on, in the notes to his collected poems, Yeats includes the following:

In this edition of my poems I have adopted Lady Gregory's spelling of Gaelic names, with, I think, two exceptions. The "d" of "Edain" ran too well in my verse for me to adopt her perhaps more correct "Etain," and for some reason unknown to me I have always preferred "Aengus" to her "Angus." In her *Gods and Fighting Men* and *Cuchulain of Muirthemne* she went as close to the Gaelic spelling as she could without making the names unpronounceable to the average reader. (447)

In both of Lady Gregory's volumes mentioned by Yeats, syllabic pronunciation is given for many Irish names, and the pronunciation guides I give are based on these wherever they accord with Yeats's meter and wherever they are not ambiguous, as syllabic pronunciation can sometimes be. I have also drawn, regarding place names and their pronunciation, upon the work of Patrick W. Joyce, whose works were well known to Yeats, revealed in Allan Wade's edition of *The Letters of W. B. Yeats* (see esp. 95, 112, and 217). Also, I received very helpful suggestions from R. J. Hayes while he was director of The National Library of Ireland, Dublin, and from the late Professor Elliott V. K. Dobbie of Columbia University.

In compiling this dictionary, I have tried to use Yeats's own words whenever possible to identify, explain, or illuminate the name word. Yeats intended that his work have organic unity, and often the best explanation of a name used in the poetry is to be found in one or another of his prose writings. Yeats's notes, found at the end of his *Collected Poems,* are used here to the fullest extent. But material drawn from all earlier editions are credited to *The Variorum Edition of the Poems of W. B. Yeats,* edited by Peter Allt and Russell K. Alspach, where the notes from all those early editions are so conveniently reprinted.

In addition to Yeats's own works, all principal critical works have been consulted and drawn upon for information that throws light upon any name in the poetry. Yeats's sources have been determined when names are involved. Thus, when Yeats speaks of "An image out of Spenser," that image has been located and indicated in the entry for Spenser. Material contemporary to Yeats, the writings and the letters of his friends and of people of his era, has been consulted and brought to bear on entries where pertinent.

Each entry is followed by its identifying material, including pronunciation guides where necessary. At the end of each entry, the reader is directed to all the poems in which that name appears. The identifying material is designed to cover the context of each use of the name. There are several ways to use this dictionary effectively; a combination is perhaps best:

1. The reader can go directly from a poem with a name in it to this dictionary for its immediate identification, pronunciation guide, etcetera.

2. The reader can then follow up on any cross references given, shown by [q.v.].

3. Those poems in which the name appears are given at the end of each entry.

4. The dictionary can profitably be read through, or browsed, because it contains helpful information that identifying a single name may not demand.

There are, of course, many individuals to thank for help, encouragement, and inspiration. I will do most of this in the page of dedication and acknowledgment. No one, however, can have given me more outright help and encouragement than Samuel Hynes, Professor Emeritus, Princeton, and I can but hope that my gratitude is as obvious as my indebtedness.

A Yeats Dictionary

A

Abbé Michel de Bourdeille. *See* **Michel.**

Abbey or **Abbey Theatre.** The legitimate theatre in Abbey Street, Dublin, and the name traditionally used to refer to the Irish National Theatre Society, which was formed and established by William and Frank Fay in 1901, with W. B. Yeats, John Millington Synge, and Lady Gregory as the first board of directors. The immediate predecessor to this group had been the Irish Literary Theatre, founded in 1899 by Yeats, George Moore, and Edward Martyn. In 1903, an Englishwoman, A. E. F. Horniman, became interested in the Irish National Theatre Society, particularly as Yeats explained to her the aims of the group: to train Irish actors and produce Irish plays. Miss Horniman purchased the lease of the old Mechanics' Institute in Abbey Street, and after reconstructing the building, a part of which had been a morgue, she gave it to the society as its home theatre. As the Abbey Theatre, it opened on December 27, 1904. On January 26, 1907, the Abbey presented the world premiere of Synge's play, *The Playboy of the Western World*. Riots followed and lasted all week. Finally, Yeats opened the theatre for a public discussion of the play. His father, John Butler Yeats, was on the Abbey stage with his son, giving him spirited support in the attempt to interpret the play to the hostile crowd. See particularly "At the Abbey Theatre" and "Beautiful Lofty Things."

Abd al-Rabban. In Yeats's poem, "The Gift of Harun al-Rashid," Abd is the treasurer to Caliph Harun and the friend of Kusta-ben-Luka.

Achilles. A great hero of Greek mythology. His parents were Peleus and Thetis. In the argument among the Greek chieftains with which Homer opens the *Iliad*, Achilles' hand is stayed from drawing his sword against Agamemnon by Athene, who held Achilles back by his long red hair. Later, Achilles is the slayer of Hector, prince of Troy. In *A Vision*, Yeats places Achilles in the hero crescent of Phase 12 of the moon. See particularly "Her Courage," which is poem VI of "Upon a Dying Lady"; and "The Phases of the Moon."

Acropolis. In Greek, the upper part of a town, where a citadel and temple were established. The most famous Acropolis, the one Yeats refers to, is the one at Athens, where once amid its famous buildings could be seen the fabled ivory statues of Phidias. See "Nineteen Hundred and Nineteen."

Adam. Yeats uses the name with specific reference to the Fall of man with the attendant ideas of original sin and expulsion from Paradise. Michelangelo's famous depiction of Adam in the Sistine Chapel in the Vatican in Rome is referred to by Yeats in "Long-Legged Fly" and in "Under Ben Bulben."

Aedh [e]. In Yeats's 1895 edition of *Poems,* he wrote of Aedh: "A God of death. All who hear his harp playing die. He was one of the two gods who appeared to Cuhoolin [*see* Cuchulain] before his death." The name is spelled Aedh in Gaelic and means a flame of fire. Originally, many of the poems in *The Wind Among the Reeds* (1899) had the names Aedh (also spelled Aed and Aodh), Hanrahan, and Michael Robartes in titles where "He," "The Lover," or "The Poet" appears in later editions. Of these three names, Yeats said in the 1895 edition, "Hanrahan is the simplicity of an imagination too changeable to gather permanent possessions, or the adoration of the shepherds; and Michael Robartes is the pride of the imagination brooding upon the greatest of its possessions, or the adoration of the Magi; while Aedh is the myrrh and frankincense that the imagination offers continually before all that it loves."

Aengus [an'gus]. A chief figure of the Tuatha De Danaan [*see* Danaan]. In Yeats's work, Aengus is the god of youth, beauty, and poetry, who reigned in Tir-nan-Og, the Country of the Young [q.v.]. Yeats also refers to Aengus as the master of love and as Hermes. In the poems "The Song of the Wandering Aengus," the figure of Aengus is that of a mortal, whereas elsewhere in Yeats he is immortal. The girl in that poem is of the Tuatha de Danaan who, as Yeats says, can take all shapes, those who live in water most often taking the shape of fish. Such figures turning from fish into human and then disappearing are popular in Irish folklore. Yeats tells of a woman he knew in Galway who told him of many such, an account to be found in early editions of his *Wind*

Among the Reeds and reprinted in Allt and Alspach, 805. [*See also* Laban.] In most of Yeats's other references to Aengus, he is the lover of Edain [q.v.]. In the poem "The Old Age of Queen Maeve," however, Aengus seeks the love of Caer, another girl of the Tuatha de Danaan, and he enlists the aid of Maeve. A full account of this episode is given in Lady Gregory's *Cuchulain of Muirthemne*, 143–47. In the story of Diarmuid [q.v.], Aengus is Diarmuid's protector. In 1893, in *The Celtic Twilight*, in the story "The Queen and the Fool" (111), Yeats wrote of Aengus as "the old Irish god of love and poetry and ecstasy, who changed four of his kisses into birds." See particularly "The Song of the Wandering Aengus"; "Under the Moon"; "The Wanderings of Oisin"; "The Old Age of Queen Maeve"; "Baile and Aillinn"; "The Harp of Aengus," which is the forepoem to *The Shadowy Waters;* and "The Shadowy Waters."

African Mountains of the Moon. The Ruwensori mountain range of central Africa, just north of the equator. Ancient writers, such as Ptolemy, referred to the range as the Mountains of the Moon. The mountains were supposed to be the source of the Nile. See "The Two Kings."

Agamemnon. Leader of the Greek forces against Troy in the *Iliad* of Homer. In Greek legend, the two daughters of Leda [q.v.] were Clytemnestra and Helen, who married respectively the brothers Agamemnon and Menelaus. Helen was carried off to Troy by Paris, the event that led to the Trojan War. Agamemnon, to avenge his brother, led the Greek forces and ultimately won, reducing Troy to the ashes of burning roof and tower. To get favorable winds for the Greek ships sailing to Troy, Agamemnon sacrificed his daughter Iphigenia, but in doing so he angered his wife, Clytemnestra, who took a lover and arranged her husband's murder when he returned home from Troy. Aeschylus in his Oresteia and Sophocles and Eruipides in their Electra plays also treat of the subject matter. See "Leda and the Swan."

Aherne, Owen. Imaginary character in Yeats's *A Vision* and in several poems, often assigned the role of taunting or deprecating Yeats himself. Speaking of Aherne and Michael Robartes [q.v.], Yeats, in notes to the poem "Michael Robartes and the Dancer" (see notes to *The Collected Poems*), considers that he used the actual names of two friends who had quarreled with him. But the essential fictive nature of Aherne, as well as Robartes and Kusta-ben-Luka [q.v.], is set forth at length by T. R. Henn, in his *Lonely Tower:*

> More subtle projections of personality were needed, puppet figures that might in their initial lives deceive the reader into thinking of them as real beings, and to whom he [Yeats] could give a licence of expression that would make them important quasi-dramatic mouthpieces. The three most important figures are Michael Robartes, Owen Aherne and Kusta-ben-Luka. The first projection, Owen Aherne, is part ascetic, part demoniacal principal. (46)

See especially "The Phases of the Moon" and "Owen Aherne and His Dancers."

Aibric [ev'rik]. A popular name in Irish mythology but here the name of a character in Yeats's play *The Shadowy Waters,* a friend of Forgael [q.v.]. See "The Shadowy Waters."

Ailell [al'yell]. The king-consort of Queen Maeve [q.v.] of Connacht Province. He possessed a famous White-horned Bull, which so filled Maeve with jealousy that she entered upon the great cattle raid of Ulster Province to gain possession of the equally famous Brown Bull. It became the Iliad of Irish mythology. See "The Old Age of Queen Maeve."

Aillinn [il'yin]. Daughter of King Lugaidh [q.v.] and the beloved of Baile [q.v.]. Aillinn and Baile died of broken hearts when each was told that the other had died, the sad news brought to each of them, in Yeats's version of the legendary story, by Aengus, the master of love. A yew tree grew up over Baile's grave, an apple tree over Aillinn's. Boards from the two trees sprang together and could not be separated and were used as tablets on which to record love stories. See "Ribh at the Tomb of Baile and Aillinn" and "Baile and Aillinn."

Alcibiades. Athenian general and statesman (ca. 450–404 B.C.). His guardian was Pericles, and Socrates was his teacher. An egoist often associated with rash and foolhardy acts, Alcibiades was banished from Athens in 415 B.C. for his suspected part in the sacrilegious defacement of the phallic symbols of Athens. In *A Vision*. Yeats lists Socrates as an example of a saint, who would, of course, wish to thrash from his flesh such worldly figures as Alexander, Augustus Caesar, Alcibiades. See "The Saint and the Hunchback."

Aleel. The name of the poet who is in the service of the countess in Yeats's play *The Countess Cathleen*. Aleel is a figure from Irish mythology and folklore. Yeats only uses the name here. See "Alternative Song for the Severed Head" in *The King of the Great Clock Tower.*

Alexander. Alexander III of Macedonia (Alexander the Great, 356–323 B.C.), the great general and conqueror. His father was Philip of Macedonia; and Aristotle [q.v.], who "played the taws / Upon the bottom of a king of kings," was his tutor. Upon Alexander's death, the great empire he had built began at once to disintegrate. See "The Saint and the Hunchback" and "On a Picture of a Black Centaur by Edmund Dulac."

Alexandria. The Mediterranean port in northern Egypt founded by Alexander the Great and the site of the famous Pharos lighthouse, one of the Seven Wonders of the World. In his *Alexandria: A History and a Guide,* E. M. Forster describes the lighthouse as having been over 400 feet high, a fortress as well as a beacon. He writes, "It beaconed to the imagination, not only to ships at sea, and long after its light was extinguished memories of it glowed in the minds of men." The lighthouse was destroyed by an earthquake in the fourteenth century. It had been built by the Kings Ptolemy I and II, completed about 280 B.C. See "Blood and the Moon." The assassination of Kevin O'Higgins in 1927 inspired this poem.

Algeciras. Seaport of southern Spain, six miles west of Gibraltar and across the Straits of Gibraltar from Morocco. Yeats visited Algeciras in the fall of 1927, when he traveled in France and Spain in search of health. See "At Algeciras—A Meditation upon Death."

Almhuin [al'lin also **al'win].** A hill in county Kildare, Leinster Province, the site in very ancient times of a hosting place or great hall of the kings of Faery. Later in the olden times, it was the principal seat of Finn [q.v.] Mac Cumaill, leader of the heroes of the White or Finian cycle of Irish mythology. In the preface to Lady Gregory's book *Gods and Fighting Men,* Yeats wrote, "A few months ago I was on the bare hill of Allen, 'wide Almhuin of Leinster,' where Finn and the Fianna lived." Yeats used the Allen spelling in some early editions of his poems. See "The Wanderings of Oisin."

Alt. The name of a cleft in the Sligo mountain called Ben Bulben [q.v.]. The word in Irish denotes a height or a cliff or the side of a glen. Visitors to Alt confirm that there is an echo there. See "The Men and the Echo."

Amrita. In Yeats's poem, the name of a woman; but in Hindu mythology, it is a name meaning the beverage of immortality or the water of life. See "Anashuya and Vijaya."

Anashuya. A Hindu name meaning charity. Various Hindu mythologies associate the name with a very pious woman given to austere devotion, given also to miraculous powers. See "Anashuya and Vijaya."

Antaeus. In classical mythology, Antaeus was a giant, son of Poseidon, the god of the sea, and Ge, goddess of the earth. As long as Antaeus touched earth, he drew new strength from his mother and was invincible. Hercules could overcome him only by lifting him into the air and squeezing him to death before he could touch the ground. See "The Municipal Gallery Revisited."

Anthony, Saint Anthony (A.D. 251?–356?). Founder of Christian monasticism. See "Mariotic Sea or Lake." He was born near Heracleopolis, in Upper Egypt. At the age of twenty, he gave away all his property and retired to live as an ascetic, moving ever deeper into the desert to be alone. When disciples gathered nearby, he finally emerged and created a community of monks; but he soon withdrew himself. Later, ca. 311, he emerged again to give strength to the Christian martyrs then undergoing the merciless persecutions of the Roman emperors Diocletian and Maximus I. See "Demon and Beast."

Antigone. The daughter of Oedipus and Jocasta. In the tragedy by Sophocles, Antigone buried her brother Polyneices in defiance of King Creon's order. Creon ordered her to be buried alive. She killed herself first, and Creon's son, Haemon, who loved her, killed himself upon her grave. Yeats did not create a version of Sophocles' *Antigone* for the modern stage, but he did stage versions of *King Oedipus,* and *Oedipus at Colonus.* See "Antigone," which is poem XI of "A Woman Young and Old."

Aoife [ee'fa]. An immortal female warrior who dwelt on Craig Liath, or the gray rock, located in Scotland. It was by Aoife that Cuchulain [q.v.] had a son, named Connla, whom he later inadvertently kills. (See the poem "Cuchulain's Fight with the Sea" and the play *On Baile's Strand.*) Yeats freely associates the name of Aoife with such stalwart lady friends as Florence Farr Emery and Maud Gonne. See "The Grey Rock."

Arcady. Any place where rustic simplicity and contentment prevail. Originally, Arcady was a district of ancient Greece and supposedly the home of pastoral poetry and of people content in their simplicity. See "The Song of the Happy Shepherd."

Archer. *See* **Great Archer.**

Ardan [ar'dan]. The name of the brother of Eochaid [q.v.]. In most accounts of the mythological story, the brother's name is Ailell, but not to be confused with Queen Maeve's consort. This may be why Yeats changed the name. Arden also occurs in mythology as a brother of Naoise [q.v.], the man who was Deirdre's lover. See "The Two Kings."

Argo. In Greek mythology, the ship that took Jason and the Argonauts on their quest for the Golden Fleece. See "Two Songs from a Play."

Aristotle. Greek philosopher (384–322 B.C.). Born at Stageira, the son of a physician, Aristotle went to Athens in 367 and studied under Plato until 347, when Plato died. In 342 he was invited to be tutor to Alexander, son of King Philip of Macedonia. [*See* Alexander.] In 335, Aristotle returned to Athens and established his Peripatetic School. When Alexander died in 323, Aristotle quit Athens and died the next year at Chalcis. For Yeats, Aristotle is one of the three philosophers who apprehend reality in different ways: Plato, seeing it in ghostly paradigms; solider Aristotle, seeing it in nature itself; and Pythagoras, seeing it in precise measurement and art. Aristotle is solider because from him, unlike from Plato, we get, as Cleaneth Brooks described in his *Well Wrought Urn*, "not speculation but application." See "Among School Children."

Armstrong. The name of paternal relatives of Yeats. Yeats's paternal great-grandfather was William Corbett (1759–1824), and Corbett's wife was a Grace Armstrong, daughter of a military family. Her father was a Captain Armstrong, who died in 1797 and who was the nephew of Major General Sir John Armstrong (1674–1742), who was Quartermaster General in Ireland and, at one time, according to the *Dictionary of National Biography,* "Chief Engineer of England." Yeats thought that some military Armstrong or, from another line of relatives, a Butler [q.v.] must certainly have been present at the Battle of the Boyne [q.v.] in 1690. See "Pardon, Old Fathers."

Arthur. King of Britain, the central figure of vast material drawn from mythology, legend, fairy lore, and historical reference. Many Arthurian stories have direct counterparts in Celtic tales, especially those dealing with Cuchulain [q.v.] and Finn [q.v.]. A traditional legend related to Arthur concerns the hunting of the white stag. Whoever could slay it had the right to kiss the fairest maiden. In Celtic lore, the stag often typifies the soul. The white stag, particularly with a cross between its antlers, is in medieval Christian Ireland a symbol of Christ. See especially "Towards Break of Day" and also the reference in *The Shadowy Waters*.

Artisson, Robert. The incubus of Dame Alice Kyteler [q.v.]. In the notes given at the end of his *Collected Poems,* Yeats says that Artisson was an evil spirit much run after in Kilkenny at the start of the fourteenth century. Artisson, also called Robin, son of Art, and Lady Kyteler figure in what is perhaps Ireland's most famous case of witchcraft. See "Nineteen Hundred and Nineteen."

Athene. Pallas Athene, the Olympian goddess of wisdom. She was a virgin goddess, the daughter of Zeus, having sprung fully grown from his brow. In the *Iliad* of Homer [q.v.], she is a supporter of the Greek cause, supposedly because she had not won the famous Judgment of Paris [q.v.]. In numerous depictions of Athene, she is wearing a helmet and carrying a shield, but often she is seen with the olive branch; for in legend she is the giver of the olive tree to man, the result of a contest with Poseidon [q.v.] to see who could do most for man. Poseidon gave man the horse; but Athene won by giving man the olive tree, symbol also of peace. She was the patroness of both art and war. Often, one of her favorite animals or birds, the owl, the serpent, or the cock is depicted with her. There are many temples dedicated to her in Greece, the most famous being the Parthenon on the Acropolis [q.v.]. The Palladium, the sacred image of Athene, was used as the guardian of the safety of a city. Troy fell only after the Palladium within its gates was removed. Yeats associates Athene with beautiful, proud women in general and with Maud Gonne [q.v.] in particular. Traditionally, Athene is described as being gray-eyed. Yeats does so in both poem and play. At the opening of the *Iliad,* it is Athene who keeps peace among the Greek chieftains by holding Achilles back by his hair when he is about to draw his sword against Agememnon. See "A Thought from Propertius"; "The Phases of the Moon"; "Michael Robartes and the Dancer"; "Colonus' Praise," which is a song of the chorus in Yeats's play *Oedipus at Colonus;* and "Beautiful Lofty Things."

Attis. A death and resurrection, or vegetation, god. Generally a Phrygian, and later a Roman deity, he was driven mad by a jealous goddess, Cybele, and he castrated himself and died; but Zeus made the pine tree of his spirit, and violets sprang from his blood. Yeats, an avid reader of Frazer's *Golden Bough,* would have come upon the lines: "On the twenty-second day of March, a pine tree was cut in the woods and brought into the sanctuary of Cybele, where it was treated as a divinity. The duty of carrying the sacred tree was entrusted to a guild of Tree-bearers. The trunk was swathed . . . with woolen bands and decked with wreaths of violets . . . ; and the effigy of a young man, doubtless that of Attis himself, was tied to the middle of the stem." See "Vacillations."

Augustine. Yeats takes his epigraph to his volume of poems entitled *The Rose,* 1893, from the *Confessions of Saint Augustine* (A.D. 354–430), specifically from book X, chapter 27. Professor Emerita Helen North of Swarthmore College provided the translation from the Latin: "Late have I loved thee, Beauty so old so new! / Late have I loved thee." See the epigraph for the volume *The Rose* in *Collected Poems.*

Augustus Caesar. The first Roman emperor (63 B.C.–14 A.D.). He was the adopted son of Julius Caesar, the actual grandson of his sister. [*See also* Caesar.] Named Caius Octavius, he received the name Augustus as a title of honor from the Roman senate, the name Caesar being his through adoption. He returned to Rome after the assassination of Julius Caesar and subsequently, after the Triumvirate with Mark Anthony and Lepidus, became emperor. His reign, a worldly and sophisticated one, was notable for buildings and road construction and for his patronage of the arts and artists, Virgil, Ovid, Livy, and Horace among them. See "The Saint and the Hunchback."

Avalon. In the Arthurian legends, a mythical ever-green land of the blessed. Arthur was taken there. See "Under the Moon," and "The Statesman's Holiday."

B

Babar. Poetic name of Zahir ud-Din Muhammad, founder of the Mogul dynasty of India. Babar (1483–1530) was a descendant of Genghis Khan and Tamerlane [*see* Timor]. After his mighty conquest of India in 1525–27, he became a great reformer and a patron of the arts. See "Her Courage," which is poem VI of "Upon a Dying Lady."

Babylon or **Babylonian.** References to the famous city of antiquity, going back to the third millennium B.C. The city was located near modern Hilla on a branch of the Euphrates River. The Hanging Gardens of Babylon, one of the Seven Wonders of the World, were located here. The science of astrology was much advanced by Babylonian scholars. In a footnote to *A Vision*, Yeats identifies "Mathematical Starlight" as Babylonian astrology, present in the friendships and antipathies of the Olympic gods. In the poem that closes his play *The Resurrection*, Yeats writes "The Babylonian starlight brought / A fabulous, formless darkness in" at the moment of Christ's death. See "The Dawn," "Two Songs from a Play," "Wisdom," "Blood and the Moon," and "Vacillations."

Baile [bal'ya]. With Aillinn, among the most famous of the star-crossed lovers in Irish mythology. Lady Gregory writes of him in her *Cuchulain of Muirthemne*, "he was of the race of Rudraige [Rury], and although he had but little land belonging to him, he was the heir of Ulster, and every one who saw him loved him, both man and woman, because he was so sweet-spoken; and they called him Baile of the Honey-Mouth." Having arranged to meet his beloved Aillinn, Baile set out from Emain [q.v.] over the plains of Muirthemne [q.v.] to the strand, or beach, where Aillinn was to join him. There he was approached by a wild-looking stranger [*see* Aengus, to whom Yeats assigns this role in his version of the story], who told Baile of Aillinn's death, causing Baile to die of a broken heart, the same fate accorded to Aillinn. The strand where the lovers were to meet is famous as Baile's Strand, the very place where Cuchulain [q.v.] engaged in his fight with the waves, depicted in the poem "Cuchulain's Fight with the Sea" and in Yeats's play *On Baile's Strand*. *See also* the entry for Aillinn and the following poems: "Ribh at the Tomb of Baile and Aillinn," which is poem I of "Supernatural Songs," and "Baile and Aillinn."

Ballinafad. The Anglicized name of a small town near Sligo; originally called Bel-an-atha-fada, meaning "the mouth of the long ford." The town, containing the ruins of an old castle and very few inhabitants, is located at the base of the Curlew Mountains which divide counties Sligo and Roscommon. See "The Ballad of Father O'Hart."

Ballylee or Thoor Ballylee. The name of Yeats's tower home, located in the townland of Ballylee, near the town of Gort and but a few miles from Coole Park, the estate of Lady Gregory. Thoor Ballylee [toor bal a lee] means the tower, or castle, of the townland of Lee. Lee itself means calves. Yeats purchased the tower in June 1917, planning to use it as a summer residence for his wife and himself, after rehabilitation made it habitable. Ballylee is also celebrated as the one-time home of the famous beauty Mary Hynes, beloved of the blind poet Raftery [q.v.]. The building itself is, of course, behind much of Yeats's tower symbolism in his poems. See "To Be Carved on a Stone at Thoor Ballylee" and "Coole Park and Ballylee."

Balor. A Formorian king who did battle for the possession of ancient Ireland with the Danann [q.v.] people. Balor had an evil eye that only opened upon the battlefield. It required four men to lift up the eyelid and place an instrument under it. But when the eye was opened, the opposing warriors that Balor looked at could not resist their enemies. Balor was carried about in the manner of many ancient kings. In his notes to the 1895 edition of *Poems* (reprinted in Allt and Alspach), Yeats calls him "the Irish Chimera, the leader of the hosts of darkness at the great battle of good and evil, life and death, light and darkness, which was fought on the strands of Moytura, near Sligo." See "The Wanderings of Oisin."

Barach or Cook Barach. A figure of Irish legend who enticed Fergus [q.v.] to a feast so that the Sons of Usna [q.v.] might be attacked and killed in Fergus's absence. Fergus was the protector of the Sons of Usna and Deirdre [q.v.]. Yeats notes in the 1895 edition of *Poems* (reprinted in Allt and Alspach, 794), "Fergus had made an oath never to refuse a feast from [Barach], and so was compelled to go, though all unwillingly." The connection with the feast accounts for Yeats's use of the epithet "Cook." See "The Wanderings of Oisin."

Barhain. An unidentified hero. The name may possibly relate to the Bahrams of Persian legend, men of great courage and heroism. Edward Fitzgerald uses one of them in his translation of the *Rubáiyát of Omar Khayyám*. But Yeats may simply have made the name up. See "Her Courage," which is poem VI of "Upon a Dying Lady."

Beauvarlet, Jacques Firmin (1731–97). Noted French engraver. Many of his subjects were shown surrounded by cherubim, in the manner of Fragonard. See "To a Young Beauty."

Ben Bulben. The beautiful, flat-topped mountain near Sligo town. It is famous in Irish legend, particularly in the story of Diarmuid [q.v.] and Grania in the Finn [q.v.] cycle of Irish mythology. Ben Bulben is actually a corruption of Binn-Gulbain, meaning "Bulgan's Peak." It had been fated from early childhood that Diarmuid would die in battle with the wild boar on Ben Bulben. He might have been saved by Finn but was not because Finn so resented that Diarmuid had eloped with Grania, who had been promised to Finn. Ben Bulben is one of two mountains that guard the harbor of Sligo, the other being Knocknarae [q.v.]. Lisadell, the ancestral home of the Countess Markiewicz, is located close by Ben Bulben. Yeats remembered years later, when the countess was a political prisoner, how as a girl she had ridden near Ben Bulben on her way to meets. Also nearby is the waterfall Glen-Car. Yeats, of course, is buried in the shadow of Ben Bulben. See "On a Political Prisoner," "Towards Break of Day," "The Tower," "Alternative Song for the Severed Head" in *The King of the Great Clock Tower*, and "Under Ben Bulben."

Bera. The island of Bere, located in Bantry Bay, county Cork. In Irish Oilean Beare [el'on bar' a, the island of Beara] is from a personal name. See "The Wanderings of Oisin."

Berenice or **Berenice's Hair.** The constellation Coma Berenices. Berenice II of Cyrene (d. 217 B.C.) was the wife of Ptolemy III. When her husband departed on an expedition to Syria from Egypt, Berenice made a votive offering of a lock of her hair for her husband's safe return. The lock disappeared mysteriously and became, according to legend, the aforementioned constellation. See "Veronica's Napkin"; and "Her Dream," which is poem XIII of "Words for Music Perhaps."

Berkeley, George (1685–1753). Anglican bishop of Cloyne [q.v.]. Berkeley, famous as an educator and as a philosopher associated with subjective idealism, devoted much of his life to the economic and spiritual betterment of Ireland. In a letter to Joseph Hone, who with M. M. Rossi had written *Bishop Berkeley,* for which Yeats was to provide an introduction, Yeats said: "You have set Berkeley in his Irish world, and made him amusing, animated and intelligible. He is of the utmost importance to the Ireland that is coming into existence, as I hope to show in my introduction. I want Protestant Ireland to base some vital part of its culture upon Burke, Swift, and Berkeley." In the introduction to that book, reprinted in Yeats's *Essays and Introductions,* Yeats pointed out Berkeley's response as a young man: that Irishmen thought otherwise. And Yeats also noted the special qualities of his favorite Protestant Irish literary forebears:

> Berkeley with his belief in perception, that abstract ideas are mere words, Swift with his love of perfect nature, of the houyhnhnns, his disbelief in Newton's system and every sort of machine, Goldsmith and his delight in the particulars of common life that shocked his contemporaries, Burke with his own conviction that all States not grown slowly like a forest tree are tyrannies, found in England the opposite that stung their own thought into expression and made it lucid.

See "Blood and the Moon."

Bethlehem. The town five miles south of Jerusalem where Christ was born. For Yeats, Bethlehem also symbolizes the birthplace of any new cycle in civilization. See "The Second Coming."

Billy or **King Billy.** King William III of England (1650–1702); reigned as joint British sovereign with Queen Mary from 1688–1702. Dutch-born and known as William of Orange, he used "bomb-balls," that is, artillery, against the Irish in the Battle of the Boyne [q.v.] in 1690. Yeats, no doubt, intended King Billy to serve simultaneously as a reference to Kaiser Wilhelm II (1859–1941), whose planes and zepplins bombed England in World War I. See "Lapis Lazuli."

Biscay, Bay of. A bay of the Atlantic Ocean between Spain and France that is famous for its storms. Yeats's grandfather, William Pollexfen [q.v.] had long profited from trade with Spain and had even won the freedom of a Spanish city. Sligo was, of course, his home port. Yeats tells of this and of his grandfather's leap into the Bay of Biscay to recover an old hat in "Reveries," a section of his *Autobiography*. See "Pardon, Old Fathers."

Bishop or **The Bishop.** In Yeats's "Crazy Jane" poems, he depicts a bishop with a skin wrinkled like a goose's foot and hunched like a heron. The caricature recalls Swift's depictions of contemporary churchmen, but Yeats would also have been familiar with the Bishop O'Dea whom Augustus John, painter of a famous portrait of Yeats, refers to in his book *Chiaroscuro* as the "author of the celebrated phrase, 'the degrading passion of Love.' " See "Crazy Jane and the Bishop," "Crazy Jane Talks with the Bishop," and "Crazy Jane on the Mountain."

Bishop of Cloyne. A reference to George Berkeley, who was appointed bishop of Cloyne in 1734. See "The Seven Sages."

Bishops or **The Bishops.** A reference to the Roman Catholic bishops who turned against the Irish leader Charles Stewart Parnell [q.v.], when he was named as co-respondent in the divorce of Kathleen and William O'Shea, whom writers termed the husband that sold his wife. See "Come Gather Round Me, Parnellites."

Black Pig, the Valley of. The site of a great coming battle in which all the enemies of Ireland will be routed. In the notes to *Collected Poems*, Yeats explains this and the symbolism of the Black Pig. In *Autobiography*, Yeats writes of Macgregor [q.v.] Mathers, his friend of occult studies, that Mathers began announcing in 1893 or 1894 that immense wars were soon to come. And Yeats says that this talk of Mathers may have made him write this poem: See "The Valley of the Black Pig."

Blake, William (1757–1827) English poet, artist, and mystic to whom Yeats was both devoted and indebted. Yeats was coeditor with Edwin John Ellis of *The Works of William Blake: Poetic, Symbolic and Critical* (1893); and was himself the editor of *The Poems of William Blake* (1893), for which he also did the introduction. The epigraph to Yeats's poems collected as "Crossway," 1889, seems to be misquoted from

Blake's "Vale" in volume 3 of the Yeats-Ellis edition, where the lines appear in "Night," IX, stanza 645:

> The morning dawned. Urizen rose, and in his hand the flail
> Sounds on the floor, heard terrible by all beneath the heavens.
> Dismal, loud, redounding, the nether floor shakes with the
> sound, And all the Nations were threshed out, and the stars
> threshed from their husks.

Blanaid [blan'id]. Also spelled Blanad, she was a legendary heroine of Ireland. The sad story of her love for Cuchulain and her sad death is told briefly in Lady Gregory's *Cuchulain of Muirthemne.* See a mention of the name in "The Wanderings of Oisin."

Boar or **the Boar Without Bristles.** The animal that killed Diarmuid [q.v.] in one of the most famous of Irish mythological tales. Donn, the father of Diarmuid, resented that Aengus was raising his, Donn's son, along with the son of a steward. When the steward's son rushed between his legs to escape some fighting hounds, Donn squeezed him to death between his knees. The steward demanded satisfaction from their leader Finn [q.v.] and forced Finn to discover who had killed the boy. When the steward learned it was Donn, he took a Druid rod and struck his dead son and made of him a wild boar without bristles, ear, or tail, and he charged the boar to bring Donn's son, Diarmuid, to his death. The wild boar ran out of the place, but years later when Diarmuid was fleeing the wrath of Finn for having eloped with Grania, Finn's betrothed, Diarmuid came at last to Ben Bulben, where he was run to death by the boar. Finn might still have saved Diarmuid but failed to do so, and the steward's curse finally took its effect. See "He Mourns for the Change That Has Come upon Him and His Beloved, and Longs for the End of the World."

Bourdeille, Abbé Michel de. *See* **Michel.**

Boyne. River in Ireland. In 1690, at the river site, occurred the famous Battle of the Boyne, in which the forces of the exiled James II were routed by those of William III of England. [*See also* Billy; Dutchman.] Although the river's name probably means "cow river" from its stem of *bo,* the word for cow, in Irish mythology the river is said to have been formed by Roann and to have taken its name from Boann, the mother of Aengus. Of the famous battle, Yeats wrote [*see Explora-*

tions] that it "overwhelmed a civilization full of religion and myth, and brought in its place intelligible laws." See "Pardon, Old Fathers."

Brahma. In Hinduism, Brahma means "creator" and is the creative force in the Hindu Trinity, later represented in a three-fold personification of Brahma (Creation), Vishnu (Preservation), and Siva (Destruction). See "Anashuya and Vijaya."

Brahmin. The meaning of the word *Brahmin* is teacher or priest, and in ancient times when the Indian caste system was a functional one, Brahmin indicated those professions. In later times of hereditary caste system, the name indicated any descendant of a one-time functional Brahmin. In modern times, both applications are used, as in the case of the Hindu teacher, Mohini Chatterjee [q.v.]. See also "Mohini Chatterjee."

Bran. The name of a legendary hound. According to Irish legend, a Sidhe [q.v.], jealous because her sweetheart married Finn's aunt, changed the woman into a beautiful hound who then gave birth to two whelps. Finn named the whelps Bran and Sceolan, and they were the great hunting dogs of the Fianna, and followers of Finn. Bran, the hound, should not be confused with Bran, the Welsh fertility god, who was the brother of Branwen. For Bran the hound, see "The Wanderings of Oisin."

Branwen. A Welsh goddess of love. Branwen was the daughter of Llyr, the Welsh sea god, comparable to the Irish sea god Lir. She was the sister of the fertility god Bran, who died rescuing her from the torture of her husband, Matholwych, a king of Ireland. The story, part of the collection of Welsh tales called *The Mabinogion,* is one of the great medieval allegories. Her name, which can mean white crow or white breast, is later associated with that of Brangwaine, a figure in the Tristan legend. See "Under the Moon."

Brown Bull. The great bull of Ulster. The fight over this bull forms the central epic of the Red Branch or Ulster cycle of Irish mythology. The story is called *Tain Bo Cuailgne* [ton' bo hoo' alnya]; *The Cattle-Raid of Cooley.* The story has its beginnings in the great contest between Maeve, Queen of Connaught, and Ailell, her consort, to see which of them had the greater possessions. A great White-horned Bull that had belonged to Queen Maeve had left her service and entered that of

Ailell, leaving Maeve short a great bull in the contest. Then she heard that in Ulster there was a great Brown Bull, and she determined to have it. When peaceful means failed, the war between Connaught and Ulster broke out. Cuchulain was the great Ulster hero, pitting himself against Maeve's wiles and her hordes. Ultimately, the White and the Brown Bulls met in head-on battle. The Brown Bull emerged victorious and returned to Ulster where, with a great bellow of victory, his heart burst and he died. [Other related references can be found in Ailell, Cuchulain, Fergus, Maeve, and the White-horned Bull.] The *Tain Bo Cuailgne*, dating to accounts in the earliest Irish chronicles, has been retold countless times. Full accounts are given by Lady Gregory in her *Cuchulain of Muirthemne* and in Thomas Kinsella's *Tain Bo Cuailgne*. Some of it is given in the more recent account *Over Nine Waves* by Marie Heaney. See also "The Old Age of Queen Maeve" and "Baile and Aillinn."

Browning, Robert. Yeats's reference to the English poet (1812–89) is in connection with a line from Browning's earliest published work, the poem "Pauline." In the poem, Browning is recalling early years "passed alone with wisest ancient books" wherein he encountered gods and giants and "an old hunter talking with gods." See "Are You Content?"

Brycelinde. In Arthurian legend, the region adjoining Brittany, usually given as Broceliande. Merlin lived in the forest of Broceliande, and it was there that the sorceress Viviane cast a spell upon him. Yeats is listing magical lands and the magical women whose spells upon men constitute "a burden not to be borne." See "Under the Moon."

Bual [boo'al]. Shortened by Yeats from Ethal Ambual, Bual is the father of Caer [q.v.]. See "The Old Age of Queen Maeve."

Buan [boo'an]. Father of Baile [q.v.]. See "Baile and Aillinn."

Buddha. Gautama Buddha, a fifth-century noble who formulated the principles that came to be the basis of Buddhism. The image of Buddha, various in pose and conception, has been widely used in sculpture and painting. See "The Statues."

Bull, John. Popularly, a name for England, supposedly personifying the English character as one of robust solidity and forthrightness. The image of John Bull was established by Dr. John Arbuthnot in

The History of John Bull, published in 1727, with a preface by Pope and Swift. In more recent times, the name is frequently used pejoratively. See "The Ghost of Roger Casement."

Burke. Edmund Burke (1729–97), Irish-born statesman who championed self-government for Ireland. Although his mother was a Catholic, Burke was raised as a Protestant. To Yeats, this statesman and renowned orator was one of the greatest men of Anglo-Irish history. [For further comment on Burke, *see* Berkeley.] Also, especially for the reference to the trees, see "The Tower," "Blood and the Moon," and "The Seven Sages."

Butler or **Butlers.** Butler is a family name in Yeats's paternal ancestry. [*See* Genealogical Information.] The name goes back to the twelfth century, when Theobald Walter was named by King John to the hereditary office of Butler to the lord of Ireland. In the fourteenth century, a descendant was created an Irish earl with the title of Ormonde [q.v.], a name with which the Butler family is thereafter associated, always as loyal followers of the English throne. There is, however, nothing to confirm that the paternal family of Butlers, from whom the poet gets his middle name, is in any direct line descendant from the Butler-Ormondes. In 1773, Yeats's great-great grandfather married Mary Butler. She was the great granddaughter of Edmond Butler, who, in 1696, had married Mary Voisin of French Huguenot stock, a heritage that Yeats was wont to refer to. See "Pardon, Old Fathers" and "Are You Content?"

Byrne, Billy, and **Byrnes** and **O'Byrnes.** An illustrious family name in Irish history, in all its variations. Yeats gives his beggar, Billy Byrne, the same name as that of one of the great heroes of the Insurrection of 1798. The name is also found in stories and tales, one of which Yeats himself tells in *The Celtic Twilight:* "The Three O'Byrnes and the Evil Faeries." See "Under the Round Tower."

Byzantine. *See* **Byzantium.**

Byzantium. Ancient city on the site of present day Istanbul. Yeats had a profound fascination for the Byzantine city, which he sets forth in *A Vision* as follows:

> I think if I could be given a month of Antiquity and leave to spend it where I chose, I should spend it in Byzantium a little

before Justinian [Byzantine emperor 527–565] opened St. Sophia and closed the Academy of Plato. I think I could find in some little wine-shop some philosophical worker in mosaic who could answer all my questions, the supernatural descending nearer than to Plotinus even, for the pride of his delicate skill would make what was an instrument of power to princes and clerics, a murderous madness in the mob, show as a lovely flexible presence like that of a perfect human body.

I think that in early Byzantium, maybe never before or since in recorded history, religious, aesthetic and practical life were one, that architect and artificers—though not, it may be, poets, for language had been the instrument of controversy and must have grown abstract—spoke to the multitude and the few alike. The painter, the mosaic worker, the worker in gold and silver, the illuminator of sacred books, were almost perhaps without the consciousness of individual design, absorbed in their subject-matter and that the vision of a whole people.

For Yeats's use of Byzantine and Byzantium in the poems, see "The Old Age of Queen Maeve," "Sailing to Byzantium," "Byzantium," and "The Gift of Harun al-Rashid."

C

Caer [ker]. Daughter of Ethal Ambual [*see* Bual]. Caer appeared to Aengus in a dream, and he became sick with love of her. He searched everywhere to find her and enlisted the help of mortal and immortal figures alike. In the traditional story, told at length in Lady Gregory's *Cuchulain of Muirthemne,* he finally learns that she becomes a swan for every other year. When, at last, he finds her, she agrees to marry him if he will be a swan too, which he agrees to. Yeats's treatment of the story of Aengus and Caer is much condensed from the traditional. See "The Old Age of Queen Maeve."

Caesar or Caesars. The name of the famous Roman family and later part of the title of Roman emperor. The most famous Caesar was Julius (100–44 B.C.) The Caesar name was passed on to his adopted son Augustus and was continued in use by Tiberius, Caligula, Claudius, Nero, and thereafter, without family connection, by succeeding emperors. The name in the plural form is used by Yeats only to suggest the emptiness of power, but he uses it differently in the singular. Here it suggests isolation and the need of silence: "His eyes fixed upon nothing . . . His mind moves upon silence." For Caesar, see "Long-Legged Fly." For Caesars, see "Demon and Beast."

Caliph. *See* **Harun al-Rashid.**

Callimachus. Athenian sculptor of the fifth century B.C., Callimachus is credited with the invention of a drill that enabled him to make diaphanous draperies in marble. He also fashioned a golden lamp, shaped like a palm and designed to shed perpetual light on the Erechtheum, the Ionic temple of Athene on the Acropolis. In one of his essays, Yeats wrote "In half Asiatic Greece Callimachus could still return to stylistic management of the falling folds of drapery, after the naturalistic drapery of Phidias." See Yeats's essay "Certain Noble Plays of Japan" and the poem "Lapis Lazuli."

Calvert, Edward (1799–1883). English painter and engraver. Calvert was a close friend and great admirer of William Blake. Calvert's work has been likened to Blake's, and the influence is evident. It should be noted that Calvert, whose name occurs in only one poem, along with Wilson [q.v.], Blake, and Claude [q.v.], carries on Blake's tradition just as Richard Wilson carried on the tradition of the landscape artist Claude Lorrain. In his *Autobiography,* Yeats lists "Calvert in the woodcuts" and Blake among "The great myth-makers and, the men of aristocratic mind." See "Under Ben Bulben."

Caoilte [kweel'tcha]. Legendary Irish hero. There are variant spellings of his name: Caolte, and Yeats once used Coulte. In notes to the poem "The Hosting of the Sidhe" in the volume of his poems called *The Wind Among the Reeds* (reprinted in Allt and Alspach), Yeats writes of Caoilte that he "was a companion of the Fianna [*see* Finn]; and years after his death, he appeared to a king in a forest, and was a flaming man, that he might lead him in the darkness. When the king asked him who he was, he said, 'I am your candlestick.' " In some accounts, Caoilte is Finn's nephew, especially renowned for his long red hair and his fleetness of foot, supposedly having won a race against Finn's black horse. Whenever he ran, his red hair blazed out behind him. In the poem "The Secret Rose," Yeats refers to a man "who drove the gods out of their liss," or fort. In a note to that poem, Yeats says that this was something he read about Caoilte, who was so enraged after the Battle of Gabhra [q.v.] when almost all his companions of the Fianna were killed. See "The Hosting of the Sidhe" and "The Wanderings of Oisin."

Casement or **Roger Casement.** Roger David Casement (1864–1916), Irish Protestant and devoted nationalist. Yeats regarded Casement as being in the tradition of such Protestant patriots as Robert Emmet, Wolfe Tone, and Henry Grattan. Casement had served with distinction in the British Consular Service—his reports on the Congo and on the atrocities at Putumayo, Brazil, attracted worldwide attention and acclaim, services for which he was knighted. He retired to Ireland in 1913 and soon took up the cause of Irish nationalism, finally journeying to Berlin, via Norway, to enlist German aid in an Irish uprising against the English in the midst of World War I. Disillusioned with the Germans, Casement returned to Ireland via German submarine, landing on shore in county Kerry in hopes of being in time to stop the planned uprising, which he was now certain would fail. He was betrayed and arrested shortly after he landed and taken at once to England to be tried for treason. Shortly thereafter, copies of certain obscene, personal diaries, supposedly in Casement's handwriting, were circulated among influential people to dissuade them from signing a petition for Casement's reprieve. Among those persons was the English poet Alfred Noyes (1880–1958), then engaged in teaching at Princeton as well as assisting the British embassy in Washington. Sir Cecil Spring-Rice [*see* Spring-Rice] was the British ambassador to the United States at that time. As a result of the circulation of the diaries, no Irish-American protest, which had been anticipated, was forthcoming, the diaries being generally accepted as authentic. Casement was convicted of treason and hanged. Still, among some people, the feeling persisted that the diaries were forgeries, designed to assure Casement's conviction and death. In 1936, there appeared a book by William J. Maloney called *The Forged Casement Diaries*. It was this book that aroused Yeats's anger and gave rise to his two Casement poems. When the poem "Roger Casement" was first published with great prominence in *The Irish Press,* the line that later became "Come Tom and Dick, come all the troop" read "Come Alfred Noyes and all the troop." Noyes immediately responded with what Yeats called a "noble" letter, in which Noyes explained why he had assumed the diaries to be authentic. He said that he hoped Yeats would consent to be on a committee to examine the original documents. Yeats amended the line, removing Noyes's name, but would never consent to withdraw the poem. The British have rarely permitted the original Casement diaries to be seen, and in 1957, Alfred Noyes, acknowledging that "the ghost of Roger Casement is beating on the door," wrote a stinging rebuke of British policy in *The Accusing Ghost or Justice for Casement* (London, 1957). Some scholars who have seen the original diaries have attested to the homosexual content therein. Years later, Casement's bones were dug up from the lime pit where they had been buried and were returned to Dublin, where they were received with great honor and interred in Glasnevin Cemetery. The portrait of Roger Casement described by Yeats in "The Municipal Gallery Revisited" actually hangs in the Royal College of Law in Henrietta Street, but it has on occasion been on loan

to the Municipal Gallery. In addition to the books by William J. Maloney and Alfred Noyes, see chapter 22 of Alfred Noyes's *Two Worlds for
Memory* (Philadelphia, 1953), and see *Letters* (in Wade), 667, 868–
70, 875, 880–84. But see especially "Roger Casement," "The Ghost
of Roger Casement," and "The Municipal Gallery Revisited."

Cashel. Site of the celebrated Rock of Cashel. The city of Cashel is located
about seventy-five miles southwest of Dublin in county Tipperary,
Munster Province. The Irish word caiseal [cash'al] indicates a stone
building, particularly a circular stone fort; and the ruins of such a fort
can be seen on the Rock of Cashel, sometimes called the Irish Acropolis
with its 360 degree view of the land. Among the impressive ruins is
also the chapel of Cormac [q.v.] MacCarthy, king of Munster in the
twelfth century. See "The Double Vision of Michael Robartes."

Castle Taylor. The name of the estate of the Shawe-Taylor [q.v.] family.
Elizabeth Persse, a sister of Lady Gregory, married the Shawe-Taylor
heir. Castle Taylor was located about fifteen miles from Galway. See
"In Memory of Major Robert Gregory."

Cathleen. The name of the woman symbolizing Ireland. In Yeats's work,
this symbol of Ireland is found in poem and play. In his play *Cathleen
ni Houlihan,* she is an old beset woman in need of help from an enemy
who has taken her land. When a strong young Irishman deserts all to
come to her aid, she is seen as a young girl, "and she has the walk of a
queen." It is also a reference to Maud Gonne, for whom the play was
written and who played the role of Cathleen when the play was first
produced in 1902. In his *W. B. Yeats: Man and Poet,* A. Norman
Jeffares quotes Stephen Gwynn's reaction to the first production:

> The effect of Cathleen ni Houlihan on me was that I went
> home asking myself if such plays should be produced unless
> one was prepared for people to go out to shoot and be shot.
> Yeats was not alone responsible; no doubt but Lady Gregory
> had helped him to get the peasant speech so perfect; but above
> all Miss Gonne's impersonation had stirred the audience as I
> have never seen another audience stirred.

Yeats himself wondered, in his poem "The Man and the Echo," if this
play had "sent out / Certain men the English shot?" Yeats's other
Cathleen, the Countess Cathleen, is the heroine of his play *The Countess*

Cathleen (1892). Here, the countess, crazed with pity for the starving peasants and fearful that they will sell their souls to the devil, sells hers that the peasants might have bread. "But masterful Heaven had intervened to save it," as Yeats puts it in his poem "The Circus Animals' Desertion." But this intervention caused much controversy in Dublin when the play was first produced. See also "Red Hanrahan's Song About Ireland."

Catullus, Gaius Valerius (847–854 B.C.), Roman lyric poet, who addressed many of his poems to a woman named Lesbia. It is interesting to note that Yeats, speaking of his friend Arthur Symons, said, "nor shall I ever know how much my practice and my theory owe to the passages that he read me from Catullus and from Verlaine and Mallarmé." Symons dedicated to Yeats his book *The Symbolist Movement in Literature,* 1899. See "The Scholars."

Cephisus. The sacred river of Delphi, where was located the oracle of Apollo. The river takes its name from Cephisus, or Caphissus, a Greek river god. See "Colonus' Praise."

Chang, the prince of. A name included in a quotation taken from the Chinese philosopher Confucius. [*See* Khoung-Fou-Tseu.] Richard Ellmann, writing about the Yeats of 1909, in *Yeats, the Man and the Masks,* says, "He needed still a fresh impetus. . . . The visions which he could produce through symbolic meditations were limited. . . . Then too, they became difficult for him to evoke. He admits as much in the epigraph . . . where he quoted Khoung-fou-tseu" (191). See the epigraph to Yeats's book of poems called *Responsibilities.*

Charlemagne. Charles the Great (742–814), king of the Franks and emperor of the West. Charlemagne's parents were Pepin III and Berta, daughter of Chaubert of Laon. Yeats, as in "Leda and the Swan" and other poems, is interested in unions that produce "world-transforming" offspring. See "Whence Had They Come?" poem VIII of "Supernatural Songs."

Chatterjee, Mohini. Brahmin theosophist. Yeats met the Bengali sage when he went to Dublin in 1885 to assist in the founding of the Dublin Theosophical Lodge. For Yeats, the meeting was unforgettable. He first attempted to put into verse what he learned from Mohini in the poem "Kabva on Himself." This poem was published in *The Wanderings of Oisin and Other Poems,* (London, 1889), and was never thereafter reprinted until *The Variorum Edition*, 1956, where it is given as one of the poems not in the definitive edition. But in 1908, Yeats was still recalling in *The Collected Works in Verse and Prose of William Butler Yeats*, vol. 8, where he wrote:

> Somebody asked him [Mohini] if we should pray, but even prayer was too full of home, of desire, of life, to have any part in that acquiescence that was his beginning of wisdom, and he answered that one should say, before sleeping: 'I have lived many lives, I have been a slave and a prince. Many a beloved has sat upon my knees, and I have sat upon the knees of many a beloved. Everything that has been shall be again.' Beautiful words that I spoilt once by turning into clumsy verse.

Nearly forty years later, this became the basis of his poem on Mohini. See "Mohini Chatterjee."

Cheshire Cheese. The ancient eating-house in Fleet Street, London, and the meeting place of the Rhymers' Club. Writing in his *Autobiography*, about Ernest Rhys, a Welsh poet and translator, Yeats noted:

> Between us we founded The Rhymers' Club, which for some years was to meet every night in an upper room with a sanded floor in an ancient eating-house in Fleet Street called the Cheshire Cheese. Lionel Johnson, Ernest Dowson, Victor Plarr, Ernest Redford, John Davidson, Richard Le Gallienne, T. W. Rolleston, Selwyn Image, Edwin Ellis, and John Todhunter came constantly for a time, Arthur Symons and Herbert Horne, less constantly, while William Watson joined but never came and Francis Thompson came once but never joined; and sometimes if we met in a private house, which we did occasionally, Oscar Wilde came. (101)

Yeats more fully described some of his fellow members on a dispatch that appeared in the Boston *Pilot*, April 23, 1902, reprinted in *Letters to the New Island*, edited by Horace Reynolds. See "The Grey Rock."

Chou. A Chinese dynasty holding sway from 1027–256 B.C., named for its ruling family. Later, the Chou lost their military power. The period, however, is considered the Chinese classical age, marking the first appearance of progress and of such arts as carving jade, lacquering, gold and bronze ornamentation. It was also the period of such Chinese philosophers as Lao-tzu and Confucius. See poem VI of "Vacillations."

Christ Church Bell. The bell of Christ Church College in Oxford, where Yeats was when he composed "All Souls' Night," as the dateline at the end of the poem indicates. See "All Souls' Night."

Chronos. Legendary Greek god of the Titans. Chronos is associated with time, and his name is the Greek word for time. See "The Song of the Happy Shepherd."

Cicero, Marcus Tullius (106–43 B.C.). also called Tully. The great orator of Roman antiquity, Cicero was also eminent as politician and philosopher and as the purist of prose stylists. Yeats kept images of the great classical authors in his study. He felt that his own experience of passion must have been felt by them as well. See "Mad as the Mist and Snow," which is poem XVIII of "Words for Music Perhaps."

City Hall. The city hall in Dublin. Located just outside Dublin Castle on Cork Hill, an extension of Dame Street, the building is famous for its Corinthian columns. It was constructed in 1769–79 by Thomas Cooley. The fighting in the Easter Uprising of 1916 took place mainly at the General Post Office, but skirmishes occurred at many different places. Though the labor leader James Connolly was one of the organizers and leaders and martyrs of the uprising, the Connolly referred to as dying close to City Hall was an actor named Sean Connolly, whom Yeats would have known from the theatre. See poem III of "Three Songs to the One Burden."

Clare. One of the western counties of Ireland, located in Munster province. The Irish word clar means a board, and probably the county got its name from a board used to ford a river, but one of the great treasures of county Clare is rocky, glacial hills known as The Burren. See "In Memory of Major Robert Gregory."

Claude Lorrain. (1600–1682). French landscape painter. (Lorrain was a pseudonym for Gelée.) Claude's landscapes are in the best classical tradition and are among the most influential on the art of landscape painting. Richard Wilson [q.v.], an eighteenth-century English landscape artist, is among those who have carried on Claude's tradition. See "Under Ben Bulben."

Clifton, Harry. A friend of Yeats who had given him a piece of carved lapis lazuli, which in turn inspired a poem: See "Lapis Lazuli," below the title of which appears "For Harry Clifton."

Cloone. A bog near Ballylee [q.v.]. The name comes from the Irish word clusin [kloo'an], meaning a meadow, a fertile piece of land among bogs, marshes, or woods. Yeats in his use of the name is referring to a popular old story relating to Mary Hynes, the beautiful peasant girl of Ballylee, celebrated in verse by the blind poet Raferty [q.v.]. In his book called in Irish *Abráin atá leagtá ar an reactúire* (Dublin, 1902) Douglas Hyde [q.v.] gives the story as follows: "There was a number of young men sitting up drinking one night, and they fell to talking about Mary Hynes, and a man of them stole away to go to Ballylee to see her, and when he came to the Bog of Cloon he fell into the water and was drowned." Yeats retells much the same story in his poem "The Tower," which see.

Clooth-na-Bare [klooth'no bar']. A legendary woman whom Yeats first wrote of in the story "The Untiring Ones," in *The Celtic Twilight,* where he noted that Clooth-na-Bare "went all over the world seeking a lake deep enough to drown her faery life, of which she had grown weary, leaping from hill to hill, and setting up a cairn of stones wherever her feet lighted, until at last, she found the deepest water in the world in little Lough Ia, on Bird Mountain in Sligo." There are many accounts of Clooth-na-Bare to be found, among them those of Lady Gregory in *A Book of Saints and Wonders* and Patrick W. Joyce's *Old Celtic Romances.* The name means the old woman of Bare but may be a corruption of a variation meaning the old woman Bare. Her name came to be used also as the place name for the mountain where she drowned herself. See "The Hosting of the Sidhe" and "Red Hanrahan's Song About Ireland."

Cloyne. Town located in county Cork, Munster Province. The original Irish name from which it was shortened and Anglicized Clusinnuamadh, meaning the meadow of the cave. George Berkeley [q.v.] was the most famous bishop of Cloyne, so appointed in 1734. See "The Seven Sages."

Colonus. Ancient town north of Athens, Greece. It was to Colonus that the self-blinded Oedipus went in his exile from Thebes, and at Colonus he died. See "Colonus' Praise," (from Yeats's play *Oedipus at Colonus,* after Sophocles.

Colooney. Town located about five miles south of Sligo town. In the original Irish, of which Colooney is an Anglicized adaptation, the name meant the angle or recess of the bald or horned cow. Father O'Hart [q.v.] served in the parish of Kilvarset [q.v.], of which Colooney is a part. See "The Ballad of Father O'Hart."

Conan. A legendary figure associated with Finn [q.v.] and the Fianna. Conan Mail, or Conan the Bald, was a large-bodied man known, according to P. W. Joyce in his *Old Celtic Romances,* as " a great boaster, a great coward and a great glutton. He had a venomous tongue and hardly ever spoke a good word of anyone." Conan was often the butt of the jokes of the Fianna, followers of Finn, yet all dreaded his tongue. Along with Goll [q.v.], Conan was a leader of the Clan Morna that often rivaled and fought with Finn. See "The Wanderings of Oisin."

Conchubar [kon'a har]. Lady Gregory gives "Conachoor" with the "ch" as in "loch," but either is close enough. Conchubar was the legendary warrior-king of the Ulster or Red Branch cycle of Irish mythology. Son of Nessa [q.v.], Conchubar is supposedly of virgin birth, although Cathbad the Druid is called his father in some accounts. Fergus [q.v.], who later married Nessa, gave up his throne of Ulster in favor of his young stepson, through Nessa's influence in some accounts, through Fergus's own choosing in others. The Ulster cycle deals with the warriors of Conchubar, principally with Cuchulain [q.v.], Conchubar's nephew. The position of Conchubar in the cycle suggests a parallel with King Arthur. In one famous episode in the cycle, however, Conchubar wishes to marry the beautiful maiden Deirdre [q.v.] and is enraged when she runs off with Naoise [q.v.], never resting until he is revenged. Yeats's version of this story is given in his play *Deirdre* (1907). Conchubar possessed a great sword called the Corm Olas, the Blue Green. Another story of Conchubar recounts that he was told of Christ's Crucifixion and became so enraged that he rushed into a wood and slashed at the trees with his sword. In the process, he dislodged a ball from his head that had once been imbedded there, thrown from a sling. The ball came out, followed by brains, and thus Conchubar died. See "Fergus and the Druid," "Cuchulain's Fight with the Sea," and "The Wanderings of Oisin." See also the lines in "The Secret Rose" that refer to Conchubar:

> and the King whose eyes
> Saw the Pierced Hands and the Rood of elder rise

In Druid Vapour and make the torches dim;
Till vain frenzy awoke and he died

Connemara. A district bordering on the Atlantic Ocean, in county Galway, in the west of Ireland. The area gets its name from mara, the genitive of sea, plus the family name indicating the descendants of Cormac, an early king. Yeats always assumed that Connemara cloth came from this district; and in his *Autobiography,* he confesses his surprise when a letter from his tailor, apologizing for the delay in completing his suit, explained: "It takes such a long time getting Connemara cloth as it has to come all the way from Scotland." Nevertheless, it is the make of clothes that Yeats gives his characters. See "The Dedication to a Book of Stories Selected from the Irish Novelists," "The Fisherman," and "The Phases of the Moon."

Connolly, James (1870–1916). One of the prominent revolutionaries in the disastrous Easter Uprising of 1916. A self-educated man, Connolly founded the newspaper *The Harp* in America in 1903 and, on his return to Dublin, *The Irish Worker,* in 1910. He was a trade union organizer and took an important part in the great strike of 1913 in Dublin, a strike in which Yeats, like Connolly, favored the workers against the middle class employers. (See Yeats's poem "September 1913.") Connolly, commanding forces in the General Post Office, was severely wounded in the Easter Uprising of 1916. He was summarily tried and shot, strapped in a chair because he was unable to stand. See "Easter 1916," "The Rose Tree," and "The O'Rahilly."

Connolly, Sean. An Abbey actor shot and killed in the Easter Uprising of 1916, referred to by Yeats as the "player Connolly" so as to distinguish him from James Connolly. Though he already had "carriage and voice," he had not yet his full skills in the theatre, and Yeats pays tribute to him as a famous, brilliant actor that might have been. See poem III of "Three Songs to the One Burden."

Cook Barach. *See* **Barach.**

Coole or **Coole Park.** The estate of Lady Gregory near the town of Gort in County Galway, it consisted of nearly four thousand acres. Yeats first went to Coole when he was thirty years old (1895), and was a frequent caller and resident thereafter. The Georgian-styled house was surrounded by great wooded acres, seven such areas bearing separate names. Yeats lists the seven names in the opening lines of the dedicatory poem to his play, or dramatic poem, *The Shadowy Waters*. On the Coole property, there was also a great lake, not far from the house. From the edge of the lake, Yeats could see and count the numerous swans that frequented the locale. In his *Autobiography*, he writes, "In later years I was to know the edges of that lake better than any spot on earth, to know it in all the changes of the seasons, to find there always some new beauty." The lake further fascinated Yeats because its only drain was a narrow subterranean passage which caused the lake to double and treble its size in winter. In addition, the lake was fed from the stream that ran by Yeats's tower at Ballylee, disappearing underground near the tower in what was known as Raftery's cellar [*see* Raftery], to rise again at Coole, forming the lake there. Amid the beauty of Coole, Yeats worked, frequently guarded from interruption by Lady Gregory. He also enjoyed there on occasion the company of illustrious countrymen, such as Douglas Hyde, John Synge, and Lady Gregory's estimable nephews, John Shawe-Taylor [q.v.] and Hugh Lane [q.v.]. See "In the Seven Woods"; "The Wild Swans at Coole"; "Coole Park, 1929"; "Coole Park and Ballylee"; and "I Walked Among the Seven Woods of Coole," which is the dedicatory poem to Yeats's play *The Shadowy Waters*.

Corbets or **Sandymount Corbets**. Paternal relatives of Yeats. In 1836, William Butler Yeats, grandfather of the poet, married Jane Corbet of Sandymount, a near suburb of Dublin in county Dublin. Her brother, Patrick Corbet, was at one time the governor of Penang. Her brother Robert was the owner of Sandymount Castle, with its great clock tower. At a house very near this castle, the poet was born. Later, Robert Corbet went bankrupt and lost Sandymount. See "Are You Content?"

Cordelia. The faithful, tragic daughter of King Lear in Shakespeare's play *King Lear*. See "Lapis Lazuli."

Cormac. MacCarthy. King of Munster Province in the twelfth century. The ruins of Cormac's chapel, dedicated in 1134, may still be seen at Cashel in county Tipperary. Yeats associates Cormac's ruins with his own ruined tower at Ballylee. See "The Double Vision of Michael Robartes."

Cosgrave, William Thomas (1880–1965). Irish patriot and political leader. Cosgrave was a member of Sinn Fein, meaning "we ourselves," organized to further the ideal of Irish rights. Cosgrave fought in the Easter Uprising of 1916. In 1922, he was elected president of the executive council of the Irish Free State, after the sudden death of Arthur Griffith [q.v.]. Cosgrave held this office until 1932, when Eamon de Valera [q.v.] won the election. Cosgrave continued as opposition leader until 1944, when he resigned his party leadership. Yeats regarded both Cosgrave and De Valera as lacking in the kind of leadership of a Parnell [q.v.]; and he further blamed the administration for the assassination of Kevin O'Higgins [q.v.], whom Yeats respected more than any political figure in Ireland since Parnell. See "Parnell's Funeral."

Cosimo de'Medici (1389–1464). Sometimes referred to as Cosimo the Elder, was the first Medici to rule in Florence. Previously, Cosimo had been banished from the city. He returned in 1434 and became a popular ruler, lavishing great sums on the state, on charitable works, on arts and learning. His generosity to and protection of artists has assured his fame as a great patron. Among the many works commissioned by him was the reconstruction of the San Marco [q.v.] library by Michelozzo [q.v.], some of the planning made even during his exile. See "To a Wealthy Man Who Promised a Second Subscription to the Dublin Municipal Gallery If It Were Proved the People Wanted Pictures."

Countess or **The Countess Cathleen.** The central figure of Yeats's play *The Countess Cathleen* (1892). In the play, the countess sells her soul to the devil so that the starving peasants in the famine need not sell their souls for money to buy bread. Katherine Tynan, poet and friend of Yeats, had told the story in her poem "The Charity of the Countess Kathleen," in *Ballads and Lyrics* (1891) and in a note to the poem, she says it is "an authentic folk-story of the West of Ireland." Yeats included in his *Irish Fairy and Folk Tales* (1893) an account of "The Countess Kathleen O'Shea." In a footnote to the tale, which is precisely the same story told in the play, Yeats says, "I am unable to find out the original source." At the end of the play, when the countess has died and presumably gone to fulfill her bargain, Aleel, a poet in her service, extracts from an angel an assurance that the Countess has gone to heaven and has been kissed by Mary for

> The Light of Lights
> Looks always on the motive, not the deed,
> The Shadow of Shadows on the deed alone.

There was much dissension at the first performance because of un-founded rumors that the play was anti-Catholic and because many Irish could not accept the idea of a woman going to heaven who has sold her soul to the devil. There was much booing and counter cheering. Yeats regarded the attack as public ignorance of the literary method but blamed himself for using as symbols what were realities in Ireland, as he duly explained in his *Autobiography.* The play was dedicated to Maud Gonne, who Yeats hoped would play the title role; but it was played at the first production by May Whitty, and the part of Aleel was played by Florence Farr [q.v.], a favorite chanter of poetry of Yeats. See the poem "Alternative Song for the Severed Head" in *The King of the Great Clock Tower,* "The Countess Cathleen in Paradise," and note that the title of the play appears in the poem "The Circus Animals' Desertion."

Country of the Young. A literal translation of the Irish Tir-nan-Og. The name in legend referred to the land of the immortal Tuatha de Danaan, the fairy folk of Danu [*see* Danaan]. Country of the Young is fairyland; it is the land beyond the sea; it is paradise. See "He Thinks of His Past Greatness When a Part of the Constellations of Heaven."

County Down. A county in the southeast section of Northern Ireland. Yeats's grandfather, also named William Butler Yeats, occupied a rec-tory in county Down, and the poet's father was born there. See "Are You Content?"

Craoibhin Aoibhin or, in full, **An Craoibhin Aoibhin [en kre'ven e'vin].** The Irish pen name of Douglas Hyde [q.v.], meaning "the delightful [or pleasant] little branch." The name is formed from the definitive article an, which Yeats does not use; the diminutive form of the Irish word for branch; and the adjective meaning pleasant or de-lightful. By his pen name, Hyde was well known all over Irish-speaking Ireland. A gold branch with golden apples on it was the logo that appeared on the cover of his books. Yeats hoped that Douglas Hyde, with his overwhelming influence on the Irish people (later Hyde be-came the first president of the Irish Republic, 1938–45), would help the Irish writers who were writing in English but using the same ancient and common materials of Ireland, toward a similar influence, instead of the rejection and riot with which their works were so often greeted by the Irish people. Yeats has in mind the first presentation at the Abbey Theatre of John Synge's *Playboy of the Western World,* and, earlier, his own *Countess Cathleen.* In this effort to secure Hyde's secret of appeal and influence, Yeats was reminded of a similar effort made by Pierre de Ronsard [q.v.] on behalf of the group of writers known as the Pléiade, in sixteenth-century France. Ronsard wrote the poem (reprinted is the Ronsard entry), which Yeats imitates, to Pontus de Tyard (or Thiard), an older member of the Pléiade who had a much wider influence and appeal than any of the others. See "At the Abbey Theatre."

Crazy Jane. Central figure in a series of poems by Yeats. In a note to his play *The Pot of Broth,* Yeats wrote, "The words and air of "There's Broth in the Pot" were taken down from an old woman named Cracked Mary, who wanders about the plain of Aidhne, and who sometimes sees riders on white horses coming through stony fields to her hovel door in the night." Later, as Richard Ellmann points out, Yeats "returned to Cracked Mary, combining her apparently with another old woman who lived near Lady Gregory. . . . He changed the name from Cracked Mary to Crazy Jane because of possible invidious religious implications" (275). In a letter to his friend Olivia Shakespeare, Yeats wrote that

> Crazy Jane is more or less founded upon an old woman who lives in a little cottage near Gort. She loves her flower-garden —she has just sent Lady Gregory some flowers in spite of the season—and [has] an amazing power of audacious speech. One of her great performances is a description of how the meanness of a Gort shopkeeper's wife over the price of a glass of porter made her so despair of the human race that she got drunk. The incidents of that drunkenness are of an epic magnificence. She is the local satirist and a really terrible one.

With regard to the changing of the name, several reasons are advanced "to avoid giving offense because of the candid nature of her remarks, to avoid any attempt to associate the character with Queen Mary of

England." A. Norman Jeffares reports that, at the time when King George V, Queen Mary's husband, opened the new wing of the Tate Gallery in London, where the controversial pictures that had belonged to Hugh Lane [q.v.] were being displayed, rather than in Dublin where Yeats and Lady Gregory so strongly felt they belonged, Yeats wrote an unpublished poem called "Cracked Mary's Vision." With regard to literary sources for Crazy Jane and Yeat's treatment, one might look first at a dream that Yeats reported that he had, in a letter of March 1929, to Olivia Shakespeare:

> Last night I saw in a dream strange ragged excited people singing in a crowd. The most visible were a man and woman who were I think dancing. The man was swinging around his head a weight in the end of rope or leather thong—I know that he did not know whether he would strike her dead or not, and both had their eyes fixed on each other, and both sang their love for one-another. I suppose it was Blake's old thought "sexual love is founded on spiritual hate."

A very likely influence that Yeats would have known is found in John Synge's *Poems and Translations,* in his translation of François Villon's "Old Woman's Lamentations": "The man I had a love for—a great rascal would kick me in the gutter—is dead thirty years and over it, and it is I am left behind, gray and aged. When I do be minding the good days I had, minding what I was one time, and what it is I'm come to, and when I do look on my own self, poor and dry, and pinched together, it wouldn't be much would set me raging in the streets." Also, Yeats may well have been aware of the poem called "Crazy Jane," by M. G. "Monk" Lewis, from his volume *Poems* (1912), and herewith the last three stanzas:

> Dost thou weep to see my anguish?
> Mark me, and escape my woe:
> When men flatter, sigh, and languish,
> Think them false—I found them so!
> For I loved, Oh! so sincerely,
> None will ever love again
> Yet the man I prized most dearly
> Broke the heart of Crazy Jane.

Gladly that young heart received him,
Which has never loved but one;
He seemed true, and I believed him—
He was false, and I undone!
Since that hour has reason never
Held her empire o'er my brain.
Henry fled!—With him for ever,
Fled the wits of Crazy Jane.

Now forlorn and broken-hearted
Still with frenzied thoughts beset,
Near the spot where last we parted,
Near the spot where first we met,
Thus I chant my lovelorn ditty
While I sadly pace the plain;
And each passer by, in pity,
Cries "God help thee, Crazy Jane!"

Yet another possibility of indebtedness is to Robert Burns's "Jolly Beggars," for example in the beginning, "I once was a maid, tho' I cannot tell when, / and still my delight is in proper young men." Or again in "There's not a lad in a' the lan' / was match for my John Highlandman." [see Jack or Jack the Journeyman.] Yeats's great familiarity with Burns's work is attested to in Yeats's essay "The Symbolism of Poetry," in *Essays and Introductions*. [For a comment on Crazy Jane's Bishop, see Bishop.] Yeats's Crazy Jane poems are "Crazy Jane and the Bishop," "Crazy Jane Reproved," "Crazy Jane on the Day of Judgment," "Crazy Jane and Jack the Journeyman," "Crazy Jane and God," "Crazy Jane Talks with the Bishop," "Crazy Jane Grown Old Looks at the Dancers," "Crazy Jane on the Mountain," and a reference in poem I of "Three Songs to the One Burden."

Cretan or **Cretan Barb.** An allusion to mythological material related to ancient Crete and to fifth-century coins of Crete that picture this material. In "Notes to 'The Trembling of the Veil,' " a section of his *Autobiography,* Yeats discusses a number of Cretan references. In one section of these notes, entitled "The Woman Who Shot the Arrow," Yeats says:

She was, it seems, the Mother-Goddess whose representative priestess shot the arrow at the child whose sacrificial death symbolized the death and resurrection of the free-spirit, or Apollo. She is pictured upon certain Cretan coins of the fifth century B.C. as a slightly draped, beautiful woman sitting in the heart of a branching tree. (G. F. Hill, *A Handbook of Greek and Roman Coins*, p. 163.) She goes back to the very earliest form of the religion of Crete, and is, it seems probable, the Tree as Mother killing the Tree as Son.

Yeats also reports in his *Autobiography,* that he had seen the woman in a dream shooting an arrow at a star. In addition, he says that Arthur Symons, who was with him in Ireland, returned to London to find awaiting him a story by Fiona MacLeod [pen name of William Sharpe], wherein someone had a vision of a woman shooting an arrow into the sky. Yeats, returning to London a few weeks later, encountered a woman whose little child, "perhaps at the same time of my vision, perhaps a little later—had come running in from the garden calling out, 'oh, mother, I have seen a woman shooting an arrow into the sky and I am afraid that she has killed God.' " Yeats associated this material with the phenomena that occurred in the sky at the funeral of Charles Stewart Parnell [q.v.]. He writes of this event in the notes to the first publication of his poem "Parnell's Funeral," in the volume called *The King of the Great Clock Tower* (1934) in which he says: "I did not go to the funeral, because being in my sensitive and timid youth, I hated crowds, and what crowds implied, but my friend [Maud Gonne] went. She told me that evening of the star that fell in broad daylight as Parnell's body was lowered into the grave—was it a collective hallucination or an actual event." Standish O'Grady [q.v.], Yeats continues, wrote of the event, saying thousands witnessed the event, that the sky was bright with strange lights and flames. Yeats then makes his association with the Cretan material, "I think of the symbolism of the star shot with an arrow, described in the appendix of my book *Autobiographies.* I asked if the fall of a star may not upon occasion, symbolize an accepted sacrifice." See "Parnell's Funeral."

Crevroe. A mountain in Ireland in a simplified spelling of Creeveroe. The name means Red Branch [q.v.], and is said to mark the spot where the heroes of the Red Branch resided. See "The Wanderings of Oisin."

Cromwell, Oliver (1599–1658). Lord Protector of England during most of the years of the English Commonwealth government (1649–60). His reign was known as the Protectorate. His expedition to Ireland in 1649 remains one of the most hated of English colonial actions in Ireland. The cruelty of the massacres, such as those at Drogheda and Wexford has never been erased from Irish memory. Cromwell sought to gain Irish submission to his regime and to transfer dispossessed Irish lands to English and Scottish subjects. In this, he followed the practice of James I (1556–1625), a practice completed by William III [*see* Billy] after the famous Battle of the Boyne [q.v.]. In *Autobiography,* Yeats speaks of "Cromwell's warty opinionated head." On January 8, 1937, Yeats wrote to his friend Dorothy Wellesley, "At this moment I am expressing my rage against the intelligentsia by writing about Oliver Cromwell who was the Lennin [*sic*] of his stay—I speak through the mouth of some wandering peasant poet in Ireland." Some of Yeats's lines in the Cromwell poem are taken from the poem "Last Lines" by the wandering bard Egan O'Rahilly (1670–1726). See "The Curse of Cromwell."

Crooked Plow. Ursa Major, or the constellation of the Great Bear. Yeats writes of the association in many countries of the Tree of Life with the Seven Lights [q.v.], yet another name for Ursa Major. And in his notes to the first publication of *The Wind Among the Reeds* in 1899, (reprinted in Allt and Alspach), Yeats says: "It is this Tree of Life that I have put into the "Song of Mongan" [later retitled "He Thinks of His Past Greatness When a Part of the Constellations of Heaven"] under its common Irish form of hazel; and because it had sometimes the stars for fruit, I have hung upon it 'the Crooked Plough' and the 'Pilot' star [q.v.], as Gaelic-speaking Irishmen sometimes call the Bear and the North star." Also called the Big Dipper, this constellation has seven prominent stars. See "He Thinks of His Past Greatness When a Part of the Constellations of Heaven."

Cro-Patrick. A mountain, more commonly spelled Croagh Patrick, though pronounced pretty much the same, located near Clew Bay in county Mayo. The mountain rises to a height of over 2,500 feet and is considered a holy mountain. Its name means the rick or hill of Saint

Patrick, the patron saint of Ireland. Every July especially, it is the scene of Ireland's most famous holy pilgrimage as thousands climb the mountain from the summit of which, according to legend, Saint Patrick banished the snakes from Ireland. See "The Dancer at Cruachan and Cro-Patrick."

Cruachan [krok'en, as Yeats gives it and therefore what is used; but more properly **kroo'nan].** A hill with a surrounding plain in county Roscommon. The name is the diminutive form of cruach, a hill or rick, generally of a round, stacked, or piled up appearance. Yeats, in his preface to Lady Gregory's *Cuchulain of Muirthemne*, writes, "What beauty was lost to me, what depths of emotions is still lacking in me, because nobody told me . . . that Cruachan of the Enchantments lay behind those long, blue, ragged hills." (He is referring to hills that could be seen from heights in Sligo.)

Cruachan was also the seat of Maeve [q.v.], the queen of Connacht, from which site she led her invasion of Ulster in her attempt to win the famous Brown Bull [q.v.]; her chief opponent would be Cuchulain. Yeats gives his pronunciation of Cruachan in footnotes to poems where the name occurs. See "The Hour Before Dawn," "The Dancer at Cruachan and Cro-Patrick," and "Tom at Cruachan," the latter two being respectively poems XXI and XXIII of "Words for Music Perhaps"; also "The Old Age of Queen Maeve."

Cuchulain [koo'hoo'lin]. [Lady Gregory also gives **koo'hull'in].** The great hero of Irish legend and the central figure of the Ulster or Red Branch cycle of Irish mythology. Cuchulain was the son of Dechtire [deh'ti ra], sister of King Conchubar of Ulster. There is some disagreement in the old legends about Cuchulain's father. The oldest manuscripts advance three possibilities, but the most frequent one is that he was the son of Lugh [loo], a fairy god who enters Dechtire in the form of a mayfly, which she takes in a drink. Lugh, king of the Sidhe [q.v.], the fairy folk, is also known as Lugh of the Long Hand. On her wedding night to a warrior named Sualtim, Lugh changed Dechtire and her fifty handmaidens into birds, and they disappeared. A year later, the birds returned and resumed human form; and the next day, Dechtire gave birth to a boy who was at first called Setanta, son of Sualtim. Setanta was brought up on the great plain of Muirthemne [q.v.] with the most illustrious of the Ulster knights as his tutors. When he was still a boy, he was already much admired for his character and his athletic prowess. One day he arrived late at a feast given by Culain, the great smith of Ulster. Because the boy did not arrive with the others, he was regarded as an intruder and attacked by the great, ferocious hound owned by Culain. But the boy, showing astounding strength and ingenuity—he hurled his ball down the hound's throat—won the battle. All the great men of Ulster rushed out and were proud of his feat, except Culain who moaned that now he had no hound to protect his property. The young boy then said that while he raised and trained a new whelp for Culain, he would remain there and he himself would be Culain's watchdog. At this, Cathbad [kah'vah], the famous Red Branch Druid, said, "And from this time out your name will be Cuchulain, the hound of Culain." This latter is from Lady Gregory's full account of his life and times in her *Cuchulain of Muirthemne.*

Cuchulain, arguably the greatest hero of all Irish mythology, has some times been called roughly the equivalent of Achilles in Greek mythology. Certainly, Cuchulain is the central figure of Yeats's Irish material, the hero of five of his plays and a presence in many poems and prose writings. Yeats, however, is concerned in his work more with the nature of heroism than with the character and life of the Ulster champion. But Cuchulain was not merely a great hero, famous for his fighting skill, as in his feats against Maeve and her forces; he was also a great lover of many women, but associated particularly with Emer [q.v.], whom he courted and married; Fand [q.v.]; and Aoife [q.v.]. In his poem "Cuchulain's Fight with the Sea," Yeats makes Emer the mother of Cuchulain's only son. In his play *On Baile's Strand,* on the same subject, as also in most mythological accounts, Aoife, the warrior, is the mother. Yeats regarded Cuchulain's love affair with Fand, a queen of the Danaan [q.v.] and wife of Manannan [q.v.] the Irish sea god, as one of the most beautiful of the old tales. In his notes to the first publication of *The Wind Among the Reeds,* Yeats says, "I have imagined Cuchulain meeting Fand 'walking among the flaming dew.' "

The image of Cuchulain fighting the waves in anger and frustration, after he has inadvertently killed his only son, is perhaps the most forceful in Yeats's Cuchulain material, symbolizing as it does man's anguish in the face of destructive life. This legend, ending with Cuchulain's death in the waves, Yeats drew from an account given him by Jeremiah

Curtain, author of *Myths and Folk-Lore of Ireland* (1890). In his later work, Yeats changed Cuchulain's death to a death resulting from battle wounds and treachery. Yeats also suggests that Cuchulain changes to a bird after death (as his mother had been in pregnancy), but in this Yeats departs from legend. In a letter to Dorothy Wellesley, August 15, 1938, Yeats wrote of his champion, saying, "Cuchulain seemed to me a heroic figure because he was creative joy separated from fear." A famous statue of Cuchulain stands in the General Post Office, principal site of the 1916 Easter Uprising. Erected in 1934, it is the work of the sculptor Oliver Sheppard. It shows Cuchulain tied to a pillar, in his death throes. A hawk is perched on his shoulder, quite as described in old accounts. In a letter to Edith Shackleton Heald (June 28, 1938), Yeats wrote, regarding his poem "The Statues," "Cuchulain is in the last stanza because Pearse [q.v.] and some of his followers had a cult of him. The Government has put a statue of Cuchulain in the rebuilt post office to commemorate this." See "To the Rose upon the Rood of Time," "Cuchulain's Fight with the Sea," "Alternative Song for the Severed Head" in *The King of the Great Clock Tower*, "The Statues," "Crazy Jane on the Mountain," "The Circus Animals' Desertion," and "Cuchulain Comforted." The five plays that Yeats devoted to Cuchulain should also be referred to: *At the Hawk's Well, The Green Helmet, On Baile's Strand, The Only Jealousy of Emer*, and *The Death of Cuchulain*.

Cumhal [koo'al]. The father of Finn [q.v.] and grandfather of Oisin [q.v.]. Cumhal was head of the Fianna of legendary Ireland and was killed in battle by the sons of Morna, who were fighting with him for leadership. The sons of Morna were Conan [q.v.] and Goll [q.v.]. See "The Blessed."

Cummen Strand. Part of the shoreline of Sligo Bay at the point where one looks down from Knocknarea [q.v.]. See "Red Hanrahan's Song About Ireland."

D

Dan. A name Yeats uses, along with that of Jerry Lout, to depict ordinary man. See "His Bargain," which is poem XIV of "Words for Music Perhaps."

Danaan or **De Danaan.** The fairy folk of Ireland. The name for the Danaan in full is Tuatha de Danaan [too' a ha' da' dan'en], meaning the folk of the goddess Danu. They are also called the Sidhe [shee] [q.v.] . They were driven underground into little fields or fairy mounds, sometimes referred to as Tir-nan-Og, or the Country of the Young. In his notes to the 1895 edition of *Poems* (reprinted in Allt and Alspach), Yeats says: "Tuatha De Danaan means the Race of the Gods of Dana. Dana was the mother of all the ancient gods of Ireland. They were the powers of light and life and warmth and did battle with the Fomoroh, or powers of night and death and cold. Robbed of offerings and honour, they [the Danaan] have gradually dwindled in the popular imagination until they have become the Faeries." Yeats continues, saying that the Danaan can "take all shapes, and those that are in the waters take often the shapes of birds and are as white as snow." See "The White Birds," "To Some I Have Talked with by the Fire," "The Unappeasable Host," "The Withering of the Boughs," and "The Wanderings of Oisin."

Danes or **The Danish Troop.** The Scandinavian invaders of Ireland, active from 800–1014, by which time the Irish kings and heroes overthrew the tyranny and regained control of Ireland. Edmund Curtis writes in *A History of Ireland* that "the traditional name for our Scandinavian invaders is 'the Danes,' but it is accepted that the greater part of them were Norwegian." See "The Grey Rock."

Dante Aligheri (1265–1321). In *A Vision*, Yeats places Dante in Phase 17 of the moon, where creative imagination is realized through antithetical emotion. This is the same phase in which Yeats places himself; it is the ideal phase, where Unity of Being is most possible. In his *Autobiography,* Yeats also wrote, "I thought that in man and race alike there is something called 'Unity of Being,' using that term as Dante used it when he compared beauty in the Convito to a perfectly proportioned body." In his poem "Ego Dominus Tuus" [*see* the entry for this Latin phrase drawn from Dante's *Vita Nuova*], Yeats associates Dante, "the chief imagination of Christendom," with the use of the poetic mask, the calling forth of one's opposite self, similar to Yeats's own use of mask. In his essay "Per Amica Silentia Lunae," Yeats says of Dante that "he celebrated the most pure lady poet ever sung and the Divine Justice, not merely because death took that lady and Florence banished her singer, but because he had to struggle in his own heart with his unjust anger and his lust." Further in the same essay, Yeats cites Boccaccio's remark that Dante found room for lechery among his virtues; and Guido Cavalcanti found too much baseness in his friend Dante. Dante exchanged sonnets with his friends, among them Lapo [q.v.], Gianni, and Guido [q.v.] Cavalcanti. Among these sonnets is one of Dante's subtitled, in the Rossetti translation which Yeats read, "He imagines a pleasant voyage for Guido, Lapo, Gianni, and himself, with their three ladies."

Yeats is especially fascinated with several of Dante's sayings: In the essay "A General Introduction to My Work," reprinted in *Essays and Introductions,* he again speaks of "that Unity of Being Dante compared to a perfectly proportioned human body." And Yeats says that that is part of his conception of "my Christ." And elsewhere he says it is his own definition of beauty. See the essay "A People's Theatre" in *Explorations.* Another of Dante's sayings that fascinated Yeats is "His Will is our Peace," a line that Spenser [q.v.] never equaled nor could Shelley [q.v.] ever say.

In his poem "Why Should Not Old Men Be Mad?" Yeats mentions, "A girl that knew all Dante once / Live to bear children to a dunce." This is often thought to be a reference to Maud Gonne and to her marriage to Major John MacBride, whom Yeats disliked and whom he called, in the poem "Easter 1916," a "drunken, vainglorious lout." But others think it may refer to Maud Gonne's daughter, Iseult, who had also rejected a marriage proposal from Yeats and married, unhappily, the writer Francis Stuart. See "Ego Dominus Tuus" and "Why Should Not Old Men Be Mad."

Daphne. A name Yeats uses for an ordinary woman who, nevertheless, may have her day with love or lovers. See "His Phoenix."

Dathi [do'he]. In Irish history, he is accounted the last king of pagan Ireland, reigning in the fifth century, A.D. According to legend, he died at the foot of the Alps, struck by lightning while on a foreign expedition, A.D. 428. His body was supposedly returned to Ireland and buried in Roscommon under a great pillar-stone which still stands. In the poem, Yeats uses only the name and gives the character a mystic and religious role. See "The Blessed."

Davis, Thomas Osborne (1814–45). A poet and essayist, Davis was one of the founders of the influential newspaper, *The Nation,* leader of the Young Ireland Party, and always a great inspiration to Irish nationalists. Yeats at one time hoped to edit the poems of Davis, as he indicated in a letter (June 1888) to his friend Katherine Tynan. In the essay "A General Introduction to My Work" (reprinted in *Essays and Introductions*) Yeats says it was John O'Leary [q.v.], Yeats's dear friend and mentor, who gave him the poems of Thomas Davis and who "spoke of other poets associated with Davis and *The Nation* newspaper, probably lent me their poems." Yeats did not have the highest regard for Davis's poetry and says it was their Young Ireland Society's criticism that "set Clarence Mangan [q.v.] at the head of the Young Ireland poets in place of Davis, and put Sir Samuel Ferguson [q.v.] next. On November 20, 1914, Yeats gave a lecture on Davis (Later published as *Tribute to Thomas Davis* [1947]) before the Students' National Literary Society at the Ancient Concert Rooms, after Trinity College had banned the program because Patrick Pearse was also scheduled to speak. In a pointed rebuke of the vice-provost who had banned the talks, Yeats made as his main point that Davis "was the foremost moral influence on our politics," a more real contribution than his poetry. He reiterated this in saying, in his essay "The Cutting of an Agate" that "Thomas Davis . . . had the moral simplicity which can give to actions the lasting influence that style alone can give to words." It is with these precepts in mind that Yeats expressed his desire to be counted one with Davis, Mangan, and Ferguson in the treatment of Irish subjects in an Irish fashion. (See Yeats's letter to the editor of *United Ireland* [September 10, 1892].) See "To Ireland in the Coming Times."

Dectora. A name found in Irish mythology, but used by Yeats as the name for a character in his play *The Shadowy Waters.* Dectora, in the play, is

the beautiful woman found on the captured ship and subdued by Forgael [q.v.], who finds himself in his love for Dectora. See "I Walked
Among Shadowy Waters" and the play itself.

De Danaan. *See* **Danaan.**

Deirdre [dear'dra]. The heroine of one of the great romances and trage-
dies of Irish legend, a vital episode in the Ulster, or Red Branch, cycle
of Irish mythology. At her birth, it was predicted that Deirdre's beauty
would one day bring death and sorrow to Ulster. Instead of being put
to death, however, she was shut away from the world. Later, Conchubar learned of her beauty and desired her to be his queen, but Deirdre
had fallen in love on sight with a young warrior named Naoise [q.v.].
Naoise consented to elope with her before she could be married to
Conchubar. Naoise and his two brothers, known as the children of
Usna [q.v.] carried Deirdre to Alba (Scotland). Later, persuaded by
Fergus that Conchubar had forgiven them, they returned to Ireland,
where Conchubar treacherously slew the children of Usna, and Deirdre
died of a broken heart. Because of this, Fergus broke with Conchubar;
and in the war that followed, huge numbers of warriors were killed,
fulfilling thus the dire prophecy of Deirdre's birth. Yeats wrote a play
on the subject, *Deirdre* (1907); and with Lady Gregory, he helped
finish *Deirdre of the Sorrows,* the play John Synge had left unfinished at
his death. See also "Baile and Aillinn."

Delacroix, Ferdinand Victor Eugene (1798–1863). Delacroix is generally considered to be among the greatest of French artists, especially
for color, composition, and draughtsmanship. His paintings are noted
as well for their sense of energy. See "A Nativity."

Delphic Oracle. The most famous oracle of the classical world, located in
Delphi, in Greece, at the foot of Mt. Parnassus. The oracle was housed
in Apollo's temple, constructed in the sixth century B.C. The prophecies are spoken by a priestess while in a trance and were interpreted
by temple priests, appropriate sacrifices accompanying the ritual. The
prophecies were famous for their ambiguity, being capable of more
than one interpretation. Yeats's poem "The Delphic Oracle upon Plotinus" is drawn from Stephen MacKenna's translation of Porphyry's *Life
of Plotinus.* See "The Delphic Oracle upon Plotinus" and "News for
the Delphic Oracle."

De Valera, Eamon (1882–1975). Irish statesman, born in New York of an Irish mother and a Spanish father, but raised in Ireland. Imprisoned for his part in the Easter Uprising of 1916, De Valera later became president of the extreme nationalist Sinn Fein; and in 1932 he became president of the Executive Council of the Irish Free State. In 1938, under the new constitution of the Irish Republic, he became prime minister, maintaining Ireland's strict neutrality in World War II. His party lost the election of 1948. Later, De Valera became president of Ireland. At first, Yeats did not have a high regard for de Valera, considering him a "loose-lipped demagogue" responsible for the civil war that broke out in the early twenties, when opposing factions of the Irish could not agree on the nature of the Irish Free State. Yeats, however, changed his opinion of De Valera, saying in a letter to Olivia Shakespeare (March 9, 1933), "I was impressed by his simplicity and honesty." See "Parnell's Funeral" and "The Statesman's Holiday."

Diarmuid [der'mid]. Yeats's spelling of the name in early editions of his work. Hero of one of the great but tragic romances of Irish legend, a vital story in the Finn, or White, cycle of Irish mythology. Diarmuid was the son of Donn and grandson of Duibhne [dwe'ne], but he was raised by Aengus, who protected him whenever he could. Diarmuid became a member and outstanding champion of the Fianna, the followers of Finn. According to legend, he had a "love-spot" on his forehead, which he usually kept covered, but no woman that saw it was able to refuse him her love. When the beautiful Grania saw the love-spot accidentally, she forsook her betrothal to Finn and eloped with Diarmuid, after she and some leading members of the Fianna talked him into it. Finn pursued them mercilessly across the countryside for sixteen years before making peace; and even then, years later, he lured Diarmuid into a fatal hunt for the Boar Without Bristles [q.v.], who was charged by a curse to bring Diarmuid to his death. Though Finn might have saved him but did not, Diarmuid was in effect killed by the boar. This myth parallels that of Adonis and of Attis in classical mythology. See "A Faery Song" and "Her Courage," which is poem VI of "Upon a Dying Lady."

Dick. A name used by Yeats, along with the name Tom, to suggest all the unthinking people who accepted without question the authenticity of the supposedly obscene personal diaries kept by the Irish nationalist Roger Casement [q.v.]. Many people have believed the diaries to be forgeries, but the British government has rarely permitted the originals to be seen, and questions remain. But so that Casement would receive little support in any effort to gain a reprieve before his execution (he was convicted of treason and hanged), copies of the diaries were circulated among certain eminent people, especially in America, where the strong Irish-American community might have pushed for a reprieve. The English poet Alfred Noyes, then teaching at Princeton, aided the British ambassador in showing the copies around. When interest in the case was revived in 1936, Yeats wrote his ballad "Roger Casement," in the original version of which there appeared the line "Come Alfred Noyes, come all the troop"; however, when Noyes responded in the Irish press with a letter explaining why he assumed the diaries to be authentic, Yeats called it a noble letter and immediately changed the line in the poem to "Come Tom and Dick, come all the troop." See "Roger Casement" and "The Ghost of Roger Casement."

Dionysius. God of vegetation and of wine and also patron of choral song and the drama. Sir James George Frazer, in *The New Golden Bough*, writes, "Like the other gods of vegetation . . . Dionysius was believed to have died a violent death, but to have been brought to life again; and his sufferings, death and resurrection were enacted in his sacred rites" (352). Frazer also recounts the Cretan myth wherein the young Dionysius is left by his father, Jupiter, in care of guards because of his wife Juno's jealous dislike of the child who was not her own. But Juno bribed the guards and lured the child into an ambush, where the Titans rushed upon him and cut him limb from limb and boiled and ate him. His virgin sister Minerva (Athene) [q.v.], who had shared in the murder, kept his heart and gave it to Jupiter on his return. Jupiter built a temple in the boy's honor. In other accounts, Dionysius arises from the dead and ascends to heaven, or Zeus (Jupiter) swallows his heart and begets him again by Semele [q.v.]. See song I in "Two Songs from a Play."

Donne, John (1572–1631). English poet and Dean of Saint Paul's, London. On November 14, 1912, Yeats wrote to Professor H. J. C. Grierson, editor that year of an edition of Donne's poetry. In the letter, Yeats said, "I want to thank you for your edition of Donne. It was very generous of you to send it to me. I have been using it constantly and find that at last I understand Donne. Your notes tell me exactly what I

want to know. Poems that I could not understand or could but understand are now clear and I notice that the more precise and learned the
thought the greater the beauty, the passion; the intricacy and subtleties
of his imagination are the length and depths of the furrow made by his
passion. His pedantry and his obscenity—the rock and the loam of his
Eden—but make me the more certain that one who is but a man like
us all has seen God." From this on, Donne is an important influence
on Yeats, no where more so than in poems collected in the volume
called *Responsibilities*. See also "To a Young Beauty."

Dooney. A country area, near Sligo town, located on the southwest shore
of Lough Gill, the lake in which the isle of Innisfree [q.v.] is situated.
The most notable feature of the Dooney area is a great rock. Though
fiddlers were to be found everywhere in the Irish countryside, there is
no available record of a particular one associated with Dooney. See
"The Fiddler of Dooney."

Doric. The oldest and most severely simple of the Greek orders of archi-
tecture. See song II of "Two Songs from a Play."

Dorothy. In Yeats's poem *His Phoenix,* he lists names, such as Dorothy,
for ordinary women, each of whom has had the privacy of her love. See
"His Phoenix."

Dowson, Ernest Christopher (1867–1900). English poet, good friend
of Yeats, and fellow member of the Rhymers' Club [*see* Cheshire
Cheese]. Of Dowson, Yeats wrote in his *Autobiography*, "I think Dowson's best verse immortal, bound, that is, to outlive famous novels and
plays and learned histories and other discursive things, but he was too
vague and gentle for my affections. I understand him too well, for I
had been like him but for the appetite that made me search out strong
condiments." Dowson, like his friend Lionel Johnson [q.v.], died very
young of gross self-neglect and dissipation. Yeats attempted to explain
some part of their misfortune in his lines:

> What portion in the world can the artist have,
> Who has awakened from the common dream,
> But dissipation and despair.

Those lines are from "Ego Dominus Tuus," but see also "The Grey
Rock."

Dromahair. The nearest town to Innisfree, eight miles from Sligo town.

The name is from the Irish, meaning the ridge of the air-demons. Dromahair was the village to which Yeats's grandfather, William Pollexfen [q.v.], came to join the milling and shipping enterprises of his widowed cousin, Mrs. William Middleton, marrying her daughter Elizabeth [q.v.] and becoming a partner in the Middleton-Pollexfen interests. See "The Man Who Dreamed of Faeryland."

Druid. The ancient order of Celtic priests. The Druids believed in the transmigration of souls and were versed in magic and the ability to prophesy. Every great chieftain of Irish legend maintained at least one Druid in his company. Fergus [q.v.] turns to his Druid when he wishes to abandon his kingship. The presence of the Druids is equally dominating in much of Yeats's early poetry. See "To the Rose upon the Rood of Time," "Fergus and the Druid," "Cuchulain's Fight with the Sea," "The Dedication to a Book of Stories Selected from the Irish Novelists," "To Ireland in the Coming Times," "The Secret Rose," "The Wanderings of Oisin," "The Old Age of Queen Maeve," "The Harp of Aengus," and "The Shadowy Waters."

Drumcliff. A large parish in county Sligo, less than four miles from Sligo town. The parish is a wide green valley at the foot of Ben Bulben. Yeats's great-grandfather, John Yeats [q.v.], was appointed to be rector at Drumcliff in 1805. The Church of Ireland church at Drumcliff had been built on the site of an old monastery, and the area is repeatedly mentioned in the oldest Irish records. The churchyard contains a sculptured Celtic cross, restored by John Yeats; and the cemetery there is, as he requested, the final resting place of the poet. The name Drumcliff is from the Irish, meaning the hill ridge of the baskets, after the cleeve, or basket, which from ancient times was used to carry turf or potatoes. See "Are You Content?" and "Under Ben Bulben."

Duddon. The name of a character appearing in old Hibernian tales. Yeats uses the name, along with Huddon and Daniel O'Leary, in two poems, one of which appeared only in *A Vision* as the forepiece to "Stories of Michael Robartes and His Friends: An Extract from a Record Made by His Pupils" in which the three appear as characters. The opening lines of the poem are "Huddon, Duddon and Daniel O'Leary / Delighted me as a child." And in a footnote, Yeats says that as a child he pronounced O'Leary to rhyme with dairy. But in an early Hibernian tale, which Yeats included in his *Irish Fairy and Folk Tales*, the names are given as "Hudden and Dudden and Donald O'Nery." The story is called "Donald and His Neighbours," and is a humorous account of how O'Nery outwits Hudden and Dudden in their efforts to ruin him, rob him, and kill him. In the opening section of the Michael Robartes piece in *A Vision*, Duddon is the narrator. See "Tom the Lunatic."

Dulac, Edmund. Artist and musician (1882–1953), close friend of Yeats and coworker with him on many projects. Of French origin, Dulac became an illustrator of English books and was particularly well-known for his illustrations for *The Arabian Nights' Entertainments* and for the *Rubáiyát of Omar Khayyám*. Dulac designed the masks for Yeats's play *At the Hawk's Well*, and other of Yeats's plays bear his contributions. Yeats's book *A Vision* is illustrated by a woodcut of the so-called medieval face of Giraldus which is actually a portrait of Yeats himself but with a beard. Dulac also did the diagram of the Great Wheel in *A Vision*. Dulac's painting of a centaur inspired Yeats's poem "On a Picture of a Black Centaur by Edmund Dulac."

Dutchman. A reference to William III of England (William of Orange), who defeated the exiled James II [q.v.] at the famous Battle of the Boyne in 1690. [*See* Billy.] See also "Pardon, Old Fathers."

E

Eade or **Eade's Grammar School.** The Church of Ireland's diocesan school in Sligo town near the Mall [q.v.]. William C. Eade was the principal during the years of Yeats's childhood. See "In Memory of Alfred Pollexfen."

Early or **Biddy Early.** A famous witch of county Clare. In his *Autobiography,* Yeats says that he would often mention Biddy Early's name to get peasants to talk freely to him when he was going about the countryside collecting their anecdotes. In *The Celtic Twilight,* Yeats writes of visiting Ballylee to ask residents about Biddy Early, "a wise woman that lived in Clare some years ago." See the dedicatory poem to *The Shadowy Waters* entitled "I Walked Among the Seven Woods of Coole."

Echtge [eht'ye]. Refers to Sliabh Echtge [slee'av eht'ye], a range of mountains on the borders of Galway and Clare. According to legend, the name of the range comes from Echtge, a lady of the Danaan [q.v.] folk. She married the cupbearer to the king of Connaught and brought with her two cows, remarkable for their milk-giving faithfulness. They were put to graze near a stream that rises on the slope of the mountain and flows into a lake near Gort in Galway. From this circumstance, the stream was called Abhainn-da-loilgheach [owen da lu lah], the river of the two milk cows. And the mountain took its name from the lady. See "The Withering of the Boughs."

Edain [aid'in]. A lovely lady of Irish legend. In old accounts of Edain, she was taken as wife by Midhir [me'yir], a king of the Sidhe [shee]. This aroused the jealousy of his first wife Fuamach [foo'a moy], who with the help of a druid, cast spells on Edain and drove her away. Aengus [q.v.] took her into his keeping and would not give her up to Midhir. In fact, he took such loving care of her that this too aroused the jealousy of Fuamach, who now arranged a peace meeting between Aengus and Midhir. While Aengus was at the meeting, Fuamach went

52

to his house and turned Edain into a fly, and with a blast of wind blew her away through the window. Aengus killed Fuamach, but he could not find Edain, who was blown about for seven years until she fell from a beam into a golden cup of wine and was swallowed by the wife of Etar, a king in Ireland. Nine months later, Etar's wife gave birth to a girl whom they chose to name Edain. Later, as a beautiful young lady, she was seen by Eochaid [yoh'ee], the high king of Ireland at Tara, who made her his queen. In Lady Gregory's account in her *Gods and Fighting Men*, it is Midhir who attempts to win back Edain through the ruse of making King Eochaid's brother fall in love with her—the substance of Yeats's poem "The Two Kings." Yeats, however, does not name the man of "Unnatural majesty" who comes for Edain, and in fact it is with Aengus that Yeats always associates Edain. In "The Wanderings of Oisin," Edain and Aengus are mentioned as the parents of Niamh [q.v.]; In "Baile and Aillinn," Edain is named as Midhir's wife, but the harp that Aengus plays was woven for him by Edain from Aengus's own hair, which is the account given of it by Yeats in "The Harp of Aengus." Aengus played this harp while Edain was a fly blown about on the wind, so that she would know he wept. It is this harp that Forgael [q.v.] plays in "The Shadowy Waters," where the vision of the wandering lovers, Aengus and Edain, appears to the sailors. See "The Wanderings of Oisin," "Baile and Aillinn," "The Harp of Aengus," "The Shadowy Waters," and "The Two Kings."

Edward or **Lord Edward Fitzgerald.** *See* **Fitzgerald.**

Ego Dominus Tuus. A sentence taken from Dante's *Vita Nuova* and translated as "I am Your God." Yeats would have known D. G. Rossetti's use of the words, in Latin, in Rossetti's *Poems and Translations,* but he would also have known Dante's context. See "Ego Dominus Tuus."

Eire [air'ah]. A mythical queen of the Danaan [q.v.] who gave her name to Ireland and from whom the present Irish Republic takes its Irish name. See "To the Rose upon the Road of Time" and "The Dedication to a Book of Stories Selected from the Irish Novelists."

Ellis, Edwin J. (1848–1918). Painter and poet and fellow member of the Rhymers' Club. Ellis was a friend of Yeats's father and shared a studio with him at one time. Also deeply interested in Blake, Ellis became collaborator with Yeats on *The Works of William Blake,* published in three volumes in 1893. In his essay "Ireland and the Arts," collected in *Essays and Introductions,* Yeats writes, "I once heard my friend Mr. Ellis say, speaking at a celebration in honor of a writer whose fame had not come till long after his death, 'It is not the business of a poet to make himself understood, but it is the business of the people to understand him. That they are at last compelled to do so is the proof of his authority.' " In his *Autobiography,* Yeats indicates no interest in Ellis's painting, but as to Ellis the poet, he says, "he had at times a nobility of rhythm—an instinct for grandeur." Yeats included Ellis's poem about Christ, entitled "Himself," in *The Oxford Book of Modern Verse, 1892–1935,* which he edited. Yeats dedicated "The Wanderings of Oisin" to Ellis.

Emain [avvin]. The capital of ancient Ulster, in full Emain Macha [avvin mah'a]. The name comes from the Irish eo, meaning pin, and muin, meaning neck, hence a neck pin or brooch. The name goes back to the limits of authentic Irish history. Three kings ruled, each for seven years in turn. When one of them died, his daughter, the celebrated Macha of the Golden Hair, insisted his turn of rule become hers. She was opposed by one of the remaining kings and his sons. She fought and won several battles with them, in one of which the opposing king was killed, and she assumed sovereignty, afterwards marrying the one surviving monarch. Instead of killing the sons of the king who had opposed her, she condemned them instead to slavery and ordered them to raise a rath, a circular fort, around her that would forever be the chief city of Ulster. In some old accounts, she herself marked out the area for the palace with the brooch of gold from her neck, and the name was thereafter applied to the palace. Patrick W. Joyce, in his *Irish Names of Places,* indicates that the remains of it are situated about a mile and a half west of Armagh. The great rath, or rampart of earth, is known today as Navan fort. See "The Madness of King Goll" and "Baile and Aillinn."

Emer [eem'er]. Some Irish speakers give the name as Eve'er, but Yeats rhymes it with schemer, so that is that. Emer became Cuchulain's wife. Lady Gregory, in her *Cuchulain of Muirthemne,* writes that Cuchulain thought Emer worth courting because she had the six gifts—"the gift of beauty, the gift of voice, the gift of sweet speech, the gift of needlework, the gift of wisdom, the gift of chastity." Yeats, in his poem "Crazy Jane on the Mountain," refers to "Great-bladdered Emer," and this is explained in a footnote in the "On the Boiler" section of *Explorations:* "In a fragment from some early version of, 'The Courting of Emer', Emer is chosen for the strength and volume of her bladder. This strength and volume were certainly considered signs of vigour. A woman of divine origin was murdered by her jealous rivals because she made the deepest hole in the snow with her urine." In his poem "Cuchulain's Fight with the Sea," Yeats makes Emer the mother of his son, but in his play *On Baile's Strand,* he has Aoife [q.v.] as the mother, which is in accord with traditional accounts. Again in his preface to *Cuchulain of Muirthemne,* Yeats writes, "And yet I think it may be proud Emer, Cuchulain's fitting wife, who will linger longest in the memory. What a pure flame burns in her always, whether she is the newly married wife fighting for precedence, fierce as some beautiful bird, or the confident housewife, who would awaken her husband from his magic sleep with mocking words; or the great queen who would get him out of the tightening net of his doom, by sending him into the Valley of the Dead, with Niamh [q.v.], his mistress [Yeats changes this name in his play *The Only Jealousy of Emer,* but it is Niamh in Lady Gregory's account.], because he will be more obedient to her; or the woman whom sorrow has sent with Helen and Iseult and Brunnhilde and Deirdre, to share their immortality in the rosary of the poets." See "Cuchulain's Fight with the Sea," "The Secret Rose," and "Crazy Jane on the Mountain."

Emery, Florence. The noted actress Florence Farr (1860–1917). Also an occultist, Florence Farr (Mrs. Edward Emery) was a leading actress of the London stage. Yeats said of her, in his *Autobiography,* that she had one great gift, "the most perfect poetical elocution." Among her famous roles was that of Mary Bruin in Yeats's play *The Land of Heart's Desire.* She also played Aleel, the poet, in his play *The Countess Cathleen;* and she was the star of George Bernard Shaw's *Arms and the Man* when it was first presented in London. Later, producers found it difficult to meet her salary demands, and she appeared infrequently, devoting more of her time to occult studies and to reciting poetry while accompanying herself on the psaltery. The musician Arnold Dolmetsch had made a version of this ancient instrument; and in his essay "Speaking to the Psaltery" [in *Essays and Introductions*], Yeats writes that Miss Farr "has sat with a beautiful stringed instrument upon her knee, her

fingers passing over the strings, and has spoken to me some verses from
Shelley's Skylark and Sir Ector's lamentations over the dead Launcelot
out of *Morte d'Arthur* and some of my own poems." When her looks
faded and illness began to ravage, she left England for Ceylon, where
she pursued Indian studies and taught in a native school, Ramanathan
College, where she died of cancer in 1917. In his volume entitled *Poems
1899–1905,* published in London and Dublin in 1906, Yeats included
the following dedication at the beginning of the "In the Seven Woods"
section [reprinted in Allt and Alspach]:

TO FLORENCE FARR

The only reciter of lyric poetry
who is always a delight, because
of the beauty of her voice and
the rightness of her method.

See "All Souls' Night."

Emmet, Robert (1778–1803). Great Irish patriot. Exiled because of his
nationalistic activities, Emmet returned to Ireland from France to lead
an abortive uprising against the English. When he went to Dublin to
be near his beloved, Sarah Curran, he was captured, brought to trial,
and sentenced to be hanged, his head to be severed from his body. His
courageous speech from the dock inspired generations of Irishmen and
made Emmet a great national hero. Unlike Parnell [q.v.], whom Yeats
felt was "murdered" by his own people, Emmet, as also Fitzgerald
[q.v.] and Tone [q.v.], met death at the hands of "strangers," that is,
the English. Emmet's last words at his trial were:

Let no man write my epitaph; for as no man who knows my
motives now dares vindicate them, let not prejudice or ignorance asperse them. Let them rest in obscurity and peace. Let
my memory be left in oblivion, and my tomb remain unin-
scribed, until other times and other men can do justice to my
character. When my country takes her place among the nations
of the earth, then, and not till then, let my epitaph be written.
I have done.

On the gallows he added, "My friends, I die in peace, and with senti-
ments of universal love and kindness toward all men." Yeats wrote in

his *Autobiography*, "My great-grandfather [*see* John Yeats] had been Robert Emmet's friend and was suspected and imprisoned though but for a few hours." The exact spot of Emmet's execution is still marked in Thomas Street in Dublin. The epitaph still remains unwritten. See "Pardon, Old Fathers," "September 1913," "Parnell's Funeral," "Three Songs to the Same Tune," and "Three Marching Songs."

Empedocles (ca. 495–ca. 435 B.C.). Greek philosopher who taught that the four elements—fire, water, earth, and air—were composed of material particles that were indestructible. He believed that harmony and discord worked on all the elements as opposing forces, resulting in change and in the phenomena of the world. Yeats refers to Empedocles frequently in *A Vision*, where the words suggest elements of Yeats's ideas of the mask and the gyres. He writes: "Empedocles and Heraclitus thought that the universe had first one form and then its opposite in perpetual alteration." (See particularly "Book I: The Great Wheel," in *A Vision*.) Empedocles is said to have ended his life by throwing himself into the crater of Mt. Etna. See "The Gyres."

Eochaid [yo'hee]. A king of Ireland at Tara [q.v.], sometimes referred to in old accounts as Eochaid the Ploughman, to distinguish him from others of that name. The pronunciation of his name given here is the one given by Yeats in a footnote to the earliest version of his poem "The Two Kings." [*See also* Edain.] And see "The Two Kings."

Ephesian. A reference to the Seven Sleepers of Ephesus. Ephesus, an ancient Greek city in Lydia, was renowned as a center of early Christian activity. In A.D. 250, Decius Caius Messius Quintus Trojanus began his persecutions of Christians; and according to legend, seven young men fled the city and hid in a nearby cave, where they slept for two hundred years, when they suddenly awakened. It was claimed that God had caused the sleep as proof of resurrection, and the incident is said to have kept Theodosius II from losing his faith. If the seven sleepers had a barrel of wine in the cave with them, as Yeats indicates, there is no indication of it in the usual accounts. For a further reference by Yeats to the Seven Sleepers of Ephesus, see the letter he wrote to Henry James on August 20, 1915 (in the Wade edition of the Yeats letters). See "On a Picture of a Black Centaur by Edmund Dulac."

Ercole. The duke of Ferrara [q.v.]. Both Ercole d'Este I (1431–1505) and Ercole d'Este II (1508–1559) were friends and patrons of the poet

Lodovico Ariosto (1474–1533), as were other members of the Este
family of Ferrara, including Alfonso I d'Este (1486–1534) and
Cardinal Ippolito d'Este (1479–1520). Ariosto, most famous for his
Orlando Furioso (first published in 1516), was also translator of Plautus
[q.v.] and Terence, the Roman dramatists; and Ariosto often made
plays of his own from parts of the earlier dramatists' works. For his
work in the drama, Ariosto is often credited with reviving theatre in
Italy. His play *I Suppositi,* a patchwork from the comedies of Plautus
and Terence, influenced Shakespeare's *Taming of the Shrew,* by way of
George Gascoigne's adaptation called *The Supposes.* Other artists who
received the patronage of the dukes of Ferrara are Petrarch, Boiardo,
and Tasso. The rulers of Ferrara are frequently referred to in Baldasar
Castiglione's *Book of the Courtier,* which Yeats's great friend Lady Gregory read to him at the end of each day's work in the summer of 1904.
It was Duke Ercole I who had five plays of Plautus performed during
the wedding celebrations of his son Alfonso I to Lucrezia Borgia in
1502, the plays translated for his patron by Ariosto. Yeats regarded
such patrons of the arts as Ercole, Guidobaldo [q.v.], and Cosimo [q.v.]
with respect for the manner in which they used their wealth for the
higher good without concession to public taste. Thus the contempt he
expressed in a letter to Hugh Lane [q.v.], dated January 1, 1913 (in
Wade), for the general argument of a wealthy man (such as Lord Ardilaun) "that they should not give unless there is a public demand." The
reference to Lord Ardilaun is to Sir Arthur Guinness, second baronet,
first Baron Ardilaun (1840–1915) who was head of the famous Guinness brewery, founded by his grandfather. Actually, he was a famous
philanthropist and public benefactor. Dublin owes him its St. Stephen's
Green, a truly handsome public park, where a statue of him was erected
in 1891 by public subscription. But when asked for a second subscription to the fund that would have brought Hugh Lane's art collection
permanently to Dublin and housed in a new museum that would span
the Liffey River, he said no, unless there was a public demand for the
art. This occasioned Yeats's bitter but triumphant poem; yet in that
same letter to Hugh Lane, Yeats says that "the 'correspondent' to
whom the poem is addressed is of course an imaginary person." See
that poem entitled "To a Wealthy Man Who Promised a Second Subscription to the Dublin Municipal Gallery if It Were Proved the People
Wanted Pictures."

Esserkelly. The name of a parish in county Galway, usually spelled Isert-kelly, as in *Lady Gregory's Journals*. The name Isertkelly means Kelly's hermitage. The term isert actually derives from the Latin desertum. It came to mean in Irish a sequestered place or a desert wilderness. In an ecclesiastical sense, it was used to denote a hermitage, the kind of secluded spot the early Irish saints loved to select for their little, remote dwellings. Isertkelly was an ancient church that subsequently gave its name to the parish. See "In Memory of Major Robert Gregory."

Europa. A Phoenician princess to whom Europe owes its name. Zeus fell in love with the beautiful Europa and approached her as a white bull, so that his wife Hera could not discern his activities. He enticed Europa on to his back and carried her off from Phoenicia to Crete, where he ravished her. Two of her sons by Zeus became famous, Minos [q.v.] and Rhadamanthus [q.v.], and after judicial lives on earth became the judges of the dead in Hades. See "Crazy Jane Reproved," poem II of "Words for Music Perhaps."

Eurotas. River of ancient Sparta in Greece. On the banks of the Eurotas, Leda [q.v.], wife of Tyndareus, king of Sparta, was visited by Zeus in the form of a swan. [*See* "Leda and the Swan."] From their union, according to mythological accounts, Leda brought forth two eggs. From the eggs came Helen [q.v.] of Troy and Clytemnestra, who became the wife of Agamemnon [q.v.], and the twin heroes Castor and Pollux, who became the sign of Gemini in the zodiac. See "Lullaby," which is poem XVI of "Words for Music Perhaps."

Everest, Mount. The highest peak on earth. Located in the northeastern Himalayan Mountains on the Tibet-Nepal border, the mountain is over 29,000 feet high. It was named for a famous surveyor, Sir George Everest. Religious pilgrimages to both Mount Everest and Mount Kailas, also known as Mount Meru [q.v.], still occur. See "Meru," which is poem XII of "Supernatural Songs."

Ezekiel. The prophet of the Old Testament who had a vision of the throne-chariot of God. In the vision, he sees the magnificence of the cherubim who are guiding the chariot: "Then the glory of the Lord went forth from the threshold of the house, and stood over the cherubim. And the cherubim lifted up their wings and mounted up from the earth in my sight as they went forth, with the wheels beside them; and they stood at the door of the east gate of the house of the Lord' and the glory of the God of Israel was over them. (*Ezekiel* 10:18–19, but *see also Ezekiel* chap. 1 and all of chap. 10, King James Version). It may be of interest to note that in his poem "Vacillations" VIII, where it now reads "Isaiah's coal," Yeats had "Ezekiel's coal," changing it after the first publication. See "To a Young Beauty."

F

Falias. One of the four great legendary cities established in Lochlann, the early Irish name for Scandinavia [*see* Loughlan] by the Tuatha de Danaan [*see* Danaan], in which science and the varied arts were taught to the youth of the country. The other three cities were Findrias, Gorias, and Murias. Geoffrey Keating in *The History of Ireland* explains that after they had been in these cities for a while, they proceeded to the north of Scotland, and thence to Ireland, bringing with them the treasured cauldron, spear, stone, and sword. The stone, called Lia Fail (stone of destiny), was brought from Falias. Later, this stone was taken back to Scotland from Ireland so that Fergus, son of Earc, could sit on it and be proclaimed king of Scotland. Still later, it was forcibly taken from the Abbey of Scone and brought to England by Edward I, to be used as the coronation seat. The Stone of Scone, as it then came to be called, is still used as the inaugural seat of English monarchs. The sword, brought from Gorias, and the spear, from Findrias, were those used by Lugh [loo], a king of the Danaan for forty years. Of the cauldron, brought from Murias, it was said that a company would never go away from it unsatisfied. From the stone Lia Fail one of the names of Ireland was derived [*see* Eire]. See "Baile and Aillinn."

Fand [fan]. A Danaan goddess, and as such capable of changing to a bird or animal or fish. Fand was the wife of Manannan [q.v.], the master of the sea and of the islands of the dead. Cuchulain was Fand's lover for a brief period. Yeats, in notes to *The Wind Among the Reeds* (reprinted in Allt and Alspach) said:

> I have imagined Cuchulain meeting Fand "walking among flaming dew." The story of their love is one of the most beautiful of our tales. Two birds, bound one to another with a chain of gold, came to a lake side where Cuchulain and the host of

Uladh [q.v.] was encamped, and sang so sweetly that all the host fell into a magic sleep. Presently they took the shape of two beautiful women, and cast a magical weakness upon Cuchulain, in which he lay for a year. At the year's end an Aengus, who was probably Aengus [q.v.], the master of love, one of the greatest of the children of the goddess Danu, came and sat upon his bedside, and sang how Fand, the wife of Manannan, the master of the sea, and of the islands of the dead, loved him; and that if he would come into the country of the gods where there were wine and gold and silver, Fand and Laban [q.v.], her sister, would heal him of his magical weakness. Cuchulain went to the country of the gods, and after being for a month the lover of Fand, made her a promise to meet her at a place called "the yew of the Strand's End," and came back to earth. Emer, his mortal wife, won his love again, and Manannan came to "the yew at the Strand's End," and carried Fand away. When Cuchulain saw her going, his love for her fell upon him again, and he went mad, and wandered among the mountains without food or drink, until he was at last cured by a Druid drink of forgetfulness.

Yeats makes further use of the material of this story in his play *The Only Jealousy of Emer.* See "The Secret Rose" and "Under the Moon."

Fenians. The name ascribed to the great military order of which Finn [q.v.] was chief. In his *Literary History of Ireland,* however, Douglas Hyde explains that the ancient bands of militia were called Fianna [fee'a na], the plural form of fian, meaning a warrior band, and that the resemblance to the proper name Finn is only accidental. The poet Thomas Moore brought the word into common use in his melody "The wine-cup is circling in Alvin's hall" [*see* Almhuin], where Moore uses the form Finnian. Hyde says that it was John O'Mahoney, of the Irish Republican Brotherhood, who succeeded in perpetuating the ancient historic memory by christening the "men of '68" the Fenians. John O'Leary [q.v.], a member of the Fenians of 1868, was exiled for this; but when allowed to return, he became a great friend of the young Yeats and a great influence upon him. See "The Wanderings of Oisin."

Fergus. Yeats, in his notes to the 1895 edition of *Poems* (reprinted in Allt and Alspach), describes Fergus as the poet of the Red Branch [q.v.] or Ulster cycle of Irish mythology. He says, "He was once a king of all Ireland, but he gave up his throne that he might live at peace hunting in the woods." In his notes to the poem "The Secret Rose," Yeats writes:

> I have founded "the proud dreaming king" upon Fergus, the son of Rogh [roy], the legendary poet of "the quest of the bull of Cualnge," [see Brown Bull, Cuchulain, and Maeve], as he is in the ancient story of Deirdre [q.v.] and in the modern poems by Ferguson [q.v.]. He marries Nessa [q.v.], and Ferguson makes him tell how she took him "captive in a single look." Presently, because of his great love, he gave up his throne to Conchobar [see Conchubar], her son by another, and lived out his days feasting, and fighting, and hunting. His promise never to refuse a feast of a certain comrade [see Barach], and the mischief that came by his promise [see Usna], and the vengeance he took afterwards, are a principal theme of the poets. I have explained my imagination of him in "Fergus and the Druid," and in a little song in the second act of *The Countess Kathleen*.

[The song was later removed from the play and is the poem "Who Goes with Fergus?" Yeats also changed Kathleen to Cathleen. See "To the Rose upon the Road of Time," "Fergus and the Druid," "Who Goes with Fergus?" "The Wanderings of Oisin," and "The Old Age of Queen Maeve."

Ferguson, Sir Samuel (1810–86). Irish poet and scholar. Ferguson is one of the three Irish poets Yeats admired for the contribution to the revival of interest in Irish literature, the other two being Thomas Davis [q.v.] and James Clarence Mangan [q.v.]. In a letter dated February 27, 1885 (in Wade), Yeats listed Ferguson's *Lays of the Western Gael* among the best books of Irish imagination. One of Ferguson's well-known poems, adapted from Irish folk material, is "Pastheen Finn," often set to music. Yeats drew upon this material and the tune in the first of his "Two Songs Rewritten for the Tune's Sake." (See that poem and also the entry here for Paistin Finn.) In his *Autobiography*, Yeats writes that his hope in founding the National Literary Society had been "to denounce the propagandist verse and prose that had gone by the name of Irish literature, and to substitute for it certain neglected writers: Sir Samuel Ferguson, a writer of ballads dry in their eighteenth century sincerity." See "To Ireland in the Coming Times."

Ferrara. A commune and city in Italy, fifty-seven miles southwest of Venice and the seat of the dukes of Ferrara, famous as patrons of Ariosto, Boiardo, Petrarch, and Tasso. [*See* Ercole.] Yeats's familiarity with Ferrara was largely derived from his knowledge of Castiglione's *Book of the Courtier,* first read to him by Lady Gregory on one of his early stays at Coole. See "The People."

Findrias. A legendary city of Lochland. [*See* Falias for a detailed account of its significance.] See also "Baile and Aillinn."

Finn. His full name is Finn MacCumhal [generally pronounced **coo'al** or **cool'**]. Finn succeeded his father Cushal [coo'al] as leader of the Fianna [*see* Fenians], and as its great hero and leader, Finn is the central figure of the Fianna or White cycle of mythological stories, quite as Cuchulain is of the Red Branch. But Finn also parallels Conchubar, especially for his role in the story of Diarmuid and Grania, the counterpart of Conchubar's role in the story of Deirdre and the Sons of Usna. Finn is the father of Oisin [q.v.]. See "The Wanderings of Oisin."

Firbolg [fir bol'leg]. An early mythological race in Ireland who warred with and lost to another mythological band called the Fomoroh. Yeats does not use the name Fomoroh in any of his poems, but they are present in his symbols of night, death, and cold, and in their connection with the Shadowy Horses [q.v.]. In his notes to the 1895 edition of *Poems* (reprinted in Allt and Alspach), Yeats says, "Fomoroh means under the sea, and is the name of the gods of night and death and cold." He says they were grossly misshapen and the giants and the leprechauns are of the Fomoroh. The Fomoroh ruled until the coming of the Danaan [q.v.]. Grave mounds of the Firbolg are still to be seen in Ireland. See "The Wanderings of Oisin."

Fitzgerald or **Edward Fitzgerald** or **Lord Edward.** Lord Edward Fitzgerald (1763–98), Irish patriot. As a member of the United Irishmen in 1798, Lord Edward went to France to secure French aid for an Irish uprising. He was betrayed and, on his return, was captured by the English, dying of the wounds he received during the capture. Yeats considered that Fitzgerald, Robert Emmet, and Wolfe Tone [q.v.] were all killed by "strangers," that is, the English, but that Parnell owed his death to the Irish themselves. See "September 1913," "Sixteen Dead Men," and "Parnell's Funeral."

Fool. Reference to a character in Yeats's play *On Baile's Strand*. In the play, the Fool steals the food which the Blind Man eats. The Fool and the Blind Man symbolize the end of a cycle. See "The Circus Animals' Desertion."

Forgael. The central character in Yeats's poetic drama *The Shadowy Waters*. Richard Ellmann, in *The Identity of Yeats*, says of Forgael that he was a sea king of ancient Ireland who was promised a love of supernatural intensity. This love was Dectora, and in some interpretations he represents the seeker of Death and she the seeker of Life. In their union is perfect humanity. See the dedicatory poem to *The Shadowy Waters*, "I Walked Among the Seven Woods of Coole," and the play itself.

The Forged Casement Diaries. The title of a book by Dr. William J. Maloney [q.v.] in defense of Roger Casement [q.v.]. On November 15, 1936, in a letter to his friend Ethel Mannin (in Wade), Yeats wrote, "I am in a rage. I have just got a book by the Talbot Press called *The Forged Casement Diaries*. It is by a Dr. Maloney. I knew him in New York and he has spent years collecting evidence. He has proved that the diaries, supposed to prove Casement 'a Degenerate' and successfully used to prevent an agitation for his reprieve, were forged." See "Roger Casement."

Foxhunter. A character in Charles Kickham's novel *Knocknagow or The Homes of Tipperary*, which Yeats acknowledges he borrowed for his ballad. (See his notes to *The Countess Cathleen* and *Various Legends and Lyrics, 1892,* reprinted in Allt and Alspach.) The incident in the novel is of an old foxhunter who takes a last look at his faithful hunting hounds until tears and sighs make it impossible. When an old, blind hound raises its head and howls and the other hounds take up the cry, the old foxhunter dies. See "The Ballad of the Foxhunter."

French, Mrs. A lady who, in the eighteenth century, lived in the vicinity of Yeats's tower, Thoor Ballylee [q.v.]. In the notes to his poem "The Tower," Yeats writes, "Mrs. French lived in Peterswell in the eighteenth century and was related to Sir Jonah Barrington, who described the incident of the ears and the trouble that came of it." The incident in Yeats's poem tells of a serving man who could divine Mrs. French's every wish, "Ran with the garden shears / Clipped an insolent farmer's ears / And brought them in a little covered dish." See "The Tower."

Fuller, Loïe (1862–1928). An American dancer, born in Illinois. Loïe Fuller achieved fame in America and abroad. With her company of dancers, she was especially noted for her serpentine and Chinese dances, for which she used colored lights, draperies, and other special effects. She taught dancing in Paris, where she was a great favorite, the subject of an illustration by Toulouse-Lautrec, and a long study by Mallarmé. Frank Kermode, whose book *Romantic Image* uses the Thomas Theodor Heine drawing of Loïe Fuller as frontispiece, writes, "Loïe Fuller was valued not only by devotees of art nouveau for the exotic naturalism of her dancing, but by Symbolists as the finest example of the use of the dance as an emblem of the Image of art." In his poem, Yeats likens the whirling of her dance to the whirling of the Platonic Year. (See "The Great Year of the Ancients" in *A Vision*.) The Toulouse-Lautrec drawing of Loïe Fuller is reproduced in *W. B. Yeats: Images of a Poet* by D. J. Gordon. Loïe Fuller's autobiography, published in 1913, is called *Fifteen Years of a Dancer's Life*. See "Nineteen Hundred and Nineteen."

Furies or **Proud Furies**. Also called the Erinyes, the Eumenides, or the Dirae, the Furies were three goddesses of Greek mythology. The three were Maegaera, the envious; Tisifone, the avenger; and Alecto, the unceasing. They were frequently pictured in black with serpents entwined in their hair and blood dripping from their eyes. Their function was to pursue and torment criminals, particularly those guilty of murder, perjury, disrespect, and disobedience. Their most famous appearance in classical literature is in the last play of Aeschylus's *Oresteia,* "The Eumenides." In his poem, Yeats seems to see them as a symbol of proud, reaching, creative women, such as his friend Dorothy Wellesley. See "To Dorothy Wellesley."

G

Gabhra [gow're]. Near Tara, the site of a bloody battle in which the Fiana and the forces of the King of Ireland slaughtered each other almost to extermination. Oscar [q.v.], son of Oisin [q.v.], and grandson of Finn, fell in the battle. Among the survivors were Caoilte [q.v.] and Oisin. Lady Gregory gives a vivid account of the battle in her *Gods and Fighting Men*. In the poem "The Secret Rose," Yeats writes of "Him who drove the gods out of their liss." This is a reference to Caoilte, who was driven mad when almost all his companions were killed at the battle of Gabhra. And in "The Wanderings of Oisin," Yeats has the lines "We think . . . on the heroes lying slain on Gabhra's raven-covered plain." See "The Wanderings of Oisin."

Gabriel. The archangel frequently depicted blowing his trumpet to announce the Second Coming and the Day of Judgment. In his *Autobiography*, Yeats writes of a time in Sligo when his uncle George Pollexfen was ill and in a state of delirium. He told Yeats that he saw red dancing figures, and Yeats immediately imagined the cabalistic symbol of water. His uncle then spoke and said that there was a river running through the room, and then said he could sleep. "I told him what I had done and that, if the dancing figures came again, he was to bid them go in the name of the Archangel Gabriel. Gabriel is angel of the Moon in the Cabbala and might, I considered, command the waters at a pinch." He further tells that "the delirium did not return." See "The Happy Townland."

Gaby (Gabrielle) Deslys (1884–1920). The *Oxford Companion to the Theatre* describes Gaby Deslys as "a celebrated French singer and music hall artist, around whom some fantastic stories have accumulated, particularly the tale of her famous pearls, said to have caused a revolution in Portugal, from whence she escaped in a haycart." Her first appearance in London was in 1906 and her last in 1917. See "His Phoenix."

Galilee and **Galilean.** The region in northern Israel, and the chief location of Christ's ministry, hence his appellation, the Galilean. Nazareth and Cana are among the towns of Galilee frequently mentioned in the Gospels. The Sea of Galilee is a freshwater lake in the region. The Galilean turbulence is Yeats's metaphor for the birth of Christ, whose life on earth ends the Greek cycle that preceded the Christian cycle. See "A Prayer on Going into My House" and song II of "Two Songs from a Play."

Gallery. A reference to the National Gallery of Ireland, in Dublin, where hang the portraits of Luke Wadding [q.v.], the Ormondes [q.v.], and the Earl of Strafford [q.v.]. The National Gallery is distinct from the Municipal Gallery [q.v.] of Dublin, now known as the Hugh Lane [q.v.] Municipal Gallery. See "Demon and Beast."

Galway. City and county in the west of Ireland. A well-known racecourse is located in Galway. The Galway races, however, that Yeats refers to, were held on the open beach, or strand, as illustrations indicate. One such illustration is by the poet's artist brother, Jack Butler Yeats. In county Galway are such places of importance to Yeats as his tower, Thoor Ballylee [q.v.]; Coole Park [q.v.], the estate of Lady Gregory, the great house of which no longer exists; and the town of Gort [q.v.]. See "At Galway Races," "In Memory of Major Robert Gregory," and "Colonel Martin." See also the footnote to the second of his "Three Marching Songs," where he indicates that "airy" may be an old pronunciation of "eerie," often heard in Galway and Sligo.

George. Yeats's preferred name for his wife. Yeats met her around 1911, after he had made the acquaintance of Olivia Shakespeare's brother, a Mr. Tucker, and his wife, the former Mrs. Hyde-Lees of Pickhill Hall, Wrexham. Later, he visited the Tuckers at Lynton in Devonshire and there met Mrs. Tucker's daughter by her first marriage, Miss Georgie Hyde-Lees. He met her with some frequency over the next five years and married her on October 21, 1917, in the Register Office at Harrow Road, London, with Ezra Pound as best man. In his biography of Yeats (*W. B. Yeats*), Joseph Hone says that shortly thereafter, in a letter to his father, Yeats wrote of his wife saying, "I call her George to avoid Georgie which she has been called hitherto in spite of her protests." It was for his wife that Yeats restored the tower residence Thoor Ballylee, close to the estate of Lady Gregory. Hone also reports a letter to Lady

Gregory in which Yeats writes: "My wife is a perfect wife, kind, wise, and unselfish. I think you were such another young girl once. She has made my life serene and full of order." See "To Be Carved on a Stone at Thoor Ballylee."

George, Saint. Supposedly an official in the army of Diocletian (A.D. 245–316), Saint George suffered martyrdom ca. A.D. 303. His most famous depiction is as the slayer of a dragon that had been molesting the people of Lydda. Two others are Bordone's in the National Gallery and the altarpiece at Ferrara by Cosimo Tuva. Patron saint of soldiers, Saint George is also patron saint of England. See "Her Triumph," which is poem IV of "A Woman Young and Old."

Gilligan, Father Peter. A character of an old folk tale. Yeats in his notes to the poem given in early editions (and reprinted in Allt and Alspach) says his ballad is "founded on the Kerry version of an old folk tale" and also says the original is a "tradition among the poeple of Castleisland, Kerry. See "The Ballad of Father Gilligan."

Giorgione. (ca. 1478–1510). Venetian painter, born in Castelfranco, also known as Giorgio Barberelli. Giorgione's influence on fifteenth-century Venetian painting was considered of great importance. Among the prints that Yeats admired in the room he occupied at Coole [q.v.] was one by Giorgione, as Yeats writes in his *Autobiography*. In *A Vision*, Yeats presents Giorgione as an example of his phase fourteen, saying that "at Phase 14 and Phase 16 the greatest human beauty becomes possible." See "Her Courage," which is poem VI of "Upon a Dying Lady."

Glasnevin. The famous cemetery of Dublin, wherein are buried some of Ireland's most famous men, among them the poet James Clarence Mangan [q.v.]; the Irish hero Daniel O'Connell [see Great Comedian]; Charles Stewart Parnell [q.v.]; many heroes of the 1916 Easter Uprising; and, in more recent times, the bones of Roger Casement [q.v.]. Glasnevin Cemetery is also famous as the locale of the "Hades" section of James Joyce's *Ulysses*. The district of Glasnevin itself was where, at one time, Addison, Steele, Swift, Sheridan, and Parnell had residences. Yeats conceives of the shade of Parnell coming from his grave only to discover an unchanged Ireland where a man such as Hugh Lane [q.v.], "Of your own passionate serving kind," receives only insult for his efforts to raise Irish cultural levels, particularly from "an old foul

mouth, brazen throat" such as William Martin Murphy, the publisher
whose newspapers attacked Lane, as earlier they had attacked Parnell.
See "To a Shade."

Glen-Car. A beautiful valley, lake, and waterfall east of Drumcliff [q.v.],
at the county borders of Leitrim and Sligo. Yeats refers to Glen-Car in
his poem "Towards Break of Day," when he says,

> I thought: "There is a waterfall
> Upon Ben Bulben side
> That all my childhood counted dear;
> Were I to travel far and wide
> I could not find a thing so dear.

The Glen-Car waterfall forms on Ben Bulben [q.v.] and comes down
into the Glen-Car lake in the valley. The name Glen-Car means Glen
of the rock. See "The Stolen Child."

Glendalough [glen da loch]. From the Irish, meaning valley of the two
lakes, Glendalough is a not uncommon name for sites with two lakes
near each other. There are places of that name in Waterford, Kerry, and
Galway, the latter familiar to Yeats. But the most famous Glendalough
is in county Wicklow, south of Dublin, where the ruins of a great
monastery, founded by Saint Kevin, remain, including a great round
tower. In October 1917, Yeats returned to Ireland with his wife, and
they visited the Wicklow Glendalough. See "Under the Round Tower"
and "Stream and Sun at Glendalough."

Goban. The smith and brewer of the Danaan [q.v.] folk. It was the ale
brewed by Goban that kept the Danaan folk perpetually young. His
name, which means smith, is also given as Goibniu [gwiv'ni u]. Yeats
seems also to associate Goban with the mountain Ben Bulben [q.v.],
which name is a corruption of Binn-Gulbain, meaning Gulban's peak.
See "The Grey Rock" and "The Hour Before Dawn."

Golden Age. The particular golden age referred to by Yeats is the Hindu
Krita Yuga, the golden part of the Hindu cycle, where all is good and
unadulterated. As explained by the Hindu scholar John Alphonso, this
is followed in the cycle by Treta Yuga, when three-fourths of all is still
unadulterated good; then follows Dwapara Yuga, the period of half
good and half bad; and finally becomes Kali Yuga, the period when the
bad dominates the good until destruction comes and a new cycle be-

gins. Nine such cycles have occurred, and the present time is in the Kali Yuga of the tenth cycle. Yeats, in his use of Golden Age, may have the golden period in an earlier Krita Yuga in mind; but because jealousy was nonexistent in the Krita, his usage may be simply to a more glorious past. See "Anashuya and Vijaya."

Golden Peak. The hamadri, or golden mountain, one of the three peaks of Mount Meru [q.v.]. The Golden Peak is said to have shone like the sunrise, and the birds upon it had feathers of gold. See "Anashuya and Vijaya."

Golden Race. The race of mighty Zeus, which include Minos, Rhadamanthus, Plato, and Pythagoras, all of whose entries here are worth referring to. See "The Delphic Oracle upon Plotinus."

Goldsmith, Oliver (1728–1774). Poet, dramatist, and novelist. Born in county Roscommon in Ireland, Goldsmith was educated in Trinity College, Dublin, following which he studied medicine in Scotland and on the Continent. His most famous works are his novel, *The Vicar of Wakefield* (1766); his play, *She Stoops to Conquer* (1773); and his long poem, *The Deserted Village* (1770). Goldsmith was of that group of Irish Protestant writers and public figures whom Yeats deeply admired and of whom he wrote that England had stung their own thought into expression and made it lucid. [*See* Berkeley and also Yeats's essay on Berkeley in *Essays and Introductions*.] See "The Seven Sages" and "Blood and the Moon."

Goll [gul]. A legendary king of Ireland. In his notes to the 1895 edition of *Poems* (reprinted in Allt and Alspach), Yeats writes of him, "In the legend King Goll hid himself in a valley near Cork, where it is said all the madmen of Ireland would gather were they free, so mighty a spell did he cast over the valley." When Yeats was twenty, his father had painted him as King Goll, "tearing the strings out [of] a harp, being insane with youth, but looking very desirable . . . with dreamy eyes and a great mass of black hair," as Yeats described it in a letter to Olivia Shakespeare, May 26, 1924 (in Wade). The illustration accompanied the poem when it was published in *The Leisure Hour* magazine in September 1887, the first poem of Yeats's to be published in England. In his preface to Lady Gregory's *Gods and Fighting Men,* Yeats writes of the great courtesy of the old heroes and notes "Goll, old and savage, and letting himself die of hunger in a cave because he is angry and sorry, can speak lovely words to the wife whose help he refuses." See "The Madness of King Goll."

Gonne, Maud. Irish patriot and actress whose famed beauty and unswerving devotion to Irish nationalism inspired and profoundly affected Yeats's entire life from the moment he met her. In his *Autobiography,* Yeats recounts the moment of their first meeting in 1889:

> Presently a hansom drove up to our door at Bedford Park with Miss Maud Gonne, who brought an introduction to my father from old John O'Leary [q.v.], the Fenian leader. She vexed my father by praise of war, war for its own sake, not as the creator of certain virtues but as if there were some virtue in excitement itself. I supported her against my father, which vexed him the more, though he might have understood that . . . a young man as I could not have differed from a woman as beautiful and so young. Today [1922], with her great height and the unchangeable lineaments of her form, she looks like the Sybil I would have had played by Florence Farr [*see* Emery], but in that day she seemed a classical impersonation of the Spring, the Virgilian commendation "She walks like a goddess" made for her alone. Her complexion was luminous, like that of apple blossoms through which the light falls, and I remember her standing that first day by a great heap of such blossoms in the window.

As early as 1892, Yeats, as correspondent for the Boston *Pilot,* did an article on Maud Gonne, saying, "Thousands who come to see this new wonder—a beautiful woman who makes speeches—remain to listen with delight to her sincere and simple eloquence." [This article is reproduced in *Letters to the New Island,* edited by Horace Reynolds.] Although Yeats mentions Maud Gonne by name only once in his poetry, her presence dominates much of his verse. She is also much written about in his autobiographical writings. See especially the chapter called "The Stirring of the Bones," in the section called "The Trembling of the Veil." Yeats continuously brought her into his poetry as his central symbol of beauty, whether he called her Helen, Leda, Pallas Athene, the Countess Cathleen, rose, phoenix, or any other named or nameless image of beauty. And Yeats wrote plays as well as poems with Maud

Gonne in mind. He finished his play *The Countess Cathleen* with the memory of their first meeting still fresh in mind, dedicated the play to her, and hoped that she would act the title role. Maud Gonne, however, chose not to appear in that play, but later took the title role in Yeats's play *Cathleen ni Houlihan* [*see* Cathleen], in which her portrayal of the Poor Old Woman, who symbolized Ireland itself, had such a profound effect on the Irish audiences that Yeats in later years was to wonder "Did that play of mine send out / Certain men the English shot?" (See "The Man and the Echo.") In the poem "Adam's Curse" the "you" of the poem is Maud Gonne, while the "beautiful mild woman" is her sister Kathleen. Howth [q.v.], whose cliff paths overlook Dublin and its harbor, was important to both Yeats and Maud Gonne. Both had at one time lived on Howth. Maud Gonne describes her childhood there in her autobiography, *A Servant to the Queen;* and it was before a day spent with her on the cliffs of Howth that Yeats first proposed to her.

One of the strangest of all the accounts of Maud Gonne is found in W. B. Yeats's *Memoirs,* edited by Denis Donoghue, largely the original, unpublished text of his *Autobiography.* Therein, Maud Gonne tells him of her affair with Lucien Millevoye, the French journalist and Boulangist. By him, she had a son who died very young and who to Yeats was always referred to as an adopted son. Yeats says that, for Maud Gonne, sexual love was only justified by children. But later, she got the idea that she could re-create the son if she once more had sex with Millevoye near the tomb of the dead child. Of this union came, instead, a daughter, named Iseult (1895–1954), usually presented as an adopted daughter. After Maud Gonne's husband, Major John MacBride (she had married him in 1903) was executed for his part in the Easter Uprising of 1916, Yeats resumed his proposals, again to no avail. Later, Maud Gonne was to say that she hurt Yeats into great poetry. To no avail too were his proposals to Maud Gonne's "adopted" daughter, Iseult, whose youthful beauty phoenix-like recalled to Yeats Maud Gonne as he first met her. (There are quite a number of poems written to and about Iseult. For a few examples, see especially "To a Child Dancing in the Wind," "Two Years Later," "The Living Beauty," and "To a Young Girl."

Yeats never could reconcile Maud Gonne's beauty with her political activities and her public haranguing on behalf of the Irish poor: "A

Helen of social welfare dream," as he puts it in "Why Should Not Old Men Be Mad?" But in her very late years, Yeats, looking at Lawrence Campbell's bronzed portrait bust of Maud Gonne, recalled her as a gentle woman full of magnanimity of light but with a wildness in her, and he thought her supernatural, as in the poem "A Bronze Head." The one poem where he mentions her by name, "Maud Gonne at Howth station waiting a train, / Pallas Athene in that straight back and arrogant head," is the poem "Beautiful Lofty Things."

Gore-Booth, Eva. The second daughter of Sir Henry Gore-Booth, fifth baronet Lissadell [q.v.]. Eva and her sister Constance [see Markiewicz] lived at Lissadell, their ancestral home near Sligo town, where Yeats spent so many of his boyhood years. The Gore-Booths represented the aristocratic tradition to Yeats. He wrote in November 1894, in a letter to his sister Lily (in Wade), "I have been staying at Lissadell for a couple of days and have enjoyed myself greatly. They are delightful people." And further in the letter he wrote: "Miss Eva Gore-Booth shows some promise as a writer of verse. Her work is very formless as yet but it is full of telling little phrases." Of the Gore-Booth sisters, though it was Con who was to become one of Ireland's most cherished patriots, it was Eva that Yeats felt in closest sympathy with. Later he was pleased with her poem called "Little Roads of Cloonagh," which dealt with places near Lissadell. Eva Gore-Booth devoted her life to women's suffrage, and she died in 1926. Yeats's elegy to her and her sister was in memory of their youth. See "In Memory of Eva Gore-Booth and Con Markiewicz."

Gorias. A legendary city. [See Falias for a detailed account of its significance.] See also "Baile and Aillinn."

Gort. A town in county Galway near Yeats's home, Thoor Ballylee, and near also to Lady Gregory's estate, Coole Park. The name Gort signifies a tilled field, and there are many such town names in Ireland; but the Galway Gort was originally Gort-innsi-Guaire, meaning the field of the island of Guaire. Patrick W. Joyce, in volume 1 of his *Irish Names of Places,* explains that it takes its name from a seventh-century king of Connaught named Guaire Aidhne [gwar'a an'ya]. It is this King Guaire [q.v.] that Yeats associates with the town of Gort. See "The Three Beggars" and "To Be Carved on a Stone at Thoor Ballylee."

Grania [gran'ya]. Central figure of one of the great love stories of Irish literature. Daughter of the high king of Ireland, Grania was betrothed to Finn [q.v.], but she thought he was too old for her because he was older than her father. When, by accident, she saw the irresistible love-spot on the forehead of Diarmuid [q.v.], she fell hopelessly in love with this handsome follower of Finn. Their elopement and Finn's relentless pursuit of them form one of the most famous episodes in the Finn or White cycle of Irish mythology, comparable to the story of Deirdre [q.v.] in the Red Branch cycle, although Grania does not die of a broken heart upon the death of her lover as Deirdre does. After Diarmuid is killed by the Boar Without Bristles [q.v.], Grania eventually heeds Finn's gentle talk and loving words and becomes his wife. In his notes to the 1895 edition of *Poems* (reprinted in Allt and Alspach), Yeats writes that "Finn won her love and brought her, leaning upon his neck, into the assembly of the Fenians, who burst into inextinguishable laughter." See "A Faery Song"; "Her Courage," which is poem VI of "Upon a Lady Dying"; and "The Wanderings of Oisin."

Grattan, Henry (1746–1820). Irish statesman and brilliant orator. Although Grattan disapproved of such rebels as Wolfe Tone and Robert Emmet, he is honored in Ireland as a man who spoke eloquently for Irish independence, devoting his life to the Irish cause. It was Grattan who led the demand for Catholic emancipation in Ireland. He is another of the illustrious Irish Protestants, so particularly important to Yeats, who contributed to the heritage of Ireland, a group that includes Bishop Berkeley, Jonathan Swift, Oliver Goldsmith, and Edmund Burke. See "The Tower" and "The Seven Sages."

Great Comedian. A reference to the Irish hero Daniel O'Connell (1775–1847), sometimes called "The Liberator." O'Connell was the leader of the movement that at last won the abolition of the Penal Laws in 1829 and the granting of Catholic emancipation. Yeats illuminates his reference to O'Connell as the "Great Comedian" when he writes in his *Autobiography*, "I had seen Ireland in my own time turn from the bragging rhetoric and gregarious humour of O'Connell's generation and school, and offer herself to the solitary and proud Parnell as to her anti-self, buskin following hard on sock." And again, in the notes to his *The King of the Great Clock Tower* (reprinted in Allt and Alspach), Yeats writes: "As we discussed and argued, the national character changed, O'Connell, the great comedian, left the scene and the tragedian Parnell took his place. When we talked of his [Parnell's] pride; of his apparent impassivity when his hands were full of blood because he had torn them with his nails, the proceeding epoch with its democratic bonhomie, seemed to grin through a horse collar." In his poem "The Three Monuments," Yeats refers to the three statues that are among Dublin's most famous landmarks, the monuments to O'Connell, Parnell, and to Lord Nelson [Nelson's Pillar is no longer there, having been dynamited out of existence in 1966.]. The words "among the birds of the air" would have well-described Nelson high on his pillar. The poem may also relate, or premediate, Yeats's unsuccessful speech in the Irish Senate [See *The Senate Speeches of W. B. Yeats*, ed. Donald R. Pearce] calling for more tolerant divorce laws in Ireland, in which he said: "I am thinking of O'Connell, Parnell, and Nelson. We never had any trouble about O'Connell. It was said about O'Connell in his own day, that you could not throw a stick over a workhouse wall without hitting one of his children [workhouse means a house for the unemployed or the unemployable], but he believed in the indissolubility of marriage." But Parnell and Nelson were involved in divorce actions, and Yeats continued, "I think I have not greatly wronged the dead in suggesting that we have in our midst three very salutary objects of meditation which may, perhaps, make us a little more tolerant." O'Connell, often a fiery man involved in a number of duels and numerous public arguments, died in 1847, and his impressive tomb is in Glasnevin Cemetery in Dublin. See "Parnell's Funeral."

Great Plain. The plain of Muirthemne [q.v.], always associated with Cuchulain [q.v.], and the site of the battle in which he fell. The great plain of Muirthemne is located in county Louth where the county borders on the sea, roughly between the Boyne [q.v.] and the town of Dundalk. See "The Old Age of Queen Maeve" and "Baile and Aillinn."

Great Questioner. A reference to God, but it follows a reference to the great questioner, Sir Isaac Newton [q.v.] whose famous metaphor is vital to the poem: "I do not know what I may appear to the world; but to myself I seem to have been only like a boy playing on the seashore, and diverting myself in now and then finding a smoother pebble or a prettier shell than ordinary, whilst the great ocean of truth lay all undiscovered before me." See "At Algeciras—A Meditation upon Death."

Green Archer. The constellation Sagittarius, or the Archer, ninth sign of the Zodiac, frequently represented as a centaur shooting an arrow. In the notes that end his *Autobiography,* in which he claims to be summarizing and commenting on notes sent him by a "man learned in East Mediterranean Antiquities," Yeats writes under the heading "Sagitta": " 'About the third century B.C. we find Apollo is closely linked with the constellation Sagitta.' I find in a book upon Astrology published this year: 'Sagittarius. The symbol is an arrow shot into the unknown. It is a sign of Initiation and Rebirth.' (*A Student's Textbook of Astrology,* by Vivian E. Robson, 178.)" See "In the Seven Woods."

Green Lands. Open fields near Sligo town at the Rosses [q.v.] over which Yeats often walked, often with his uncle, George Pollexfen [q.v.]. The sandhills of the Green Lands were familiar territory to Yeats and all his relatives, including the Henry Middleton [q.v.] named in the poem. See the song II of "Three Songs to the One Burden."

Gregory, Anne. Daughter of Robert Gregory and granddaughter of Lady Gregory. See "For Anne Gregory."

Gregory, Augusta, or **Lady Gregory.** Isabella Augusta Persse Gregory (1852–1932). Author, playwright, a guiding light of the Abbey Theatre, and great friend and patron of W. B. Yeats. They first met, briefly, in London in 1894 and met again at Edward Martyn's castle in Galway in 1896. She invited Yeats to visit her at Coole, which he did the next summer and for twenty summers thereafter. They also planned together the forming of an Irish theatre which became, first, the Irish Literary Theatre and, later, the Irish National Theatre [the Abbey Theatre]. This and the summers at Coole where he could devote himself to his poetry might well be the most crucial event in the poet's life. Yeats has described Coole House in the "Dramatis Personae" section of his *Autobiography,* its magnificent library and paintings and objets d'art. He also describes Lady Gregory at length, finding in her the pride and humility that no paint brush could show, not even the famous Mancini [q.v.] portrait of her that hangs in the Dublin Municipal Gallery. Her courage and fortitude during the Black and Tan atrocities, which she wrote about anonymously in *The Nation,* and in the equally difficult times of the Irish Civil War that followed are best seen in her journal entries, 1919–27 (*Lady Gregory's Journals;* see esp. chap. 3).

Yeats's poems are filled with tributes to his great friend, her name unmentioned, as in lines 10–16 of "Friends" and the poem "A Friend's Illness." It is to Lady Gregory that Yeats addresses his poem "To a Friend Whose Work Has Come to Nothing," referring to her work toward getting a suitable modern art gallery to house the pictures that her nephew Sir Hugh Lane [q.v.] wished to give to Dublin, a project to which the brazen throats of such as the newspaper editor William Murphy [see Glasnevin] were violently opposed. (See also the notes to Yeats's *Responsibilities: Poems and a Play;* reproduced in Allt and Alspach). Lady Gregory is also referred to in Yeats's poem "My Descendants" in the lines: "For an old neighbour's friendship chose the house / And decked and altered it for a girl's love," the girl being his bride whom he brought to Thoor Ballylee [q.v.], his tower home near Lady Gregory's estate. And in his poem "Coole Park and Ballylee," Yeats describes Lady Gregory as she was shortly before her death, when, with the aid of a cane, she struggled to move about in her house: "Sound of a stick upon the floor, a sound / From somebody that toils from chair to chair."

In his official lecture to the Swedish Royal Academy, in December 1923, in acceptance of the Nobel Prize, Yeats paid perhaps his greatest tribute to Lady Gregory and to John Synge [q.v.] as well. Later, in *Autobiography,* he recalled the occasion:

> I am speaking without notes and the image of old fellow-workers comes upon me as if they were present, above all of the embittered life and death of one, and of another's laborious, solitary age, and I say, "When your king gave me medal and diploma, two forms should have stood, one at either side of me, an old woman sinking into the infirmity of age, and a young man's ghost. I think that when Lady Gregory's name and John Synge's name are spoken by future generations, my name, if remembered, will come up in the talk, and if my name is spoken first their names will come in their turn because of the years we worked together. I think that both had been well pleased to have stood beside me at the great reception at your Palace, for their work and mine has delighted in history and tradition."

In his poem "The Results of Thought," Yeats contemplates Lady Gregory's old age, and his own. At her death in May 1932, Yeats, in a letter to Mario M. Rossi (dated June 6, in Wade), wrote, "I have lost one who had been to me for nearly forty years my strength and my conscience." Perhaps it was Lady Gregory's aristocratic tradition, descended from the family Shakespeare called Percy, that Yeats most admired and that most influenced him. In a letter to Olivia Shakespeare dated May 31, 1932, Yeats wrote of a man who, when gazing at the pictures of past greats that filled the walls of Coole, said, "All the nobility of earth," and Yeats added, "I felt he did not mean it for that room alone but for lost tradition. How much of my own verse had not been but the repetition of those words" (reprinted in *Mythologies*). Yeats sums up his feeling for Lady Gregory and the other friends who influenced his life and of whom he made poems, when he ends "The Municipal Gallery Revisited" with the lines: "Think where man's glory most begins and ends. / And say my glory was I had such friends." Yeats dedicated his poetic play *The Shadowy Waters* to Lady Gregory and his play *The Words upon the Window-Pane* bears the inscription "In Memory of Lady Gregory In Whose House It Was Written." See "Beautiful Lofty Things," "The Municipal Gallery Revisited," and the dedication of *The Shadowy Waters*.

Gregory, Major William Robert (1881–1918). Son of Lady Gregory, artist, designer, notable horseman, and aviator, killed in action over Italy. Robert Gregory had been a classical scholar in school and shared with his mother the interest in languages that led to their studying Irish together. He became a promising artist, doing designs, settings, and costumes for productions at the Abbey Theatre, among them some of Yeats's plays. Yeats's play *Deirdre* is dedicated

> TO MRS. PATRICK CAMPBELL who in the generosity of her genius has played my Deirdre in Dublin and London with the Abbey Company, as well as with her own people, and IN MEMORY OF ROBERT GREGORY who designed the beautiful scene she played it in.

Robert Gregory's excellence as a hunter and rider was well known over the Galway countryside, and like his mother he was much loved by the Kiltartan [q.v.] peasantry. Yeats saw in him the aristocratic qualities of a Sir Philip Sidney [q.v.], and at Gregory's death was moved to so commemorate him: "Soldier, scholar, horseman, he." In addition to the elegy that bears his name, Robert Gregory is the subject of two other poems by Yeats, "An Irish Airman Foresees His Death" and "Shepherd and Goatherd," the latter most reminiscent of the elegy to Sidney by Edmund Spenser [q.v.]. When "In Memory of Major Robert Gregory" first appeared, published in *The English Review,* August 1918, Yeats included a note after the title: "(Major Robert Gregory, R.F.C., M.C., Legion of Honour, was killed in action on the Italian Front, January 23, 1918)." Yeats recalls Lady Gregory's son on his revisit to the Dublin Municipal Gallery, where hangs the oil painting of Robert Gregory by C. B. Shannon. Robert Gregory married Margaret Parry in 1907; and their daughter Anne Gregory is the subject of Yeats's poem, "For Anne Gregory." Robert Gregory gave Yeats many ideas for suitable repairs to Thoor Ballylee [q.v.] and did a well-known sketch of Yeats's tower. See "In Memory of Major Robert Gregory."

Gregory's Wood. A reference to the various woods on the estate of Lady Gregory, close by Yeats's tower, Thoor Ballylee. Yeats, who had spent many summers with Lady Gregory at Coole, the Gregory estate, was intimate with the many wooded areas; and in his writings he often uses the Irish names that they bore. The seven woods, and there is an entry for each in this dictionary, were called Inchy Wood, Kyle-Dortha, Kyle-na-no, Pairc-na-Carraig, Pairc-na-Lee, Pairc-na-Tarav, and Shan-Walla. Yeats's tower had little protection from gales coming in off the Atlantic Ocean but what little Gregory's Wood could offer. See "A Prayer for My Daughter."

Grey Rock, The. The rock located in Scotland and known in Irish as Craig Liath [krag'lee'a]. It was upon this rock that Aoife [q.v.], the legendary female warrior, was supposed to have made her home. See "The Grey Rock."

Griffith, Arthur (1872–1922). Irish statesman and the founder of the Sinn Fein nationalist movement. In 1899, in his patriotic newspaper *United Irishman,* Griffith called for an organization to resist, passively, all things British and to revive the Gaelic (Irish) tongue. Thus was born Sinn Fein [shin'fain'], meaning "we ourselves," which became overtly political in 1905. The organization gained strength with the outbreak of World War I and was active in the Easter Uprising of 1916. The army of Sinn Fein, originally the Irish Republican Brotherhood, be- came known as the Irish Republican Army, the IRA. Griffith also named one of his newspapers *Sinn Fein.* He was imprisoned several times by the British, but he was set free and took over command of the uprising in 1919–20. He became the first president of the Irish Free State in 1922, but he died very suddenly soon after. Griffith had prepared and written an introduction to the *Jail Journal* by John Mitchel [q.v.], which Yeats knew. A portrait of Griffith hangs in the Dublin Municipal Gallery. Though Griffith was perhaps a too-enthusiastic supporter of Yeats's play *The Countess Cathleen,* as he explains in the "Dramatis Personae" section of his *Autobiography,* Yeats never forgave Griffith for his attacks on Hugh Lane and John Synge. See "The Municipal Gallery Revisited."

Grimalkin. A cat with the spirit of a witch. *The Dictionary of Mythology, Folklore and Symbols* explains that "in medieval demonology, a witch was permitted to assume the body of a cat nine times, hence the nine lives of a cat." Grimalkin, also Graymalkin, is a name frequently applied to old crones, as well as to witches. One of the three witches in Shakespeare's *Macbeth* (1.1.13) is addressed as Graymalkin. Yeats's Grimalkin seems to be a crone no longer capable of passion who crawls toward the empty Buddha. See "The Statues."

Guaire [gwar'a]. King Guaire the Hospitable who ruled Connaught Province in the seventh century. The fame of his generosity was widespread. King Guaire is associated with the town of Gort [q.v.] in Galway, for that Gort was originally called Gort-innsi-Guaire, the field of the island of Guaire. The king in Yeats's play *The King's Threshold* (1904) is also named Guaire. See "The Three Beggars."

Guido Calvacanti (ca. 1255–1300). Poet, philosopher, and friend of Dante [q.v.]. Along with Dante and Lapo [q.v.] Gianni, Guido Calvacanti was a poet of the "dolce stil nuova," in which sweet new style he wrote sonnets and ballads. Dante called him his "First friend," and as such he would have known Dante's good and bad qualities alike. See "Ego Dominus Tuus."

Guidobaldo. Guidobaldo of Montefeltro (1472–1508). the Duke of Urbino [q.v.]. The setting of *The Book of the Courtier* by Baldasar Castiglione is the court of Guidobaldo. Lady Gregory had read the book to Yeats at the end of each day's work during one of his summers at Coole. Of Guidobaldo, Castiglione writes, "He saw to it that his household was filled with very noble and worthy gentlemen, with whom he lived on the most familiar terms, delighting in their company; in which the pleasure he gave others was not the less than that which he had from them, being well versed in both Latin and Greek and combining affability and wit with the knowledge of an infinitude of things." Like Duke Ercole [q.v.] of Ferrara and Cosimo [q.v.] de' Medici, Guidobaldo was for Yeats an example of the wealthy patron who fostered great deeds without feeling any need first to consult public taste. See "To A Wealthy Man Who Promised A Second Subscription to the Dublin Municipal Gallery if It Were Proved the People Wanted Pictures."

Guinevere. King Arthur's queen in the great legends of the Arthurian cycle. In the stories, she carries on a secret love affair with Sir Lancelot [q.v.]. See "Under the Moon."

H

Hamlet. The hero of Shakespeare's famous tragedy. In his essay "On the Boiler," collected in *Explorations,* Yeats wrote: "The arts are all the bridal chambers of joy. No tragedy is legitimate unless it leads some great character to his final joy. Polonius may go out wretchedly, but I can hear dance music in 'Absent thee from felicity awhile' or in Hamlet's speech over the dead Ophelia . . . Lear's rage under the lightning." Thus Yeats sees the great tragic heroes as finally emblematic of tragic joy. Richard Ellmann, in his *The Identity of Yeats,* points out that "Christianity has no Hamlets, full of their own selves, passionate for knowledge, but only monks with empty eyeballs, contemplating, like the Buddhists, nothingness." See "Lapis Lazuli" and "The Statues."

Hanrahan or **Red Hanrahan.** An Irish character created by Yeats himself for his *Stories of Red Hanrahan,* published in 1897. In his *Autobiography,* Yeats expressed the hope that his invention, Red Hanrahan, "Might pass into legend as though he were a historical character." In his notes to *The Wind Among the Reeds* (reprinted in Allt and Alspach) Yeats typified Hanrahan [*see* Aedh] as "the simplicity of an imagination too changeable to gather permanent possessions." In the Hanrahan stories, Red Hanrahan is a schoolteacher, based on the hedge school masters of Penal times, who is always losing his school because of his troubles with women. There are five stories of Red Hanrahan, collected now in Yeats's *Mythologies.* His song about Ireland is in the third story, "Hanrahan and Cathleen, the Daughter of Houlihan." See "Red Hanrahan's Song About Ireland," "The Tower," and "Alternative Song for the Severed Head" in *The King of the Great Clock Tower.*

Hart Lake. Sometimes spelled Heart Lake, located southwest of the town of Sligo. In his story "Kidnappers," in *The Celtic Twilight,* collected in *Mythologies,* Yeats describes such a lake: "Some five miles southward of Sligo is a gloomy and tree bordered pond, a great gathering place of water-fowl." The place is haunted by fairy folk as well. See "The Heart of the Air."

Harun al-Rashid. The most celebrated of the Abbasid caliphs, the caliphs of Baghdad, and Islam's most famous dynasty. Harun was born in March 763, in some accounts; February, 766, in others. He died in 809. In volume 2 of *The Encyclopedia of Islam,* Harun is thus described: "Harun took a great interest in art and science and his brilliant court was a centre for all branches of scholarship. In spite of occasional outbursts of Oriental despotism, he was undoubtedly one of the best of the Abbasids; nevertheless it is from his reign that the beginning of the decline of the dynasty dates. In legend and tradition however he has always been looked upon as the personification of Oriental power and splendor and his fame has been spread through East and West by the *Arabian Nights.* In *A Vision,* Yeats writes, "When in the *Arabian Nights* Harun al-Rashid looked at the singer Heart's Miracle, and on the instant loved her, he covered her head with a little silk veil to show that her beauty 'had already retreated into the mystery of our faith.' " See "The Gift of Harun al-Rashid."

Heber. One of the first of the human settlers of Ireland and therefore a first ancestor of the Irish people. The ancient name for Ireland, Hibernia, derives from his name, according to ancient accounts. [*See* Eire]. See "The Wanderings of Oisin."

Hector. Prince of Troy and its chief hero. Son of King Priam and Queen Hecuba of Troy, and husband of Andromache, Hector is depicted as the ideal warrior in the *Iliad* of Homer. Hector nearly succeeded in driving the Greeks to their ships and ending the Trojan War in victory; but his killing of Patroclus, friend of Achilles, aroused Achilles to revenge. Achilles killed Hector and dragged his body behind his chariot. Priam prevailed on Achilles to give him his son's body, and Hector was buried with great honor. Yeats places Hector in Phase 12 of the moon, the hero's crescent. See "The Phases of the Moon"; "His Memories," which is poem VI of "A Man Young and Old"; and "The Gyres."

Helen. In legend and literature, the most beautiful of women, and Yeats's favorite symbol of beauty. Helen was the daughter of Zeus and Leda [q.v.] and sister of Clytemnestra and Castor and Pollux. She was the wife of Menelaus, one of the most famous of leaders of Greece and brother of Agememnon. While her husband was away, Paris [q.v.], prince of Troy, abetted by Aphrodite because Paris picked her as the fairest of goddesses, persuaded Helen to flee with him to Troy. To retrieve her, the Greeks launched their thousand ships, and thus Helen was the cause of the Trojan War, the focal point around which the action of the *Iliad* of Homer takes place, the Trojans opting for war rather than return Helen to her husband. In the phases of the moon set forth by Yeats in *A Vision*, Phase 14 is the phase of "many beautiful women." He says: "Here are born those women who are most touching in their beauty. Helen was of the phase, and she comes before the mind's eye elaborating a delicate personal image . . . .While seeming an image of softness and of quiet, she draws perpetually upon glass with a diamond." He adds, "Is it not because she desires so little, gives so little that men will die and murder in her service?"

In Yeats's poetry, Helen of Troy is almost always equated with Maud Gonne [q.v.], his image of beauty. Yeats was disappointed in Maud Gonne's marriage to John MacBride in 1903 and wary of her participation in the social and political uprisings in Ireland: "A Helen of social welfare dream, / Climb on a wagonette to scream," as he puts it in "Why Should Not Old Men Be Mad." See "When Helen Lived," "A Prayer for My Daughter," "The Tower," "Lullaby," "Three Songs to the Same Tune," "Three Marching Songs," and "Why Should Not Old Men Be Mad?"

Helicon. In Greek legend, Mount Helicon, located in central Greece, was the home of Apollo and the Muses, the nine patron goddesses of the arts and sciences. Their temple was located on the eastern part of the mountain, abounding in fountains and streams. See "The Leaders of the Crowd."

Henry Street. A Dublin street close to the General Post Office which was the scene of much fighting in the Easter Uprising of 1916. It was near Henry Street that the patriot known as The O'Rahilly [q.v.] died in the fighting, much as Yeats describes it: "They that found him found upon / The Door above his head / 'Here died the O'Rahilly. / R. I. P.' writ in blood." See "The O'Rahilly."

Herodias. Wife of Herod and mother of Salome. But Yeats uses the expression "the daughters of Herodias"; and in his notes to "The Hosting of the Sidhe," at the end of *Collected Poems,* he explains:

The gods of ancient Ireland, the Tuatha de Danaan [q.v.], or the Tribes of the goddess Dana, or the Sidhe [shee], from Aes Sidhe, or Sluagh Sidhe, the people of the Faery Hills as these words are usually explained, still ride the country as of old. Sidhe is also Gaelic for wind, and certainly the Sidhe have much to do with the wind. They journey in whirling wind, the winds that were called the dance of the daughters of Herodias in the Middle Ages, Herodias doubtless taking the place of some old goddess. When old country people see the leaves whirling in the road, they bless themselves, because they believe the Sidhe to be passing by.

Yeats was doubtlessly familiar with his friend Arthur Symons's use of the image in a poem called "The Dance of the Daughters of Herodias," which appeared in Symons's 1901 volume of verse called *Images of Good and Evil.* See "Nineteen Hundred and Nineteen."

Himalay. The Himalaya, so named from a Sanskrit word meaning abode of snow. It is the great mountain system of India, Nepal, Tibet, and adjacent lands. Its highest peak is Mount Everest, and its most sacred is Mount Meru [q.v.]. See "Anashuya and Vijaya."

Historia Mei Temporis (The history of my time). The title of a work Yeats credits to the Abbé Michel de Bourdeille [*see* Michel]. See "The Three Bushes."

Holy Joe. There is no reference to Holy Joe in *A Vision* or in Yeats's *Irish Fairy and Folk Tales,* where references are made to his associates [*see* Duddon]. Holy Joe is, however, a popular epithet for beggars with long beards. See "Tom the Lunatic," which is poem XXII of "Words for Music Perhaps."

Homer. The blind epic poet of classical Greece. His exact dates are unknown, but he is often said to have flourished in the ninth century B.C. The two great epic poems attributed to him are the *Iliad* and the *Odyssey,* poems that explore the limits of human action and feeling. His characterization of Helen of Troy as the paragon of beauty has made her a universal symbol of beauty, just as his Achilles and Hector symbolize great heroes and his Odysseus the great wanderer. Yeats associates Homer with the blind Irish poet Raftery [q.v.], who wanders about Ireland, especially in the Galway area near Thoor Ballylee [q.v.], singing the praises of Mary Hynes, the local peasant girl of renowned beauty, as Homer had sung of Helen. No doubt that Yeats felt at times a similar kinship between Homer and himself, as Yeats's Helen was Maud Gonne, another celebrated beauty. See "A Woman Homer Sung"; "Peace"; "The Double Vision of Michael Robartes"; "The Tower"; "Ancestral Houses," which is poem I of "Meditations in Time of Civil War,"; "Coole Park and Ballylee; poems VII and VIII of "Vacillations," and "Mad as the Mist and Snow."

Horace. Quintus Horatius Flaccus (65–8 B.C.), Roman poet and satirist. His odes, satires, and epistles make of him a most mature and polished lyric poet and an important critic and philosopher. Yeats, glancing at the books on the shelves of his tower, sees his volume of Horace standing next to Homer, with Plato on the shelf below and his Cicero opened before him—all of them of supreme importance to him; yet all began as unlettered lads. See "Mad as the Mist and Snow."

Horses of Disaster. *See* **Shadowy Horses,** with which the Horses of Disaster are synonymous. See "He Bids His Beloved Be at Peace."

Horton, Willliam Thomas (1864–1919). Artist, visionary, and mystic, for whose first book of drawings, *A Book of Images* (Unicorn, 1898), Yeats wrote an introduction. Letters from Yeats to Horton are preserved in Wade and in Kelly (vols. 1 and 3). Horton is among those friends of Yeats he summons to his side on All Souls' Night, all of them friends who shared his interests in the occult, yet living very sad or strange lives of their own. See "All Souls' Night."

Houlihan. The father of Cathleen [q.v.]. Cathleen ni Houlihan is a legendary personification of Ireland. Yeats writes of this in his story "Kathleen the Daughter of Hoolihan and Hanrahan the Red," contained in the volume *The Secret Rose,* where an earlier version of "Red Hanrahan's Song About Ireland" appears. The poet James Clarence Mangan [q.v.] had treated the theme earlier in his poem "Kathleen ni Houlihan," itself a translation from the Irish. See "Red Hanrahan's Song About Ireland."

Hound of Uladh [oo'la]. A reference to Cuchulain [q.v.], whose name means "the hound of Culain." Cuchulain is the great hero of the Red Branch or Ulster cycle of Irish mythology, and Uladh is the name of ancient Ulster. See "Baile and Aillinn."

Howth [hoeth]. A headland about ten miles from the center of Dublin, overlooking Dublin Bay. Howth gets its name from the Old Scandinavian word *hofud,* meaning head. The promontory runs into the Irish Sea, forming the northeast part of the bay. In 1880, John Butler Yeats, the poet's father, took his family to live at Howth. In Yeats's *Memoirs,* edited by Denis Donoghue, Yeats talks of his first proposal of marriage to Maud Gonne and of her refusal, she asking instead for his friendship: "We spent the next day upon the cliff paths of Howth and dined at a little cottage near the Bailey Lighthouse . . . . At the day's end I found I had spent ten shillings, which seemed to me a very great sum." See "Beautiful Lofty Things."

Huddon. One of the characters in "Stories of Michael Robartes and His Friends: An Extract from a Record Made by His Pupils," which forms a section of *A Vision.* There he is referred to as Peter Huddon, "that tall fair young man." Huddon is also the name of a character in an old Hibernian tale that Yeats included in his *Irish Fairy and Folk Tales.* In the story, Huddon and his friend Duddon are defeated in their plotting against their neighbor Donald O'Nery [*see* Daniel O'Leary]. See "Tom the Lunatic."

Hyde, Douglas (1860–1949). Educated at Trinity College, Dublin, he became an eminent Irish folklorist and published translations from the Irish. He also wrote much loved poems and plays in Irish. In 1893, Hyde helped found and became first president of the Gaelic League, to promote the study and use of the Irish language. The pen name under which he wrote his Irish works, and the name by which he was famous all over Ireland, was *An Craoibhin Aoibhin,* meaning sweet or delightful or pleasant little branch [*see* Craoibhin Aoibhin]. Hyde became the first president of Ireland (Eire) in 1939, holding that position until 1946. In the summer of 1899, Hyde was a guest of Lady Gregory's at Coole, along with Yeats. Yeats writes of Hyde in his *Autobiography* that he marveled at Hyde's ability to write all day without apparent effort. He found Hyde's English style without charm; but his Irish "had charm, seemed all spontaneous, all joyous, every speck born out of itself. Had he shared our modern preoccupation with the mystery of life, learnt our modern construction, he might have grown into another and happier Synge." Yeats regretted Hyde's abandonment of his folklore poetry, "being neither quarrelsome nor vain, he will not be angry if I say—for the sake of those who come after us—that I mourn for the 'greatest folk-lorist who ever lived,' and for the great poet who died in his youth." For more on Hyde and Yeats's regard for him, see "At the Abbey Theatre." And see "Coole Park, 1929."

Hysterica Passio. A disease also called The Mother. Yeats, no doubt, draws the name from Shakespeare's Lear, where Lear has become aware of the treachery of his daughters Goneril and Regan:

> O! how this mother swells up toward my heart;
> Hysterica Passio! down, thou climbing sorrow;
> Thy element's below. (2.4.56–58)

In the G. B. Harrison edition of Shakespeare, *The Complete Works,* the term is explained: "The mother, also called hysterica passio, was an overwhelming feeling of physical distress and suffocation. Lear's mental suffering is now beginning to cause a physical breakdown."

A description of the disease occurs in Yeats's story "Rosa Alchemica," in *Mythologies:* "I would half-remember with an ecstasy of joy or sorrow, crimes and heroism, fortunes and misfortunes . . . and then I would awake shuddering at the thought that some great imponderable had swept through my mind . . . I also have felt fixed habits and principles dissolving before a power, which has hysterica passio, or sheer madness, if you like." It is more in the sense of sheer madness that Yeats uses the phrase in his poems. See "Parnell's Funeral" and "A Bronze Head."

I

"Il Penseroso" or Il Penseroso's Platonist. A reference to the poem of John Milton [q.v.]. Yeats, making this reference, has himself and his tower, Thoor Ballylee [q.v.], in mind. The specific lines from Milton's poem are:

> Or let my lamp at midnight hour,
> Be seen in some high lonely Tow'r,
> Where I may oft out-watch the Bear,
> With thrice great Hermes, or unsphere
> The spirit of Plato to unfold
> What Worlds, or what vast Regions hold
> The immortal mind that hath forsook
> Her mansion in this fleshly nook;
> And of those Daemons that are found
> In fire, air, flood, or under ground,
> Whose power hath a true consent
> With Planet, or with Element.

In his poem "The Phases of the Moon," Yeats refers to Milton's Platonist and to the engraving by Samuel Palmer [q.v.], which is entitled "The Lonely Tower," one of the illustrations Palmer did for an edition of Milton's poetry. Milton's lines on Plato refer to the afterlife, as indicated in the myth of Er, as found in Plato's *Republic;* but a good consulting source on this would be Merritt Y. Hughes's edition of John Milton, *Paradise Regained, The Minor Poems and Samson Agonistes* (198). See "My House," which is poem II of "Meditations in Time of Civil War."

Inchy Wood. The name of one of the seven wooded areas of Coole, the estate of Lady Gregory, the other six being Kyle-Dortha, Kyle-na-no, Pairc-na-Carraig, Pairc-na-Lee, Pairc-na-Tarav, and Shan-walla. Inchy takes its name from the Irish word for island, inish, meaning island or land beside a river. See "I Walked Among the Seven Woods of Coole," which is the dedicatory poem to *The Shadowy Waters*.

Inishmurray. A small island located beyond Sligo Bay in the Atlantic Ocean. The island takes its name from the Irish word for island, inish, and from Muireadbach [the pronunciation is closely approximated in the anglicized Murray, or its variant Murry], the name of the first bishop of Killala who flourished in the seventh century. See "The Ballad of Moll Magee."

Innisfree [in ish free]. An island in Lough [loch] Gill, the lake at the eastern end of Sligo town, taking its name from innis or inish, Irish for island, and the anglicized form fraoch [freh], the common heath, and thus meaning "heathy island." In a letter dated November 30, 1922, Yeats replied to the girls of the Northgate School, Ipswich, who had written asking if Innisfree were a real island:

> Dear Ladies,
>
> Yes, there is an island called Innisfree, and it is in Lough Gill, Co. Sligo. I lived in Sligo when I was young, and longed, while I was still as young as you, to build myself a cottage on this island and live there always. Later on I lived in London and felt very homesick and made the poem, "The Lake Isle of Innisfree."

A treatment of Innisfree in prose, strongly suggestive of the poem, was given by Yeats in his short novel called *John Sherman*, published a few months after the poem. Yeats used the pseudonym Ganconagh when the novel was published in 1891. In his *Autobiography*, Yeats writes that the inception of the poem came about when he was walking through Fleet Street in London and saw a little fountain in a shop-window and recalled lake water and Innisfree. See "The Lake Isle of Innisfree."

Inver Amergin [in'ver avar'gin]. A reference to a river mouth or bay, which is what Inver means in Irish, named for Amergin, the poet of the early Milesian invaders of Ireland. However, it may have been named for another Amergin, an Ulster warrior who was married to the sister of Conchubar. There is an Inver in Donegal, Ulster Province. See "The Madness of King Goll."

Irregular. A member of the Irish Republican Army, in opposition to the Irish National Army during the years of the Irish Civil War. The Republicans blew up the bridge leading to Yeats's tower, Thoor Ballylee [q.v.]. See "The Road at My Door," which is poem V of "Meditations in Time of Civil War."

Irving, Sir Henry (1838–1905). Famous English actor, noted for his Shakespearian roles, particularly his Hamlet, and known as well for his majestic, grand manner. He was England's first actor to be knighted (in 1893). In his autobiographical writings, Yeats speaks of Irving as "an actor personified again and again . . . . Irving, the last of the sort on the English stage, and in modern England and France it is the rarest sort, never moved me but in the expression of intellectual pride." See "A Nativity."

Isaiah. Perhaps the greatest of the Old Testament prophets. His dates go back to as early as ca. 740 B.C. The incident of the coal, referred to in Yeats's poem, is recorded in the Book of Isaiah, 6:6–7: "Then flew one of the seraphim to me, having in his hand a burning coal which he had taken with tongs from the altar. And he touched my mouth, and said: 'Behold, this has touched your lips; your guilt is taken away, and your sin forgiven.' " See poem VII of "Vacillations."

Ith. Ancient place-name in Munster Province, taken from the name of Ith, one of the Milesians who came to Ireland and settled ca. 1234 B.C. See "The Madness of King Goll."

J

Jack or **Jack the Journeyman.** The wild lover in Yeats's Crazy Jane [q.v.] poems. Even before these poems, Jack the Journeyman appeared in Yeats's 1902 play called *The Pot of Broth,* where the name occurs in the tramp's song:

> There's broth in the pot for you, old man,
> There's broth in the pot for you, old man,
> There's a cabbage for me
> And broth for you,
> And beef for Jack the journeyman.
>
> I wish you were dead, my gay old man,
> I wish you were dead, my gay old man,
> I wish you were dead
> And a stone at your head,
> So I'd marry poor Jack the journeyman.

In a note to that play, Yeats explained that the words and air of the song were taken down from an old woman called Cracked Mary, who years later was to contribute to the character of Crazy Jane. Robert Burns's John Highlandman from his poem "The Jolly Beggars" may also have influenced Yeats. In the poem "To a Young Beauty," of course, the name Jack is used to refer simply to anyone not of a select circle. See "To a Young Beauty," "Crazy Jane and the Bishop," "Crazy Jane and Jack the Journeyman," and "Crazy Jane and God."

Jaffer or **Vizir Jaffer.** The vizir or vizier was a high official in certain Muslim states. Vizir Jaffer was minister of state to the Caliph Harun al-Rashid [q.v.]. Harun murdered Jaffer and then rejoiced by taking a new wife to himself and giving a new wife to his poet-philosopher, Kusta-ben-Luka. To a note to his book *The Cat and the Moon and*

93

Certain Poems (reprinted in Allt and Alspach), Yeats said: "After the murder for an unknown reason of Jaffer, head of the family of the Barmecides, Harun al-Rashid seemed as though a great weight had fallen from him, and in the rejoicing of the moment, a rejoicing that seemed to Jaffer's friends a disguise for his remorse, he brought a new bride into the house." See "The Gift of Harun al-Rashid."

James II (1633–1701). King of England from 1685 to 1688. In 1688, William [*see* Billy and Dutchman] and Mary took the throne of England after the so-called Glorious, or Bloodless, Revolution. Mary was James's daughter; but the English, fearing that James, who had become a Catholic, might pass the throne on to his son James Edward Stuart, also a Catholic, acted to ensure a Protestant rule by inviting Protestant William and Mary to the throne. James escaped to France and later tried to reestablish himself by leading a Catholic uprising in Ireland. This resulted in his overwhelming defeat by William at the Battle of the Boyne in 1690. In the original version of "Pardon, Old Fathers," Yeats had his Butler ancestors fighting on the side of James; the poem was changed to its present form when it was brought to Yeats's notice that his Butler ancestor had fought on William's side. See "Pardon, Old Fathers."

Jane. *See* **Crazy Jane.**

Jill. The Jack and Jill of nursery rhyme serve Yeats as a symbol of the common mob. It expresses his anxiety when Iseult Gonne, daughter of Maud Gonne, came to Dublin and started going about in Bohemian circles. See "To a Young Beauty."

John. *See* **Pollexfen, John.**

Johnson, Lionel Pigot (1867–1902). Poet and friend of Yeats and fellow member of the Rhymers' Club [*see* Cheshire Cheese]. Yeats writes of Johnson at some length in his *Autobiography,* saying of him, "Nor was there any branch of knowledge Johnson did not claim for his own." He quotes Johnson as replying to a question concerning his strange hours (he slept in the daytime) and whether this did not separate him from men and women: "In my library I have all the knowledge of the world that I need." Johnson, who first drank because of insomnia and then because he wished to, amazed Yeats with his recollections of conversations with famous people, which Yeats later learned were all imagined conversations. Yeats discovered the uncontrollable nature of

Johnson's excessive drinking only when Johnson arose from a conversation and fell to the floor. It was such a fall that led finally to Johnson's death. Yeats considered Johnson one of the "Tragic Generation," the title of that section of his *Autobiography* where he speaks at length of Johnson. Speaking of Johnson and of Ernest Dowson [q.v.], Yeats says their dissipation brought them to tragic ends. He felt he could explain this in part by quoting the lines from "Ego Dominus Tuus," which Johnson and Dowson obviously inspired:

> What portion in the world can an artist have
> Who has awakened from the common dream
> But dissipation and despair?

See also "The Grey Rock" and "In Memory of Major Robert Gregory."

Jonson, Ben (1573?–1637). English poet and dramatist and poet laureate 1619–37. Yeats much admired Jonson and the phrase he credits to him —"Beyond the fling of the dull ass's hoof"—which is to be found in the last stanza of Jonson's poem "An Ode. To Himselfe," poem XXIII of *The Underwood*, 1640 (reprinted in *Poems of Ben Jonson*):

> And since our Daintie Age
> Cannot endure reproofe,
> Make not thyselfe a Page,
> To that strumpet the Stage,
> But sing high and aloofe,
> Safe from the wolves black jaw, and the dull Asses hoofe.

Armed thus by Jonson's words, Yeats defended himself against attacks made upon him and Lady Gregory in George Moore's *Ave.* Yeats's admiration for Jonson increased when he saw Allan Wade's production of Jonson's *Volpone* in 1921. In Wade's collection of Yeats's letters (664–65), Yeats says, *"Volpone* was even finer than I expected. I could think of nothing else for hours after I left the theatre." In 1939, in Yeats's very last essay "On the Boiler," collected in *Explorations,* his final tribute to Jonson appears: "In Jonson's *Volpone,* one of the greatest satiric comedies, *Volpone* goes to his doom, but innocence is not rewarded, the young people who have gone through so much suffering together leave in the end for their fathers' houses with no hint of marriage, and this excites us because it makes us share in Jonson's cold implacability. His tribunal is private, that of Shakespeare public." See "While, I, from That Reed-Throated Whisperer," the epilogue poem to Yeats's *Responsibilities*.

Joyous Isle. The name by which Sir Lancelot calls the Castle of Blyante, where he was brought to recover after he had been wounded and was out of his mind. See "Under the Moon."

Juan. A reference to Don Juan Tenorio, a nobleman of fourteenth-century Spain, Yeats being inspired by the painting of Don Juan by his friend Charles Ricketts. As a symbol of the great, if dissolute, lover, Don Juan has been a figure of commanding interest to writers and composers, as well as artists—Molière, Corneille, Byron, Dumas, and Shaw and Purcell, Gluck and Mozart among them. Ricketts painted Juan nobly, riding a white horse through Hell, stared at by inferior eunuchs. The painting inspired Yeats to use this Juan as his symbol of the artist beset by the eunuchs or howling mobs, quite as he saw John Synge [q.v.] in relation to those who rioted at *The Playboy of the Western World* at the Abbey Theatre in 1907. And Yeats recalled the symbolism when he later wrote in his *Autobiography* (from a diary dated 1909):

> The root of it all is that the political class in Ireland—the lower-middle class from whom the patriotic associations have drawn their journalists and their leaders for the last ten years —have suffered through the cultivation of hatred as the one energy of their movement, a deprivation which is the intellectual equivalent to a certain surgical operation. Hence the shrillness of their voices. They contemplate all creative power as the eunuchs contemplate Don Juan as he passes through Hell on a white horse.

Yeats, following the manner of Byron, uses the regular English pronunciation of the *j*, making two syllables of Juan. See "On Those That Hated *The Playboy of the Western World*, 1907."

Juliet. A reference to Shakespeare's heroine as played by the American actress Julia Marlowe (Sarah Frances Frost, 1866–1950, a famous star as early as 1888.) Joseph Hone in his biography of Yeats reproduces a letter (ca. 1936) of Yeats to Miss Marlowe (now Mrs. E. H. Southern) in which he thanks her for her photograph and tells her, "My memory of the 'player in the States' in that moment when she went to meet the Friar is as vivid in my memory as when I first saw her." See "His Phoenix."

Juno. Chief of Latin goddesses, most often identified with the Greek Hera, wife of Zeus. Juno, wife of Jupiter, is especially the goddess of women, assisting at all important moments of female life. She is often depicted with the peacock, aristocratic bird of aristocratic gardens. But the scream of Juno's peacock is for Yeats a harsh symbol of the loss of self-control as well as the signal of the end of one civilization and the beginning of the next. As he writes in *A Vision:* A civilization is a struggle to keep self-control, and in this it is like some great tragic person, some Niobe who must display an almost superhuman will or the cry will not touch our sympathy. The loss of control over thought comes toward the end; first a sinking in upon the moral being, then the last surrender, the irrational cry, revelation—the scream of Juno's peacock." See "Ancestral Houses," which is poem I and "My Table," which is poem III of "Meditations in Time of Civil War."

Jupiter. The chief Roman deity, often identified with the Greek Zeus. Jupiter is also the largest planet in the solar system, followed in size by Saturn. Yeats discusses Jupiter in conjunction with Saturn at length in *A Vision* (see esp. 104, 207–8, and 302). In a letter dated August 25, 1934, to Olivia Shakespeare (in Wade), Yeats talks about the horoscopes of his children, Anne and Michael:

> I was told, you may remember, that my two children would be Mars conjunctive Venus, Saturn conjunctive Jupiter respectively; and so they were—Anne the Mars-Venus personality. Then I was told that they would develop so that I could study in them the alternating dispensations, the Christian or objective, then the Antithetical or subjective. The Christian is the Mars-Venus—it is democratic. The Jupiter-Saturn civilization is born free among the most cultivated, out of tradition, out of rule. . . . George [Mrs. Yeats] said it is very strange but whereas Michael is always thinking about life Anne always thinks of death. Then I remembered that the children were the two dispensations.

In "On A Picture of a Black Centaur by Edmund Dulac," Yeats refers to the crop of mummy wheat produced by the conjunction of Jupiter and Mars. See also "Conjunctions," which is poem X of "Supernatural Songs."

K

Kama. The god of love in Hindu literature. Yeats, in a note in the 1895 edition of *Poems* (reprinted in Allt and Alspach), calls Kama the Indian Eros. *The Dictionary of Mythology, Folklore and Symbols* describes Kama as "a beautiful youth attended by nymphs. He carries a bow of sugar cane with a bowstring of love; each of his five arrows . . . is tipped with a distinct flower to inspire love." See "Anashuya and Vijaya."

Keats, John (1795–1821). The English poet whose influence on Yeats was considerable. Yeats placed Keats in the important Phase 14 of the moon, the phase also of beautiful women; and in *A Vision*, Yeats writes:

> In the poetry of Keats there is, though little sexual passion, an exaggerated sensuousness that compels us to remember the pepper on the tongue as though that were his symbol. Thought is disappearing into image; and in Keats, in some ways a perfect type, intellectual image, where his poetry is at its best, whose subjectivity has not been heightened by its use in many great poets, painters, sculptors, artificers. The being has almost reached the end of that elaboration of itself which had for its climax an absorption in time, where space can be but symbols or images in the mind. There is little observation even in detail of expression, all is reverie.

In 1917, Yeats published his book of essays called *Per Amica Silentia Lunae* (reprinted in *Mythologies*). The essay uses Yeats's poem "Ego Dominus Tuus" as a prologue, and in the first essay called "Anima Hominis," Yeats writes: "I imagine Keats to have been born with that thirst for luxury common to many at the outsetting of the Romantic Movement, and not able . . . to slake it with beautiful and strange objects. It drove him to imaginary delights; ignorant, poor, and in poor health, and not perfectly well-bred, he knew himself driven from tangible luxury." See "Ego Dominus Tuus."

Kedron. A brook in Jerusalem that ran through the garden of Gethsemane and emptied into the Dead Sea. (See John 18:1.) And see "The Travail of Passion."

Kerry. The south-westernmost county of Ireland, in Munster Province. County Kerry takes its name from the descendants of Ciar [keer], who was one of the three sons of Fergus and Maeve. The descendants were called Ciarraidhe [kerry], and they first settled in the territory between Tralee and the river Shannon and ultimately gave their name to the whole county. See "The O'Rahilly."

Khoung-Fou-Tseu. The Chinese name of the philosopher Confucius (ca. 551–479 B.C.). Yeats uses the Chinese name as it comes down in a French transcription. The epigraph in which Yeats uses the name is to his volume of poems *Responsibilities*, first published in 1914. The two epigraphs to the book announce Yeats's turning away from the dreamy Celtic twilight of his early work to face the responsibilities of the facts and demands of present reality. Ireland's political problems, Maud Gonne's marriage and the terrible breaking up of it, the rigors of establishing and running the Abbey Theatre, with both its internal and external problems, the attacks on Lady Gregory and himself by George Moore, the Hugh Lane controversy [q.v.], and others. See the dedication page to *Responsibilities*.

Kiltartan or **Kiltartan Cross.** The name of a barony, parish, and, also a village located in county Galway. Coole, the estate of Lady Gregory, included all of Kiltartan, and thus it was the birthplace of her son, Major Robert Gregory [q.v.]. Many villages in Ireland use Cross as a termination of the town name either because of crosses erected nearby or because the village occupied a crossroads. See "An Irish Airman Foresees His Death."

Kilvarnet. A parish in county Sligo. See "The Fiddler of Dooney."

King. Yeats uses the word king with specific references in mind in King Billy, King and No King, A King Has Some Beautiful Cousins, and *The King of the Great Clock Tower*. [*See* below.]

King Billy. William III [*see* Billy and Dutchman]. *See* "Lapis Lazuli."

King and No King. From the title of a play by Beaumont and Fletcher called *King and No King* (acted in 1611, printed in 1619), wherein words are a king's enemies, specifically the words brother and sister, because the king in the play loves his sister. When he learns that he was an adopted child, he is "no kin" and can marry the girl he thought was his sister and become king in fact. See "King and No King."

A King Has Some Beautiful Cousins. " A line from the poem "Crazy Jane on the Mountain." The king is George V (1865–1936) of England, and the cousins are Czar Nicholas II (1868–1918) of Russia and his family, executed by the Bolsheviks. In the section of "On the Boiler" called "Ireland After the Revolution," (reprinted in *Explorations*), Yeats wrote:

> I have been told that King George V asked that the Russian royal family should be brought to England. The English Prime Minister refused, fearing the effect upon the English working classes. That story may be no more true than other stories spoken by word of mouth, but it will serve for an example. The average Englishman would think King George's submission, his abandonment of his relations to a fate already foreseen, if proved, a necessary, even a noble sacrifice. It was indeed his submission, his correctness, as a constitutional sovereign that made his popularity so unbounded that he became a part of the English Educational System. Some thousands of examination papers were distributed to school children in a Northern industrial district with the question 'Who was the best man that ever lived?' The vast majority answered, 'King George the Fifth.' Christ was runner-up.
>
> We [the Irish], upon the other hand, would think that he showed lack of personality, of manhood even, because he did not abdicate. No propaganda must be permitted which might recommend a sovereign who cannot boast in the words of a Sophoclean chorus:
>
>> . . . I would be praised as a man,
>> That in my words and my deeds I have kept
>>   those laws in mind
>> Olympian Zeus, and that high clear Empyrean,
>> Fashioned, and not some man or people of mankind,
>> Even those sacred laws nor age nor sleep can blind.

Indeed I beg of our government to exclude all alien appeal to mass instinct. The Irish mind has still in country rapscallion or in Bernard Shaw an ancient, cold, explosive, detonating impartiality. The English mind, excited by its newspaper proprietors and its schoolmasters, has turned into a bed-hot harlot.

See "Crazy Jane on the Mountain."

The King of the Great Clock Tower. The title of a play by Yeats written in 1933 and later revised and published in 1935 as *A Full Moon in March*. It may be worth noting that there was a great clock tower at Sandymount Castle, at Sandymount [q.v.], near Dublin, where Yeats was born. The castle was owned by Yeats's maternal uncle Robert Corbet [*see* Corbets]. See also "Alternative Song for the Severed Head" in *The King of the Great Clock Tower*.

Kinsale. A town located on the bay south of the city of Cork in county Cork at a point where the land juts out to sea. The name is from the Irish ceannsaile [kan soi' le], which means "the head of the brine." See "The Ballad of Moll Magee."

Knockashee [nok a she]. A mountain in county Sligo. The name comes from the Irish word cnoc, meaning hill, and sidhe [q.v.], meaning fairy folk. Originally, the word meant the hills or mounds or fairy mansions that the sidhe occupied. See "The Ballad of Father O'Hart."

Knockfefin. The name of a mountain in ancient Ireland. See "The Wanderings of Oisin."

Knocknarea [nok na ray]. A famous mountain near Sligo notable for its flat top on which there is a great cairn, a huge mound of stones under which, according to Irish legend, Queen Maeve [q.v.] is buried. There is a disagreement among Irish scholars about the meaning of the name. The first syllable, of course, means hill or mountain; the last syllable could have derived from a number of words of that sound, meaning variously king, executions, or smooth promontory. It is sometimes referred to on maps, however, as King's Mountain. It is one of the two mountains that guard Sligo Bay, from opposite ends, the other being Ben Bulben [q.v.]. Knocknarea, with Queen Maeve upon it, may be said to represent the Ulster or Red Branch cycle of Irish mythology, just as Ben Bulben would represent the Finian or White cycle. See

"The Ballad of Father O'Hart"; "The Hosting of the Sidhe"; "Red Hanrahan's Song About Ireland"; and "Alternative Song for the Severed Head," in *The King of the Great Clock Tower.*

Kusta-ben-Luka. A Christian philosopher at the court of Harun al-Rashid [q.v.], caliph of Baghdad. According to Joseph Hone in his biography of the poet, Yeats received help at the Bodleian Library in Oxford with reference to Arabic manuscripts and may have come upon information regarding Kusta-ben-Luka there. It is worth noting that an obvious parallel exists between Kusta and Yeats and their wives. Kusta's wife dreamed aloud and supplied him thus with great knowledge he had been unable to come upon elsewhere. Mrs. Yeats [*see* George] engaged in automatic writing and thus supplied Yeats with much material for *A Vision;* and in that work, he tells us that she talked in her sleep as well. Robert Burton, in *The Anatomy of Melancholy,* refers to a Costa ben Luca (Qusta ibn Luga of Baalbec), a ninth-century Christian Arabian writer; author of a treatise on physical ligatures; also an *Epistle Concerning Incantations, Adjurations and Suspensions from the Neck;* and a translation of Hero of Alexandria's *Mechanics.* See "The Gift of Harun al-Rashid."

Kyle-Dortha [kil' a dor' ehe]. One of the seven woods at Coole, the estate of Lady Gregory. Kyle comes from the Irish word for forest or wood, and dortha is a form of the Irish dara, meaning oak. The name, then, is the equivalent of Wood of Oak or Oak Wood. See "I Walked Among the Seven Woods of Coole," the dedicatory poem of *The Shadowy Waters.*

Kyle-na-no [kil' a na no]. One of the seven woods at Coole, the estate of Lady Gregory. The name probably means Wood of the Nuts, from kyle, meaning wood, and gno, meaning nuts. But it may have meant Wood of the Yew Trees, from *eo* [*yo*], the Irish word for the yew tree. See "While I, from That Reed-Throated Whisperer," "To a Squirrel at Kyle-na-no," and "I Walked Among the Seven Woods of Coole," the dedicatory poem of *The Shadowy Waters.*

Kyteler, Lady. Dame Alice Kyteler, convicted in fourteenth-century Ireland of being a sorceress. Three of her husbands had died of poisoning and now the fourth was deprived of his natural senses. According to the charges brought against her, as given in St. John D. Seymour's *Irish Witchcraft and Demonology,* "the said dame had a certain demon, an incubus, named son of art or Robin, son of art [*see* Artisson, Robert], who had carnal knowledge of her. . . . The sacrifice to the evil spirit is said to have consisted of nine red cocks, and nine peacocks' eyes." Dame Alice, herself, fled to England and was not put to death as were many of her followers. See "Nineteen Hundred and Nineteen."

L

Laban [lav'an]. Sister of Fand [q.v.], Laban aided Fand in casting a magical weakness on Cuchulain [q.v.], and later she assisted in healing him, as Yeats explains in his notes to *The Wind Among the Reeds* (reprinted in Allt and Alspach). In very old accounts, Laban and her lapdog are swept away by flood waters, but she survives by taking the shape of a salmon while her dog becomes an otter. See "Under the Moon."

Laighen or **Hill Seat of Laighen [lay'an].** The early form of Leinster, the province that occupies the middle and southeastern part of Ireland. In the third century, Lavra, a mariner, returned to Ireland from exile in Gaul to wrest the Irish crown from the murderers of his father and grandfather. His men used an unusual, peculiarly shaped, broad-pointed spear called a laighen; and as Patrick W. Joyce tells us in his *Irish Names of Places,* "from this circumstance, the province in which they settled, which had previously borne the name Galian, was afterwards called Laighen, which is its present Irish name. The syllable 'ster' was added in after ages, and the whole word pronounced Laynster . . . which naturally settled into the present form Leinster." See "Baile and Aillinn."

Lancelot. The famous knight of the cycle of Arthurian romances. Lancelot was the bravest of the Knights of the Round Table and the secret love of Arthur's Queen Guinevere. Because of Guinevere's jealousy when Lancelot was tricked into a love affair with the maid Elaine, Lancelot went mad and remained in exile for some years while regaining his senses [*see* Joyous Isle]. See "Under the Moon."

Land-of-the-Tower. In his poem "The Harp of Aengus," Yeats speaks of "Aengus [q.v.] in his tower of glass." It is very likely that this tower in Tir-nan-Og, the Country of the Young [q.v.], is the reference here. See "Under the Moon."

Landor, Walter Savage (1775–1864). English author and poet. Landor, with what Yeats called his "calm disdain of usual daily things," wrote much on the heroic past. Landor's *Imaginary Conversations,* prose dialogues with famous people of the ancient and modern world, is his best known work. Known as a brilliant conversationalist himself, he also had a reputation for quarrels and legal battles wherever he went; and in all these respects he became in Florence, Italy, where he lived for a long time, a legendary figure, as in the accounts set forth by Giuliana Artom-Treves in *The Golden Ring.* T. R. Henn, in *The Lonely Tower,* noting Landor as a man continually beset by every kind of domestic calamity, suggests, "Perhaps, therefore, the tarpaulin; faintly ridiculous, the temporary cover against popular ridicule." Yeats places Landor in the same phase of the moon, Phase 17, as Dante, Shelley, and himself—the total phase where Unity of Being is most possible, and he writes of Landor, in *A Vision:* "The most violent of men, he uses his intellect to disengage a visionary image of perfect sanity . . . seen always in the most serene and classic art imaginable. He had as much Unity of Being as his age permitted, and possessed, though not in any full measure the Vision of Evil." And earlier in his book of essays, *Per Amica Silentia Lunae* (reprinted in *Mythologies*), Yeats had written "Savage Landor topped us all in calm nobility when the pen was in his hand, as in the daily violence of his passion when he laid it down." See "To a Young Beauty" and "A Nativity."

Land-Under-Wave. A beautiful country situated under the sea. Gaelic tales abound in allusion to such a country, paralleling the legend of Atlantis mentioned by Plato. Patrick W. Joyce, in his *Old Celtic Romances,* tells us that in some writings this land is called Tir-fa-tonn, meaning the land beneath or under the wave. See "Under the Moon."

Lane, Sir Hugh Percy (1875–1915). Nephew of Lady Gregory. Son of Lady Gregory's sister, Frances Adelaide Persse, and the Reverend J. W. Lane, Hugh Lane was a noted art collector and dealer. He was also a much admired man. The artist Augustus John, as noted in *Lady Gregory's Journals,* said of Lane that "He was one of those rare ones who single-handed are able to enrich and dignify an entire nation." Lane's collection of French Impressionist paintings was an important one; and he wished to give the pictures to Ireland, providing the Dublin Corporation would build a gallery suitable for it. A gallery that spanned the River Liffey was designed by the architect Edwin Lutyens. The Dublin Corporation, however, did not go along with the plan, and Lane took the pictures to London and placed them on loan in the English National Gallery. In 1907, Lane had been passed over in the appointment to the curatorship of the National Museum of Ireland, though he was the perfect choice. Yeats's poem "An Appointment," published in 1909, has this incident in mind. Lane was knighted in 1909, and was named director of the Irish National Museum in 1914; but he did not change his will, which left the French pictures to the English National Gallery. Just before his departure on a wartime trip to America, however, he made a codicil to his will, revoking the bequest and leaving the pictures to Dublin after all. The codicil was signed but not witnessed. Lane, on the return trip from America, went down in the torpedoing of the Lusitania, in 1915. The controversy over the possession of the pictures began soon thereafter with both Ireland and England claiming right of possession. Despite the fact that earlier the French pictures were condemned by many a brazen throat and foul mouth in Dublin (see Yeats's poem "To A Shade," where "A man of your own passionate serving kind" is Lane), Lady Gregory, executor of Lane's estate and in full knowledge of his wishes, worked tirelessly to bring the pictures back to Ireland (see *Lady Gregory's Journals*, 283– 317, and her book *Hugh Lane's Life and Achievement*); and Yeats helped her by endless visits to people of influence in England and by the weight of his pen. (See esp. Yeats's lengthy letter to the editor of the *Observer*, published January 21, 1917 (reprinted in Wade). See also Donald T. Torchiana and Glenn O'Malley, "Some New Letters from W. B. Yeats to Lady Gregory," 8–47.)

The pictures remained in England despite all efforts, while in Dublin an empty room was maintained in the newly established Municipal Gallery of Modern Art [q.v.] to receive the paintings should they ever be returned. A compromise was reached in 1961, when half the Lane collection was handed over in trust to the Dublin Municipal Gallery. Twenty paintings would be on loan for five years in Dublin and then the collection would be exchanged for those still in London. Thus, the two parts of the collection would be exchanged every five years. Among the paintings is Daumier's *Don Quixote*, of which Yeats, in his letter to the *Observer*, said that "according to the mind of some of us a masterwork surpassing all the rest in beauty." The Dublin Municipal Gallery, renamed the Hugh Lane Municipal Gallery, was created to fulfill the codicil to Lane's will. The gallery received many other paintings from Hugh Lane, and many were secured through him and with his advice before his untimely death. Thus to Yeats, Lane is, indeed, the "onlie begetter," of the gallery and its collections; just as Mr. W. H. is the "onlie begetter of these insuing sonnets" as printed in the dedication to the 1609 edition of Shakespeare's sonnets. Yeats attacked Lord Ardilaun [see Arcole] for basing his support for the original plans for the gallery to house the Lane pictures on the taste of the people, as Yeats makes clear in the poem "To a Wealthy Man Who Promised a Second Subscription to the Dublin Municipal Gallery if It Were Proved the People Wanted Pictures."

Yeats's finest tribute to Hugh Lane is perhaps the one contained in his letter to the editor of the *Irish Times*, March 17, 1913 (reprinted in Wade), where he wrote, "We have in Sir Hugh Lane a great connoisseur, and let us, while we still have him—for great connoisseurs are as rare as any other kind of creator—use him to the full, knowing that, if we do, our children's children will love their town the better, and have a better chance of the intellectual happiness which sets the soul free from the vicissitudes of fortune." See "Coole Park, 1929"; "The Municipal Gallery Revisited."

Lapo, Gianni (ca. 1270-ca.1330). Florentine poet and, along with his friends Dante [q.v.] and Guido Cavalcanti, a follower of the "*dolci stil Nuova*," in which sweet new style he wrote some sixteen extant poems. Dante refers to him in his poem to Cavalcanti and in *De vulgari eloquentia*. See "Ego Dominus Tuus."

Lavery, Hazel. American born, second wife of the Irish artist Sir John Lavery. The Laverys were friends of Yeats. Yeats notes, in a letter to John Quinn, dated January 29, 1924, that he had Sir John's promise to act upon an Advisory Committee of Artists (in Wade). Sir John painted his wife several times, including one pose where she pretended to be dead. One of his paintings of her hangs in the Municipal Gallery [q.v.]. Lady Lavery died in 1925. See "The Municipal Gallery Revisited."

Lear. King Lear of Shakespeare's tragic drama, of whom Yeats wrote, in "Rosa Alchemica," reprinted in *Mythologies*, "There is Lear, his head still wet with the thunder-storm, and he laughs because you thought yourself an existence who are but a shadow, and him a shadow who is an eternal god." See "Lapis Lazuli"; "An Acre of Grass."

Leda; also Ledaean. In Greek mythology, Leda was the wife of King Tyndareus of Sparta. Zeus, in the form of a swan, ravished her, and from the union two eggs were hatched. Accounts vary about which of Leda's children emerged from the eggs, which were also said to represent love and war, and which were her natural children by Tyndareus. In any case, the four children were thought to be Helen [q.v.], Clytemnestra, Castor, and Pollux. Helen, symbol of the most beautiful of women, was destined to be at least indirectly responsible for the Trojan War, which ended in the destruction of Troy. Clytemnestra, wife of Agamemnon, took a lover while her husband was away at the war and murdered her husband upon his return. The two brothers, Castor and Pollux, form the zodiac sign of Gemini. Yeats's interest in Leda is not only as "that sprightly girl trodden by a bird." He is interested in the concept of annunciation being made to a mortal woman by a bird-god manifestation. He is also interested in historical cycles that begin with such annunciations. In *A Vision,* Yeats writes, "I imagine the annunciation that founded Greece as made to Leda." And he is also interested in the question of whether the wisdom of the god is transferred to the woman in the annunciation.

It has often been assumed that Yeats's description of the union of Leda and the Swan was based on Michelangelo's drawing which T. R. Henn in *The Lonely Tower* says was "always before him . . . on his desk . . . the image of Leda and the Swan, and the two eggs that were the product of that fierce union." But Charles Madge, in the *Times Literary Supplement* of July 20, 1962, points out that the British Museum owns a bas relief of Leda and the Swan, formerly displayed in the Etruscan Room, from which, he says, every detail of the poem's first six lines seems to be taken. Yeats spent a great deal of time in the British Museum, a two-minute walk from the Woburn Buildings, where he lived from 1895 to 1917. But the controversy over sources goes on. Charles B. Gullans, in the *Times Literary Supplement* of November 9, 1962, takes issue with Madge and sees Yeats's friend Thomas Sturges Moore as an even more likely source, both in his bookplate on the subject and his ode "To Leda," which first appeared in 1904 and in which Gullans finds many striking parallels.

There are other Leda legends that say she laid three eggs from her union with the swan, the third one never having been hatched but possibly containing all the knowledge of the world. In *A Vision*, Yeats has his character, Michael Robartes, telling his pupils of the lost egg of Leda, which has come into his possession. He intends to take it to the desert to be hatched by the sun's heat. See "Leda and the Swan"; "Lullaby"; and, using the adjective form Ledaean, "Among School Children."

Lissadell. The estate near Sligo of the Gore-Booth family, where Eva Gore-Booth and her sister Constance, later the Countess Markiewicz, grew up. Yeats often saw the estate, a great landmark, as a boy in Sligo; and in 1894 he was a guest at Lissadell. In his *History of Sligo*, the Reverend T. O'Rorke wrote:

> Lissadell, the seat of the Gore Booth family, stands about mid-way between Benbulben and the northern entrance of Sligo bay. It has the name in Irish Lis-an-doill, the fort of the blind man—from some blind man who formerly occupied it. . . . It was only in the first quarter of the eighteenth century the Gores began to reside at Lissadell, and only in 1837, 1838 and 1839, their present residence was built. With a fine southern aspect, with a rich soil and gently sloping surface down to the sea, and with magnificent views and surroundings, Lissadell is a most eligible site for a first-class mansion and demesne. . . . About the centre of the area, stands Lissadell House, or, as it is commonly called in the neighborhood, Lissadell Court—a name which the stately pile well deserves for the magnitude of its proportions, the beauty and finish of its building material, which is Ballysadore limestone, and the simple but classical elegance of its design. Look at it from what side you will, and you are struck with the solemn and almost conscious dignity with which it presides over the scene.

Yeats, too, was impressed when he was a house guest there, and wrote of it in a letter to his sister Lily, dated November 23, 1894 (in Wade), "An exceedingly impressive house inside with a great sitting room as high as a church and all things in good taste." See "The Man Who Dreamed of Faeryland" and "In Memory of Eva Gore-Booth and Con Markiewicz."

Loadstone Mountain. The name of a mountain in the story of Sinbad the Sailor. The mountain is inaccessible and is topped with a dome of brass, with brass pillars, and brass figures. Because of the iron in ships, no ship can safely pass. So bringing a painted chest or image from beyond the Loadstone Mountain would be a formidable task. See "A Prayer on Going into My House."

Locke, John (1632–1704). A leading British philosopher of empiricism. Though a strong influence on many subsequent philosophers, Locke was too mechanical for Yeats's taste. Yeats liked to quote the Irish philosopher George Berkeley [q.v.], who said of the philosophy of Newton and Locke that "Irishmen thought otherwise." (See Yeats's essay on Berkeley in *Essays and Introductions.*) In fact, Yeats wrote in "Pages from a Diary," in *Explorations,* that Descartes, Locke, and Newton took away the world and gave us excrement instead; but Berkeley restored the world. And again in the essay "My Friend's Book," in *Essays and Introductions,* Yeats says that Locke based himself upon the formula, "Nothing in the mind that has not come from sense—sense as the seventeenth century understood it—and Leibniz commented, 'Nothing except mind.' " And further, in his *Autobiography,* Yeats wrote: "When Locke's French translator Coste asked him how, if there were no 'innate ideas,' he could explain the skill shown by a bird in making its nest, Locke replied, 'I did not write to explain the actions of dumb creatures,' and his translator thought the answer 'very good,' seeing that he had named his book A Philosophical Essay upon Human Understanding." See "Fragments."

Lollard. The pet horse of the old Foxhunter [q.v.] in Charles J. Kickham's novel *Knocknagow or the Homes of Tipperary.* See "The Ballad of the Foxhunter."

Lomair. A legendary hound associated by Yeats with the more famous dogs of Irish mythology, Bran [q.v.] and Sceolan [q.v.]. See "The Wanderings of Oisin."

Longhi, Pietro (1702–85). A Venetian painter whose genre paintings gaily satirize Venice. His work, particularly a series of frescoes, often deals with carnival life. His son Alessandro (1733–1813) was also a painter and the author of a book on painters. See "She Turns the Dolls' Faces to the Wall," which is poem III of "Upon a Dying Lady."

Lord Chancellor. As defined in *Webster's New Collegiate Dictionary, Sixth*

Edition: "In Great Britain, the first great officer of state, whose official title is Lord High Chancellor of Great Britain. He ranks next after the blood royal and the Archbishop of Canterbury. He is keeper of the great seal, privy councilor, president and prolocutor of the House of Lords, and usually a member of the cabinet." In the House of Lords, the lord chancellor traditionally sits on a wool-stuffed Sack [q.v.] covered with red cloth. See "The Statesman's Holiday."

Lough Derg. A lake located near the town of Donegal in county Donegal. The name means Red Lake and supposedly gets its name from an ancient king who plucked out his one remaining eye to give it to a poet who had asked for it. When the king washed his bloodied face, the lake seemed to take on the red color and thus its name. Other legends credit the name to the destruction there of the serpent. But it is with Saint Patrick that the lake is most associated, for the lake site is also known as Saint Patrick's Purgatory, and it is the site of the most holy shrine in all of Ireland. The shrine itself is on the island in the lake known as Station Island. The demands on the pilgrim are very severe, but miracles are recorded there. See "The Pilgrim."

Loughlan. The name, meaning lake land, given for Scandinavia in the oldest Irish records, the Irish applying the name when the marauding Danes told them of the nature of their country. In Ireland's official work *The Annals of the Four Masters,* the earliest entry using the name, with the variant spelling of Lochlan, is for the year 851. See "The Two Kings."

Lugaidh or **King Lugaidh [loo' ee].** An Ulster warrior and early king of Ireland. He was the father of Aillinn [q.v.]. See "Baile and Aillinn."

Lugnagall [lug' na goll]. A mountain in County Sligo overlooking Drumcliffe. The name of the mountain in Irish means "the steep place of the strangers." See "The Man Who Dreamed of Faeryland."

M

MacBride, Major John. MacBride, of the Irish Brigade, married Maud Gonne [q.v.] in 1903. Yeats learned of the marriage of the woman he loved, who was also his symbol of beauty, by telegram while on an American lecture tour and was stunned, disappointed, and disapproving. Later in the same year, in a letter to Lady Gregory dated November 16, 1903 (in Wade), Yeats wrote: "I have just heard a painful rumour —Major MacBride is said to be drinking. It is the last touch of tragedy if it is true." The marriage did not last, ending in separation. MacBride, however, was one of the great heroes of the Easter Uprising of 1916, in which he had an important military role and for which he was executed by the English on May 5, 1916. MacBride, "drunken and vainglorious lout" that he may have been to Yeats, was nevertheless an authentic Irish hero. In 1899, in Africa, he had formed the Irish Brigade to aid the Boers against England. Only a year later, Yeats, working furiously to arouse the Irish party to a proper protest of the impending visit to Ireland of Queen Victoria, "tried in vain to get Harrington to resign in favour of MacBride of the Irish Brigade," as he writes in a letter to Lady Gregory, April 10, 1900 (in Wade). And Lady Gregory, examining the Boer ballads in Ireland, wrote in her *Poets and Dreamers,* "Mayo is the county to which John MacBride, the leader of the Irish Brigade, belongs; but I heard of a ballad-singer at Ballindereen, near my Galway home, the other day, whose refrain was: 'And Erin watches from afar, with joy and hope and pride, / Her sons who strike for liberty, led on by John MacBride!' " The son of John MacBride and Maud Gonne, Sean MacBride, was to become an activist in Amnesty International and later its president. He was awarded the Nobel Peace Prize in 1974. See "Easter 1916."

MacDonagh, Thomas (1878–1916). Poet, teacher, and patriot, who was executed for his part in the unsuccessful Easter Uprising of 1916. A lecturer on English literature at University College, Dublin, Mac-Donagh was the author of five volumes of verse, two of prose, and of several plays. In his critical study called *Literature in Ireland,* published shortly before his execution, MacDonagh chided Yeats, "who confesses that when he wrote the greater number of his poems, he had hardly considered seriously the question of the pronunciation of Irish words, who copied at times somebody's perhaps fanciful spelling." Mac-Donagh also taught at Saint Enda's, the school for bilingual studies that Patrick Pearse [q.v.] kept. The sixteen men who were executed by the English immediately following the Easter Uprising, MacDonagh among them, were said to have been placed in lime pits after the execution so as to dispose of the corpses, which would account for Yeats's allusion to "MacDonagh's bony thumb." About MacDonagh's potential as a literary figure, Yeats had written in his 1909 diary, a part of his *Autobiography,* "Met MacDonagh yesterday . . . a man with some literary faculty which will probably come to nothing through lack of culture and encouragement." Nevertheless, Yeats took Mac-Donagh's admonition about the spelling of Irish words seriously. The phonetic spellings of early volumes disappeared; accepted Irish spelling prevails thereafter. See "Easter 1916" and "Sixteen Dead Men."

Macgregor. Samuel Liddell Mathers (1854–1918), also known as Mac-Gregor Mathers and often simply as MacGregor. Of him Yeats wrote in his *Autobiography:*

> He was the author of *The Kabbala Unveiled,* and his studies were two only—magic and theory of war . . . . He had copies of many manuscripts on magic ceremonial doctrine in the British Museum, and was to copy many more in Continental librar-ies, and it was through him mainly that I began certain studies and experiences that were to convince me that images well up before the mind's eye from a deeper source than conscious or subconscious memory. I believe that his mind in those early days did not belie his face and body—though in later years it became unhinged, as Don Quixote's was unhinged—for he kept a proud head amid great poverty . . . . He has spoken to me, I think at our first introduction, of a society sometimes called itself—it had a different name among its members [the

different name was "The Order of the Golden Dawn"]—"The Hermetic Students," and in May or June 1887 I was initiated into that society in a Charlotte Street studio, and being at a most receptive age, shaped and isolated. Mathers was its governing mind, a born teacher and organizer. One of those who incite—less by spoken word than by what they are—imaginative action.

Although he later had a falling out with Mathers over his methods in the Hermetic Society, Yeats often stayed with Mathers and his wife in Paris, where he was much impressed with Mather's behavior—he often wore highland dress and danced sword dances, although Yeats doubted that he had ever seen the Highlands—and with Mather's ability to foresee and prophesy, particularly of the imminence of immense wars; and Yeats adds in his autobiographal writings that it may have been some talk of Mathers that made him write his poem "The Valley of the Black Pig." In "All Soul's Night," Yeats calls to his mind three friends who shared his mystical studies: Florence Farr Emery [q.v.], who was a fellow teacher of the Hermetic Society; William T. Horton [q.v.], who would have been had he not changed his mind; and, of course, Mac-Gregor. See "All Soul's Night."

Macnessa. The full name of Conchubar [q.v.] was Conchubar Macnessa, meaning son of Nessa. Nessa was his mother; Cathbadh, the Druid, was his father. Later, Nessa married Fergus [q.v.] whom she persuaded to step down from his kingship and give it over to her son Conchubar. See "The Wanderings of Oisin."

Maeve [mayv]. A legendary queen in ancient Ireland. Maeve was the daughter of a high-king of Ireland, and she became queen of Connaught Provence, in the west of Ireland, ruling jointly with her husband-consort Ailell. It was their argument over which of them had the greater possessions that led to Maeve's invasion of Ulster Province to secure a famous Brown Bull to equal the White-horned Bull that Ailell had in his herd and thus make their total possessions exactly equal. The story of this invasion—the *Tain Bo Cualnge,* translated as *The Cattle Raid of Cooley*—forms the central epic of the Ulster or Red Branch cycle, of which Cuchulain [q.v.] is the chief hero and Maeve's principal opponent. In traditional Irish folktales, Maeve is also a queen of the Sidhe [q.v.], the fairy folk of Ireland and possibly related to Shakespeare's Queen Mab in *Romeo and Juliet*. In "The Hour Before Dawn," Yeats incorrectly gives Maeve nine sons by Ailell. There were seven, as Lady Gregory indicated in her *Cuchulain of Muirthemne*, and they bore the common name of Maines [q.v.]. Maeve is believed to be buried under the cairn, or great pile of rocks, on the top of Knocknarea [q.v.] in Sligo. See "Red Hanrahan's Song About Ireland," "The Hour Before Dawn," "The Wanderings of Oisin," and "The Old Age of Queen Maeve."

Magee, Moll. The central figure of Yeats's ballad. In Joseph Hone's biography of Yeats, Yeats is quoted as saying that he wrote the poem when he was seventeen, living with his family at Howth. He further says that the poem was suggested by a sermon he heard there in the Roman Catholic church. See "The Ballad of Moll Magee."

Magh Ai [moy'we']. A great plain in county Roscommon, in Connaught Province, the lands that came to be ruled by Queen Maeve [q.v.]. The name, meaning the Plain of the Livers, got that name in ancient times when the Sidhe [q.v.] attempting to remove a Druid's spell, were instructed to kill three hundred white cows with red ears and to spread their livers on a certain plain. The heat given out by the livers melted the snow with which the Druid had blanketed the area. Lady Gregory gives this account at length in her *Cuchulain of Muirthemne*. See "The Old Age of Queen Maeve."

Magnus Annus. The Great Year, often called the Platonic Year, having been set forth in Plato's *Republic* as the year in which the heavenly bodies complete the cycle of their movements that return them to their original positions. Yeats's fullest treatment of the *Magnus Annus* is given in Book IV: "The Great Year of the Ancients," in *A Vision*. Yeats associates the year with the beginning of a cycle, the birth of a god or symbol of that cycle; and death and resurrection as in the case of both Dionysus and Christ. Yeats also has in mind Virgil's *Fourth Eclogue*, accepted in the Middle Ages as a prevision of the coming of Christ, and here quoted by Yeats: "The latest age of the Cumaean song is at hand; the cycles in their vast array begin anew; Virgin Astraea comes, the reign of Saturn comes, and from the heights of Heaven a new generation of mankind descends. . . . Apollo now is king and in your Consulship, in yours, Pollio, the new age of glory shall commence and the mighty months begin their course." In Yeats's play *The Resurrection*, songs open and close the play. These songs he has reprinted in his *Collected Poems*. See "Two Songs from a Play."

Maines [man'es]. The seven sons of Queen Maeve and Ailell, all of whom bore the name Maine in common. Yeats is in error in increasing the number of Maines to nine. (Lady Gregory's *Cuchulain of Muirthemne*, 149, gives an account of each of the seven.) See "The Hour Before Dawn," and "The Old Age of Queen Maeve."

Malachi Stilt-Jack. Yeats's metaphor, perhaps of the artist in a degenerate world, seemingly made without external reference. That name, however, suggests the possibility of allusion to Malachi, minor prophet of the Old Testament, or to Saint Malachi (1094–1148), who had been confessor to the Irish king Cormac [q.v.] MacCarthy and later was the archbishop of Armagh, a position from which he resigned in order to give his thought to his own peace. Or Yeats may have chosen the name in recollection of Lady Gregory's neighbor, Malachi Quinn, whose terrible suffering during the Irish Civil War is carefully recorded by Lady Gregory in her *Journals*, 127–65. See "High Talk."

Mall. A promenade located in the town of Sligo. Near the Mall were located the houses of Yeats's maternal relatives, the Pollexfens [q.v.], and of their friends, often visited by Yeats as a young boy. Not far from the Mall was the grammar school run by Mr. William, C. Eade [q.v.]. See "In Memory of Alfred Pollexfen."

Maloney, Dr. William Joseph (1882–1952). author, in 1936, of *The Forged Casement Diaries*. At the time of publication, Yeats wrote, in a letter to Ethel Mannin, dated November 15, 1936 (reprinted in Wade): "I am in a rage. I have just got a book published by the Talbot Press called *The Forged Casement Diaries*. It is by a Dr. Maloney. I knew him in New York and he has spent years collecting evidence. He has proved that the diaries, supposed to prove Casement [q.v.] 'a Degenerate' and successfully used to prevent an agitation for his reprieve, were forged." Dr. Maloney was born in Edinburgh and came to the United States in 1911. He was at one time professor of nervous and mental diseases at Fordham University in New York. In 1937, he was a member of a Testimonial Committee formed in America "to provide a fund to ensure that Yeats should have no financial anxieties for the rest of his life." (See footnote in Wade, 891–92.) See especially the subhead to the poem "Roger Casement."

Manannan [manan'on]. In Irish mythology, a sea god, son of Lir, principal god of the oceans, but also a legendary figure who gave his name to the Isle of Man and to descendants of that area. Manannan Mac Lir was one of the most celebrated figures among the Danaan [q.v.] people. He was also the husband of Fand, with whom Cuchulain briefly consorted. See song I of "Three Songs to the One Burden" and "The Wanderings of Oisin."

Mancini, Antonio (1852–1930). Italian artist who painted portraits of Lady Gregory and Yeats. Mancini employed a curious technique, doing a painting with a net pattern across it, as in the case of the Lady Gregory portrait that hangs in the Dublin Municipal Gallery. See "The Municipal Gallery Revisited."

Mangan, James Clarence (1803–49). Dublin-born Irish poet, much of whose poetry was based on translations from the Gaelic. Perhaps his most famous poem thus derived was "Dark Rosaleen." Another that moved Yeats as a young man was "O'Hussey's Ode to The Maguire" (see Allt and Alspach, 851). In his *Autobiography*, Yeats speaks of Mangan as "our one poet raised to the first rank by intensity." Yeats's friend Katherine Tynan, in the "Index of Authors," in her collection of *Irish Love-Songs*, wrote of Mangan that he was "esteemed the first of Irish poets . . . . His life is one long struggle of genius with misery and ill health—a gloomy and terrible story." Perhaps the most significant influence of Mangan upon Yeats was the poem "Kathleen ny-Houlihan," which Mangan had translated from the Irish of William Heffernan. (See Yeats's play *Cathleen ni Houlihan* and the poem "Red Hanrahan's Song About Ireland.") Along with Thomas Davis [q.v.] and Samuel Ferguson [q.v.], Mangan was one of Yeats's favorite poets in the nationalist tradition. Again in his *Autobiography*, Yeats tells how pleased he was on his arrival once at the Clarence Basin, a dock in Liverpool from which, Yeats says, Mangan got his middle name. See "To Ireland in the Coming Times."

Mann, Thomas (1875–1955). German novelist and essayist, often of a political bent. Mann won the Nobel Prize in Literature in 1929, six years after Yeats was so honored. Mann, however, was mentioned as a likely winner of the prize even in the year when Yeats won it, as Yeats indicates in "The Bounty of Sweden" section of his *Autobiography*. The quotation ascribed to Mann, as epigraph to the poem "Politics," was taken by Yeats from an article about himself and his poetry by

Archibald MacLeish, an article which Yeats highly praised in a letter to Dorothy Wellesley [q.v.]. (See *Letters on Poetry from W. B. Yeats to Dorothy Wellesley*, 179.) In the article, MacLeish wrote, "Thomas Mann, who has reason to know, says of the nature of our time, that in our time the destiny of man presents its meanings in political terms." (See Archibald MacLeish, "Public Speech and Private Speech in Poetry.") In a letter to this writer, Mr. MacLeish said the quotation is not from any work by Mann but is quoted from a personal conversation between himself and Mann when the Manns were staying with MacLeish. See the epigraph to the poem "Politics."

Mannion. Yeats's Roaring Tinker, whose name derives from Manannan [q.v.], a sea god and son of the Irish sea god Lir. Mannion is not a tinker, maker of pots and pans, but a lusty wanderer, scorning the "Base-born products of base beds" as Yeats puts it in "Under Ben Bulben." See song I of "Three Songs to the One Burden."

Mantegna, Andrea (1431–1506). Italian painter, whom in *A Vision* Yeats places, along with others such as Botticelli and Leonardo da Vinci, in Phase 15 of the moon, which, being a supernatural incarnation and therefore unable to find direct human expression, "it impresses upon work and thought an element of strain and artifice, a desire to combine elements which may be incompatible, or which suggest by their combination something supernatural . . . something we may call intellectual beauty or compare perhaps to that kind of bodily beauty which Castiglione called 'The spoil or monument of the victory of the soul.' " Yeats noted in his *Autobiography* that in his room at Coole a work of Mantegna was included among the Arundel prints that hung there. In *The Lonely Tower*, T. R. Henn, passim, lists a number of specific paintings by Mantegna that may have influenced Yeats. See "Her Vision in the Wood," which is poem VIII of "A Woman Young and Old."

Mareotic Sea or **Mareotic Lake.** A salt lake lying just south of Alexandria, Egypt. Alexandria is built on a strip of land that separates the Mareotic from the Mediterranean. The Mareotic is associated with both the occult, as in Shelley's "Witch of Atlas," and the founding of Christian monasticism by Anthony [q.v.]. See "Demon and Beast" and "Under Ben Bulben."

Markiewicz, Con. Constance Gore-Booth Markiewicz, first daughter of Sir Henry Gore-Booth, fifth baronet Lissadell [q.v.] in Sligo. Along with her sister Eva Gore-Booth, Constance represented to Yeats the tradition of the landed aristocracy. He observed their life when he was a young boy in Sligo and when he was a guest in their home in 1894. In 1900, Constance married a fellow art student in Paris, the Count Casimir Dunin de Markiewicz, a Polish nobleman. On her return to Ireland, she became increasingly active in Irish nationalist affairs. In 1913, during the great general strikes (that Yeats commemorated in his poem "September 1913), she ran soup kitchens and collected clothing for the locked-out workers. A great horse rider and markswoman herself, she organized the Irish boy scouts, called the Fianna, doing pretty much what the boy scouts of England were doing under Baden Powell; but in the secrecy of the Dublin mountains, she taught the Fianna how to shoot. They became the soldiers of the 1916 Easter Uprising. For her militant part in that uprising, where she and her followers held the College of Surgeons in Saint Stephen's Green for five days before surrendering, she was sentenced to death, a sentence subsequently commuted to life imprisonment, a situation that inspired Yeats's poem "On a Political Prisoner." She was, however, released from prison in 1917 and was a member of the Irish parliament from 1923 to her death in 1927. Yeats regarded ruefully these beautiful women who engaged in the shrill cries of political battle, like Con Markiewicz and Maud Gonne [q.v.]. In his poem "Easter 1916," Yeats pays Con Markiewicz this tribute along with the martyrs of that event:

> That woman's days were spent
> In ignorant good-will,
> Her nights in argument
> Until her voice grew shrill.
> What voice more sweet than hers
> When, young and beautiful,
> She rode to harriers?

See "In Memory of Eva Gore-Booth and Con Markiewicz."

Mars. In casting the horoscopes of his children, Yeats noted in a letter to Olivia Shakespeare (August 25, 1934, in Wade) that his daughter would be the conjunctive planets Mars and Venus and his son would be Saturn conjunctive Jupiter. This had been predicted, and in commenting upon it in the letter, he wrote, "Then I was told that they would develop so that I could study in them the alternating dispensations, the Christian or objective, then the Antithetical or subjective. The Christian is the Mars-Venus—it is democratic." See "Conjunctions," which is poem X of "Supernatural Songs."

Martin, Colonel. The story of Colonel Martin and the character itself are drawn from Irish legend. John Unterecker, in his *Reader's Guide to William Butler Yeats,* reports that Yeats used the Colonel Martin legend as early as 1910 as an illustration of the value of personality in dramatic art. The Colonel, "triumphs as a man of unique character" and his action "becomes one of those epiphanies that give the artist insight into man." See "Colonel Martin."

Mary or **Mother Mary.** In his play *The Countess Cathleen,* Yeats tells of the fate of Cathleen [q.v.], who had sold her soul to the devil to save the famine-ridden poor but whose soul was saved at the last moment and had risen to heaven where Cathleen was greeted by the Blessed Virgin Mary, "And Mary of the seven times wounded heart / Has kissed her lips." See "The Countess Cathleen in Paradise" and "The Uappeasable Host."

Masons. In his biography of Yeats, Joseph Hone writes that the Pollexfens, maternal relatives of Yeats, were active Freemasons, members of the "Light of the West" Lodge. The scattering of Acacia sprays or blossoms over the dead was thought to be a ritual of the masons. See "In Memory of Alfred Pollexfen."

Mayo. The western county of Ireland, in Connaught Province, bordering both county Sligo and county Galway. The name comes from the Irish magh [moy], meaning plain, and eo [yo], meaning yew. According to Patrick W. Joyce in his *Irish Names of Places,* a monastery was erected on the Plain of the Yews in the seventh century; and from this place, county Mayo derives its name. See "In Memory of Major Robert Gregory."

McTaggart, John M. E. (1866–1925). Philosopher and the author of *Studies in Heglian Cosmology.* Yeats, writing in the introduction to his play *Resurrection,* said: "All ancient nations believed in the re-birth of the soul and had probably empirical evidence like that Lafcadio Hearn found among the Japanese. In our time Schopenhauer believed it, and McTaggart thinks Hegel did, though lack of interest in the individual soul had kept him silent. It is the foundation of McTaggart's own philosophical system." See "A Bronze Head."

Meru or **Mount Meru.** Mount Kailas is the actual geographical name of the Hindu holy mountain in the Himalayas. Because it is sacred to so many millions of people, it has been called the most famous of all mountains. (See Yeats's essay called "The Holy Mountain," reprinted in *Essays and Introductions*). Pilgrimages still occur to the foot of the three peaks of Mount Meru, venerated as the dwelling place of the Hindu trinity of Brahma, Vishnu, and Siva. To Yeats, as he explains in his introduction to his play, *The King of the Great Clock Tower* (see Allt and Alspach, 837), Mount Meru "symbolizes a place where the spirits liberated from the cycle of living live in meditation." See "Meru," which is poem XII of "Supernatural Songs."

Michael. The archangel, traditionally depicted as the leader of the forces of God against Satan. Yeats depicts both Michael and Gabriel [q.v.] as trumpeters of Judgment Day. Michael is also the name that Yeats chose for his only son. See "The Rose of Peace," "The Happy Townland," "The Hour Before Dawn," and "Tom O'Roughley."

Michael Angelo. Michelangelo Buonarrotti (1475–1564). Italian sculptor, painter, architect, and poet. He was born in Tuscany and spent his early years in Florence. His decoration of the Sistine Chapel in Rome began in 1508 and was completed in 1512. Considered among the sublime masterpieces of the world, the frescoes on the Sistine ceiling represent depictions of the Creation, of which the superbly muscular Adam is the central figure; the Deluge; and the Last Judgment. The execution of the work required that Michelangelo (Yeats in his poetry spells the name as two names) lie flat on his back on scaffolding for long stretches of time, as he painted the various panels. His muscular and sensuous figures were later to serve as models for those by William Blake [q.v.]. Michelangelo's depiction of "Morning" and "Night" are also famous masterpieces and are to be found in the Medici Chapel in Florence in the New Sacristy of San Lorenzo, where, as sculptured figures, they recline on either side of the tomb. Michelangelo, like Yeats himself, wrote poetry into his very late years; in fact, he was well past fifty years of age when he began his great friendship with the lady, Vittoria Colonna, to whom he dedicated many of his poems. In his essay "Symbolism in Painting" (reprinted in *Essays and Introductions*), Yeats writes of yet another masterpiece by Michelangelo, "It is hard to say where allegory and symbolism melt into one another, but it is not hard to say where either comes to perfection; and though one may doubt whether allegory or symbolism is the greater in the horns of

Michelangelo's Moses, one need not doubt that its symbolism had helped to awaken the modern imagination." See "Michael Robartes and the Dancer," "An Acre of Grass," "Long-Legged Fly," and "Under Ben Bulben."

Michel or **Abbé Michel de Bourdeille.** A name that Yeats made up, perhaps with the help of Dorothy Wellesley (see *Letters on Poetry from W. B. Yeats to Dorothy Wellesley*), to whom he wrote, on September 14, 1936, "When we meet we will decide upon the name of the fourteenth or fifteenth (century?) fabulist who made the original story." The following November 15, he wrote again, saying, "I am describing 'The Three Bushes' as 'founded upon an incident from the *Historia mei Temporis* of the Abbé Michel de Bourdeilie.' " In the published version of the poem, Yeats changed the spelling of the abbé's name to Bourdeille. Oddly enough there was a doctor of theology at the Sorbonne named Michel Bourdeille, who died in 1694. He was the author of a number of books on moral theology, and a number of hymns are attributed to this abbé in the *Bréviaire de la Rochelle*. There is no record of any translations of this Abbé Michel's works and small likelihood that Yeats would ever have read the originals. The correspondence with Dorothy Wellesley, in which both wrote poems on the same theme, confirms a hoax after the manner of the Giraldus hoax in *A Vision*, where the woodcut on page 39 was actually done by Yeats's friend Edmund Dulac. It has also been suggested, with great doubts, that Bourdeille is a bad pun of Yeats's. This suggestion was made by Clive Driver who in turn credits Vivienne Koch for suggesting the pun on bordello. Note also that bourde is French for lie or fib. See the subtitle to and the poem "The Three Bushes."

Michelozzo Michelozzi (1396–1472). Italian sculptor, architect, and goldsmith. He was architect and advisor on art to Cosimo [q.v.] de' Medici, for whom Michelozzo enlarged and rebuilt the Monastery of San Marco [q.v.] at Florence. See "To a Wealthy Man Who Promised a Second Subscription to the Dublin Municipal Gallery if It Were Proved the People Wanted Pictures."

Middleton. Yeats's maternal relatives were Middletons and Pollexfens. [*See* Genealogical Information.] Among the Middletons referred to in Yeats's poetry are his cousin Henry Middleton and his great-grandfather and his great-uncle, both named William Middleton. [*See* below.]

Middleton, Henry. Yeats's cousin, youngest son of great-uncle William

Middleton. Cousin Henry was very little older than the poet and was a playmate of his childhood. He was a handsome, blue-eyed young boy who was the original of the character John Sherman in Yeats's novel of that name. In his biography of Yeats, Joseph Hone writes that Henry Middleton became a noted eccentric, living entirely alone at "Elsinore," one of the houses his father had built at Rosses near the Green Lands, outside of Sligo town. In 1919, when Yeats visited him there, the gate was locked; Yeats climbed the wall and walked into the sitting-room, littered with cheap novels, with a butter-churn in the middle. His cousin was there, beautifully dressed in a summer suit of white. "You see," he said, after they had exchanged a few words, "that I am too busy to see anyone.' " See "Under Saturn," "Are You Content?" and song II of "Three Songs to the One Burden."

Middleton, William. Great-grandfather of the poet, the "smuggler Middleton" of "Are You Content?" From Joseph Hone's biography of Yeats, we learn that this William Middleton "lived an early life of risk and hazard as shipowner, trader and smuggler between London, the Channel Islands and South America, where once he was placed under arrest and escaped with difficulty."

Middleton, William. Great-uncle of the poet, the "Middleton whose name you never heard of" of "Under Saturn." Yeats knew this great-uncle when the poet was a boy in Sligo and played with his cousins George and Henry Middleton, William's sons. Of this William Middleton, the Sligo historian, the Reverend T. O'Rorke, writing of the complex flour milling interests of the Middletons, adds that "Mr. Middleton, the senior partner, is also a landowner, a shipowner, a magistrate, and a Sligo harbour commissioner, and that he sees personally to the details of this multifarious business . . . and . . . if he had only the usual supply of hands and eyes . . . he must be furnished with a head to organize and to administer, such as is rarely vouch-safed to mortals." The Pollexfens were partners of the Middletons in these business ventures. Yeats's earliest autobiographical writings make frequent reference to his great-uncle William Middleton and to his Middleton cousins.

Midhir [me'yir]. A king of the Sidhe [q.v.] who lived in a fairy mound or hill that also bore his name. He took Edain [q.v.] as his second wife. Yeats, in early editions of his poems, spelled the name Meder and

Mider, suggesting his preference then for an anglicized pronunciation of the name. See "Baile and Aillinn" and "The Harp of Aengus."

Minnaloushe. The name of a black Persian cat belonging to Maud Gonne [q.v.] at the time Yeats was a house guest at her place in Calvados, France, in 1917. Writing to his friend Sturge Moore from Calvados (The letter is reprinted in Ursula Bridge, ed., *W. B. Yeats and T. Sturge Moore*, 28), Yeats said, "I am living in a house with three and thirty singing birds . . . . There is also a Persian cat, a parrot, two dogs, two rabbits and two guinea-pigs and a Javanese cock which perches on Madame Gonne's chair." In the same year, Yeats wrote, as a prologue to his essay "Per Amica Silentia Lunae" (reprinted in *Mythologies*), addressed to "Maurice," presumably a Yeatsian disguise for Maud Gonne or for her daughter Iseult, the following:

> My dear "Maurice"—You will remember that afternoon in Calvados last summer when your black Persian "Minnou-looshe," who had walked behind us for a good mile, heard a wing flutter in a bramble-bush? For a long time we called him endearing names in vain. He seemed resolute to spend his night among the brambles. He had interrupted a conversation, often interrupted before, upon certain thoughts so long habitual that I may be permitted to call them my convictions. When I came back to London my mind ran again and again to those conversations and I could not rest till I had written out in this little book all that I had said or would have said. Read it someday when "Minnoulooshe" is asleep.

See "The Cat and the Moon."

Minos. In Greek mythology, a famous king and lawgiver of Crete. Along with his brother Rhadamanthus [q.v.] (they were the sons of Zeus and Europa) and with Aeacus, Minos was one of the three judges in Hades whose duty was to pass sentence on all the dead, sending the wicked to torment and the good to Elysian Fields. See "The Delphic Oracle upon Plotinus."

Mitchel, John (1815–75). Lawyer and journalist, founder in 1848 of the *United Irishman*. Mitchel's articles called for open rebellion against England, for which he was transported to Australia on charge of sedition. He was a prisoner of the English for five years, before he escaped to the United States in 1853. During the years of imprisonment, Mitchel kept a journal, which came to be called the *Jail Journal*. His bitter outcries against the English and against Irish complacency in the fight for independence have made the journal a notable patriotic document and an Irish revolutionary classic. Mitchel returned to Ireland shortly before his death. Among other writings, he edited the poems of James Clarence Mangan and Thomas Davis. Arthur Griffith [q.v.], who was to become the first president of the Irish Free State, edited an edition of the *Jail Journal* and wrote an introduction for it. Though other editions were available, the Griffith edition was not published until 1940. The line in the journal that Yeats slightly misquotes is "Give us war in our time, O Lord!" See "Under Ben Bulben."

Mocharbuiee. A village just southwest of the town of Sligo. Yeats gives the pronunciation as Mockrabee. The name in Irish means the yellow plain and is more frequently spelled Magheraboy, Yeats's spelling being closer to his anglicized pronunciation of the name. Merville, the house of Yeats's Pollexfen grandparents, with whom Yeats so often stayed as a boy, was located very near to Mocharbuiee. See "The Fiddler of Dooney."

Mohini Chatterjee. *See* **Chatterjee.**

Molay, Jacques de (1243?-1314). The last grand master of the Knights Templars, the order of knighthood devoted to service in the Holy Land. Originally a poor order, the templars had acquired so much wealth and power that jealousy led finally to their arrest and the confiscation of their property. Jacques de Molay was tried for heresy by an inquisitorial court in France; he was tortured, confessed to certain charges, recanted his confession; he was finally burned at the stake. Yeats, in a note to the poem, found at the end of *Collected Poems,* writes, referring to the lines in the poem "Vengeance upon the murdered, the cry goes up, / Vengeance for Jacques Molay": "A cry for vengeance because of the murder of the Grand Master of the Templars seems to me fit symbol for those who labour from hatred." See "I See Phantoms of the Hatred and of the Heart's Fullness and of the Coming Emptiness," which is poem VII of "Meditations in Time of Civil War."

Montashigi. An ancestor of Junzo Sato [q.v.]. Sato, Yeats's Japanese admirer, presented Yeats with a sword encased in embroidered silk. The sword had been in Sato's family supposedly for five hundred years, when it had been fashioned by his ancestor, Montashigi of Osafume, the name that Yeats had included in the line in the poem when it appeared in *The Winding Stair* (1929), but never after. Yeats directed in his will that upon his death the sword be returned to Sato's son. In a letter to Olivia Shakespeare in October, 1927 (Wade, 729), Yeats wrote that, while the sword was in his possession, "I make my Japanese sword and its silk covering my symbol of life." See "A Dialogue of Self and Soul."

Montenegrin. The adjective form of the one-time kingdom of Montenegro, part of what was once Yugoslavia. The Montenegrin lute is described as a one-string instrument, perhaps not able to make the sweet music the poem may be ironically suggesting. Yet, perhaps in the proper hands, it might do so. See "The Statesman's Holiday."

Mooneen. More commonly Moneen, the name of many places located near small bogs, from the diminutive form of the Irish moin, meaning bog. Many so-named places are found in the west of Ireland, as well as in all the other provinces. See "In Memory of Major Robert Gregory."

Moroccan. A reference to Morocco, across the Straits of Gibraltar from Algeciras in Spain. Yeats went to Algeciras for reasons of health. See "At Algeciras—A Meditation upon Death."

Mourteen. An Irish name found commonly among the peasants and an equivalent of Martin. See "Running to Paradise."

Muirthemne [mwir hev'ne]. A great plain, located in county Louth and extending from the River Boyne to the mountains of Carlingford and from Dundalk to Drogheda. Ancient Muirthemne was the patrimony of Cuchulain [q.v.]. It was named for the son of an early Milesian invader of Ireland; but it came to be associated with Cuchulain, who was raised there and ultimately died there after the great battle of the Ulster or Red Branch cycle of Irish mythology. Cuchulain's residence is said to be the ruins of an old fort, two miles west of Dundalk. See "Baile and Aillinn."

Municipal Gallery. The Municipal Gallery of Modern Art, located in Dublin. It is entirely distinct from the National Gallery of Ireland, also located in Dublin. In 1958, Patrick O'Connor, then curator of the Municipal Gallery, published an *Illustrated Catalogue of the Gallery,* in which he wrote:

The Municipal Gallery was first temporarily housed in Clonmel House, Harcourt Street. It owes its origin to a movement initiated in 1902 by Sir Hugh Lane [q.v.] . . . . On January 20th, 1908, the Municipal Gallery was opened to the public . . . . Various controversial sites were considered for the permanent home of the Municipal Art Gallery. Eventually the choice fell on historical Charlemont House, one of Dublin's finest Georgian mansions; it was designed and built for Lord Charlemont by Sir William Chambers, 1762–5. It was reconstructed by the Dublin Corporation into a modern art gallery (1933) at the cost of £35,000.

For Yeats, the treasures of the Municipal Gallery were abundant: both his father and brother are represented there by numerous works; many of his most famous friends are to be seen there in paintings, drawings, and sculptures. Among the works of art are portraits by John Butler Yeats of Katherine Tynan, Standish O'Grady, W. G. Fay, Douglas Hyde, and John M. Synge; portraits by Antonio Mancini of Lady Gregory and Sir Hugh Lane; another portrait of Lane by John Singer Sargent; also Arthur Griffith by Lily Williams; Con Markiewicz by B. Szankowski; George Russell (pseud. Æ) by Count Markiewicz; also Sarah Purser's portraits of Edward Martyn, Maude Gonne, and Yeats himself; John Lavery's portraits of William T. Cosgrave, Eamon de Valera, Hazel Lavery, and George Bernard Shaw; also the bronzes of John O'Leary by Oliver Sheppard; Charles Stewart Parnell by Mary Grant; Lady Gregory by Jacob Epstein, and the bronzed plaster bust of Maud Gonne by Lawrence Campbell.

But for Yeats, any visit to the gallery would bring to his mind the long battle that he and Lady Gregory had waged to bring the paintings Hugh Lane's will gave to what became the Tate Gallery in London back to Dublin, in accordance with the unwitnessed codicil to the will left before Lane's trip to America, on the return from which he lost his life with the sinking of the Lusitania. The gallery is now called The Hugh Lane Gallery. See "To A Wealthy Man Who Promised a Second Subscription to the Dublin Municipal Gallery if It Were Proved the People Wanted Pictures" and "The Municipal Gallery Revisited."

Munster. The southwest province of Ireland. According to Patrick W.

Joyce's *Irish Names of Places,* it derived its name from that of an ancient monarch of Ireland named Mumha or Mumhain, whose name was pronounced moon or moun. The termination -ster was added many centuries later. See "The Dedication to a Book of Stories Selected from the Irish Novelists."

Murias. A legendary city. [*See* Falias for a detailed account of the significance of Murias.] See also "Baile and Aillinn."

Murrough. The son of the high king of Ireland, Brian Boru. In the Battle of Clontarf, on Good Friday, April 23, 1014, Brian and his forces succeeded in overpowering the Norsemen and ending forever the Scandinavian dream of conquest in Ireland. In the fierce fighting, Murrough broke the opposing Norsemen but fell in the battle. His father, Brian Boru, also gave his life in the battle. See "The Grey Rock."

N

Naoise [neesh'e]. This is the pronunciation that Yeats gives for the name where he lists the characters in his play *Deirdre*. Naoise is the young man who eloped with Deirdre [q.v.] in perhaps the most famous love story of Irish mythology. Naoise and his two brothers, known as the children of Usna [oosh' na], fled Ulster with Deirdre and set sail for Scotland to escape the wrath of Conchubar [q.v.], who had chosen Deirdre for himself. Later, the sons of Usna and Deirdre were tricked into returning to Ireland, where Conchubar arranged for the murder of Naoise and his brothers and Deirdre dies of a broken heart. See Yeats's play *Deirdre*. Also see "Under the Moon," and "Baile and Aillinn."

Nessa. The mother of Conchubar [q.v.]. In some accounts, Nessa had Conchubar in virgin birth; but in other, more frequent accounts, he was her son by her marriage to Cathbad the Druid. Later, Nessa married Fergus [q.v.] and influenced him to step down as king of Ulster in favor of her son Conchubar. See "The Old Age of Queen Maeve."

Newton, Sir Isaac (1642–1727). English physicist best known for his laws of gravitation and motion. One of the few personal quotations of Newton preserved is the famous metaphor of his life, quoted here from *John Bartlett's Familiar Quotations,* "I do not know what I may appear to the world; but to myself I seem to have been only like a boy playing on the seashore, and diverting myself in now and then finding a smoother pebble or a prettier shell than ordinary, whilst the great ocean of truth lay all undiscovered before me." Yeats obviously admired the metaphor, but he did not approve of mechanistic philosophies. In "Pages from a Diary" in *Explorations,* he writes "Descartes, Locke, Newton took away the world and gave us its excrement instead. Berkeley [q.v.] restored the world." See "At Algeciras—A Meditation upon Death."

Niamh [nee' av]. In an early edition of his poems, Yeats gives the spelling as Neave, a good approximation of the usual pronunciation. Niamh was the daughter of the king of the Country of the Young, or Tir-nan-Og. Niamh, or Niamh of the Golden Head, as she was also known, came before the Fianna [q.v.] and picked Oisin [q.v.] to be her lover from among all the men of both her country and his. Niamh and Oisin lived blissfully in the Country of the Young for many hundreds of years, until Oisin began to long for Ireland and for a glimpse of his old comrades. Despite Niamh's fears and warnings, Oisin made his way back but made the mistake he had been warned against of getting down from his horse and touching the ground. Thus time overtook him, and he became at once a withered old man. The story is told at length in Lady Gregory's *Gods and Fighting Men.* See "The Hosting of the Sidhe"; "The Lover Asks Forgiveness Because of His Many Moods"; "Alternative Song for the Severed Head," in *The King of the Great Clock Tower;* "News for the Delphic Oracle"; and "The Wanderings of Oisin."

Nietzsche, Friedrich Wilhelm (1844–1900). German philosopher and uncompromising advocate of the ideal man or superman. In *A Vision,* Yeats places Nietzsche in Phase 12 of the moon, where "there is a noble extravagance, an overflowing fountain of personal life." Yeats also says that a man true to this phase "is a cup that remembers but its own fullness. His phase is called 'Forerunner' because fragmentary and violent. . . . It is a phase of immense energy." See "The Phases of the Moon."

Ninevah. Ancient capital of the Assyrian empire. In 705 B.C., the king of Ninevah was Sennacherib, who set about to plunder and destroy that he might make Ninevah a rich city. He brought back so many riches that Ninevah became the most magnificent city of the East, so luxurious that the prophet Jonah was sent to warn its inhabitants that its days were numbered before it would become a dry waste (Jonah 1:1–13 and 3:1–10). See "Fragments," II.

No King. *See* **King and No King.**

Northern Cold. A reference to the Fomoroh. Yeats in a note to his 1895 edition of *Poems* (reprinted in Allt and Alspach, 798), describes the Fomoroh as "the powers of death and darkness and cold and evil, . . . from the north." See "The Madness of King Goll."

O

O'Byrnes. *See* Byrnes.

O'Donnell and O'Donnell Abu. Hugh Roe O'Donnell (ca. 1571–1602), also called Red Hugh and The O'Donnell, lord of Tyrconnell and an implacable foe of the English. He scored notable conquests in battles at Sligo, at the Curlews, and at Yellow Ford, and became thus a great heroic figure to the Irish. Celebrated in story and song, Red Hugh is the central figure of a famous traditional Irish song written in 1597 and credited to M. J. M'Cann. The song is called "O'Donnell Abu," *abu* being a battle cry meaning "to victory"! In the collection called *The Spirit of the Nation or, Ballads and Songs* (Dublin, 1901, 90), the first stanza is given as follows:

> Proudly the note of the trumpet is sounding,
> Loudly the war-cries arise on the gale,
> Fleetly the steed by Loc Surling is bounding
> To join the thick squadrons in Saimeer's green vale.
> On, every mountaineer,
> Strangers to flight and dear;
> Rush to the standards of Dauntless Red Hugh!
> Bonnought and Gallowglass
> Throng from each mountain pass!
> On for old Erin!—O'Donnell Abu!

See songs I and II of "Three Songs to the Same Tune," and "Three Marching Songs."

O'Driscoll. The hero of Yeats's ballad, which is based on a story told to the poet by an old woman at Balisodare, Sligo. In a note to the poem when it first appeared, in *The Bookman* in November 1883 (reprinted in Allt and Alspach, 143), Yeats wrote, "She repeated to me a Gaelic poem on the subject, and then translated it to me. I have always regret-

132

ted not having taken down her words, and as some amends for not having done so, have made this ballad. Any one who tastes fairy food or drink is glamoured and stolen by the fairies. This is why Bridget sets O'Driscoll to play cards." See "The Host of the Air."

O'Duffy, Owen [in Irish "eoin"] (1892–1944). One time chief of staff and commander of the Irish Free State forces. Later he joined the opposition party—the United Ireland Party—and became its head and head of its Fascist element, known as the Blue Shirts. Yeats became briefly interested in the Fascist movement, an interest later withdrawn, but in a letter to Olivia Shakespeare, July 23, 1933, he wrote:

> The Fascist organizer of the Blue Shirts had told me that he was about to bring to see me the man he had selected for leader that I might talk my anti-democratic philosophy. I was ready, for I had just re-written for the seventh time the part of A Vision that deals with the future. The leader turned out to be General O'Duffy, head of the Irish police for twelve years, and a famous organizer. . . . O'Duffy himself is autocratic, directing the movement from above down as if it were an army. I did not think him a great man though a pleasant one, but one never knows, his face and mind may harden or clarify.

O'Duffy's efforts in 1936 to lead an Irish Brigade supporting Franco in Spain met with defeat and disgrace, an end that Yeats wished for, as he explains in a letter to Ethel Mannin, dated March 1, 1937 (in Wade): "I am convinced that if the Spanish war goes, or if [it] ceases and O'Duffy's volunteers return heroes, my 'pagan' institutions, the Theatre, the Academy, will be fighting for their lives against Catholic and Gaelic bigotry. A Friar or a monk has already threatened us with mob violence." See "Parnell's Funeral."

Odysseus. In Greek mythology, the king of Ithaca, husband of the loyal Penelope. Odysseus is an important figure in the *Iliad* of Homer and the central figure of the *Odyssey*. After the fall of Troy, Odysseus, with twelve ships, set out on the return voyage to Ithaca. Because he was among those who had stolen the sacred statue of Athene, known as the Palladium, the loss of which led to the fall of Troy, and because he had slain Polyphemus, the son of the sea god Poseidon, his return home was delayed for a period of ten years, years of harrowing experience in which all of his ships and men were lost. He returned to Ithaca alone. See "The Sorrow of Love."

Oedipus. Sophocles told the story of Oedipus in three of the most famous tragic dramas of classical Greece: *Oedipus Rex, Antigone,* and *Oedipus at Colonus.* Of these, Yeats prepared versions of the first and last for the modern stage. He also did some passages from *Antigone.* In Greek mythology, Oedipus unknowingly kills his father and marries and has children with his mother, thus fulfilling an earlier prediction. When he learns the truth, he blinds himself in his revulsion and wanders for many years before he dies at Colonus. See Yeats's plays, Sophocles' *King Oedipus,* and Sophocles' *Oedipus at Colonus.* See also "Colonus' Praise"; and "From Oedipus at Colonus," which is poem XI of "A Woman Young and Old."

Ogham. An early form of Irish writing found chiefly on memorial stones. Notches were made on the stones for vowels and lines for consonants. See "The Wanderings of Oisin," "Baile and Aillinn," and "The Two Kings."

O'Grady, Standish (1846–1928). Irish author, historian, and a leader in the Celtic Renaissance. His *History of Ireland* remains a standard work; and his English versions of the ancient heroic legends of Ireland, including the Cuchulain saga, were well known to Yeats. The image of O'Grady that Yeats gives in "Beautiful Lofty Things" is from an actual occurrence at a dinner in Dublin, which Yeats also writes about in the "Dramatis Personae" section of his *Autobiography:*

> Towards the end of the evening, when everybody was more or less drunk, O'Grady spoke. He was very drunk, but neither his voice nor his manner showed it. . . . He stood between two tables, touching one or the other for support, and said in a low penetrating voice: "We have now a literary movement, it is not very important; it will be followed by a political movement, that will not be very important; then must come a military movement, that will be important indeed."

Yeats, in the same account, also mentions "the sweetness of that voice, the nobility of that gesture." An oil painting of O'Grady hanging in the Dublin Municipal Gallery is by Yeats's father. See "Beautiful Lofty Things."

O'Hart, Father John. An actual personage, who was priest of the parishes of Ballysadare and Kilvarnet in the early eighteenth century. Coloney [q.v.] is in the parish of Kilvarnet. Yeats, in a note to *The Ballad of Father O'Hart* in the 1895 edition of his *Poems* (reprinted in Allt and Alspach, 797), indicates that he took the story from a book by a Father O'Rorke, "from his learnedly and faithfully and sympathetically written history of these parishes." The full title of that book is *History, Antiquities, and Present State of the Parishes of Ballysadare and Kilvarnet in the County of Sligo,* by T. O'Rorke. Father O'Hart was strongly against keeping birds in cages and against the practice of keeners, the professional mourners-criers commonly employed at wakes and funerals. Yeats, in his note, continues, "Some sayings of Father John have come down. Once when he was sorrowing greatly for the death of his brother, the people said to him, 'Why do you sorrow so for your brother when you forbid us to keen?' 'Nature,' he answered, 'forces me, but ye force nature.' " See "The Ballad of Father O'Hart."

O'Higgins, Kevin Christopher (1892–1927). Lawyer and statesman. O'Higgins had fought for Irish independence and served his country as minister of justice and as minister of external affairs, a prominent figure at the League of Nations conferences at Geneva. He was vice-president of the Executive Council of the Irish Free State, and he was a much respected friend of Yeats's. Yeats in his "On The Boiler" (reprinted in *Explorations*), speaks scathingly of the ministers of the Irish Free State, noting that even "the ablest had signed the death-warrant of his dearest friend." This is a reference to O'Higgins, who signed the death-warrant for the man who had been best man at his wedding, when they were now on opposite sides in the Irish Civil War. Nevertheless, Yeats had the highest regard for O'Higgins and grieved at the news of his assassination. O'Higgins was assassinated in 1927 while on his way to mass, near Dublin. Yeats felt O'Higgins's death very deeply, as he clearly shows in a letter to Olivia Shakespeare, undated but of July or August 1927 (in Wade): "The Murder of O'Higgins was no mere public event to us. He was our personal friend, as well as the one strong intellect in Irish political life and then too his pretty young wife was our friend. We got the news just when we reached the Gresham Hotel where we were to dine and we left without dining and walked about the streets till bedtime." O'Higgins, dying, said, "I forgive my murderers," and in his notes to *The Winding Stair* (in Allt and Alspach, 831), Yeats wrote, "I think that I was roused to write "Death" and "Blood and the Moon" by the assassination of Kevin O'Higgins." A portrait of O'Higgins, painted by Sir John Lavery, hangs in the Municipal Gallery in Dublin. See "Parnell's Funeral" and "The Municipal Gallery Revisited."

Oisin [ush' een]. Son of Finn [q.v.], king of the Fianna. In notes to the 1895 and 1899 editions of *Poems* (reprinted in Allt and Alspach, 796), Yeats says that Oisin was "the poet of the Fenian cycle of legend, as Fergus was of the Red Branch cycle." Oisin is also the central figure of many of the poems dealing with the Fianna, the followers of Finn. The most famous of these is his voyage in ancient times to the Country of the Young [q.v.] led by the beautiful Niamh [q.v.], who had picked him for her husband, and his much later return to Ireland in the time of Saint Patrick. This forms the substance of Yeats's long narrative poem "The Wanderings of Oisin." See "News for the Delphic Oracle," "The Circus Animals' Desertion," and "The Wanderings of Oisin."

Old Country Scholar. A reference to the poet's great-grandfather, John Yeats, who was born in 1774. He was a scholar, receiving his B.A. degree from Trinity College, Dublin, in 1797, winning a medal in Greek. Having taken orders, he received an appointment as rector at Drumcliff [q.v.], about five miles outside Sligo town. This appointment came in 1805 and thus established the Sligo relationship of the Yeats side of the poet's family. John Yeats was a contemporary of Robert Emmet [q.v.]; and in his *Autobiography,* Yeats tells us that not only was he Emmet's friend but at the time of Emmet's arrest and sentencing, John Yeats was "suspected and imprisoned though but for a few hours." T. O'Rorke, in his history of the parishes of Sligo, writes that John Yeats was "popular amongst the Roman Catholics as well as the Anglo-Irish of the district." See "Pardon, Old Fathers."

Old Dublin Merchant. A reference to the earliest known ancestor of the poet bearing the Yeats name, Jervis Yeats, who died in 1712. According to Joseph Hone, earliest biographer of Yeats, he was in the "wholesale linen business in Dublin, and enjoyed the privilege of being exempt from certain duties by the Irish parliament"; but according to Norman Jeffares, the "Free of ten and four," stated by the poet, is, incorrect. See "Pardon, Old Fathers."

Old Merchant Skipper. A reference to the poet's grandfather William Pollexfen [q.v.]. In his *Autobiography*, Yeats says that he was a man who "thought so little of danger that he jumped overboard in the Bay of Biscay after an old hat." It was the Pollexfens who "once had their share in the old Spanish trade with Galway." And it was William Pollexfen, at whose house in Sligo the poet spent many of his childhood years, whom Yeats acknowledges as his most impressive early influence: "I think I confused my grandfather with God." See "Pardon, Old Fathers."

Old Rocky Face. This reference, being a symbol, cannot be precisely defined, but it is worth pointing out, as A. G. Stock has done in his *W. B. Yeats: His Poetry and Thought*, that there is, in fact, a sculptured stone head "set in the side of Yeats's tower facing Coole—staring, therefore, on the symbol of the glory that a turbulent age is sweeping away." But Rocky Face could be many other things as well, perhaps Ben Bulben [q.v.] itself. See "The Gyres."

O'Leary, Daniel. A character, along with Huddon [q.v.] and Duddon [q.v.], who appear in "Stories of Michael Robartes and His Friends: An Extract from a Record Made by His Pupils," which forms a section of *A Vision*. There O'Leary is introduced as the chauffeur who says his "great interest is the speaking of verse, and the establishment some day or other of a small theatre for plays in verse." In Yeats's early collection of *Irish Fairy and Folk Tales*, Huddon and Duddon appear in an old tale with their neighbor Donald O'Leary, but the name is Daniel O'Leary when Yeats uses it. In a footnote in *A Vision*, Yeats says of O'Leary, "As a child I pronounced the word as though it rhymed to 'dairy.' " See "Tom the Lunatic."

O'Leary, John (1830–1907). A leader of the Fenians [q.v.] and one of the strongest of all influences on Yeats. In his *Autobiography*, Yeats writes about the meetings of the Young Ireland Society when O'Leary presided, that from the debates there, "from O'Leary's conversation, and from the Irish books he lent or gave me has come all that I have set my hand to since." It was O'Leary, too, who was chiefly responsible for getting *The Wanderings of Oisin and Other Poems* published in 1889. Again in his *Autobiography*, Yeats writes: "I often wonder why he gave me his friendship, why it was he who found almost all the subscribers for my Wanderings of Oisin, and why he now supported me in all I did." O'Leary, born in Tipperary, became a Young Irelander in 1848 and joined the Fenian brotherhood, becoming editor of the Fenian newspaper *Irish People*. He was arrested and imprisoned in 1865, served five years of a twenty-year sentence in prison and the other fifteen years in exile, in France. He returned to Ireland in 1885 and lived with his sister Ellen in Dublin, surrounded by his books and by devoted young followers, active in many literary and political movements. Also in his *Autobiography*, Yeats says that O'Leary "had the moral genius that moves all young people," and how particularly impressed he was by O'Leary's comment that "there are things that a man must not do to save a nation." An oil painting of John O'Leary by the poet's father hangs in the National Gallery in Dublin. Yeats thought O'Leary "the handsomest old man I had ever seen." See "September 1913" and "Beautiful Lofty Things."

Ollave [ol' av]. An English adaptation of the Irish ollamh, signifying a learned man of the highest rank. See "The Madness of King Goll."

Olympus and Olympians. In Greek mythology, Mount Olympus was the home of the Olympians, the twelve most important gods and goddesses living there under the rule of Zeus. For Yeats, who felt his glory was his friends, the parallel of friends and Olympians was obvious. See "The Fascination of What's Difficult," and "Beautiful Lofty Things."

O'Neills. A reference to the heroic leaders of the O'Neill clan of Ulster, of which there were many. Shane O'Neill (ca. 1530–67) was one of the most famous, but it is, no doubt, the O'Neills who fought the Protestant forces of Elizabeth and of Cromwell that are best remembered. Hugh O'Neill (ca. 1547–1616) and his nephew Owen Roe O'Neill (ca. 1590–1649) and, in turn, his nephew Hugh O'Neill, are the leading figures of the clan. The latter O'Neill was able to throw back the Cromwellian forces in a major encounter; but it is believed that Owen Roe, who died too soon, was the one leader who might have defeated Cromwell, for which see Yeats's letter to the editor of *United Ireland*, December 17, 1892, and the accompanying note in volume 1 of *The Collected Letters*, edited by Kelly and Domville. See song II of "Three Songs to the Same Tune," and song I of "Three Marching Songs."

Ophelia. In Shakespeare's *Hamlet*, the daughter of Polonius and the beloved of Prince Hamlet. Yeats's interest is in the actress who plays the role and does not, should not, weep when the curtain falls. In Frank O'Connor's *Backward Look*, he asks Yeats if it is ever permissible for an actor to sob at the curtain of a play. Yeats replied, "Never!" See "Lapis Lazuli."

O'Rahilly, The. M. J. O'Rahilly, a hero of the Easter Uprising of 1916 who was killed in the fighting. He was the son of a wealthy publican in county Kerry. He called himself The O'Rahilly because he was the head of the old Kerry clan, and clan heads traditionally used only "The" and the surname, no first name being used. In *Protest in Arms*, Edgar Holt writes that O'Rahilly had joined in the uprising, even though he thought it was all a tragic mistake; and after the General Post Office headquarters became untenable and evacuation was ordered, the "first to leave the G. P. O. were a party commanded by The O'Rahilly, who went out by the Henry Street door and tried to make their way up Moore Street to Parnell Street; but their advance was stopped by heavy fire from a barricade farther up Moore Street, and The O'Rahilly fell mortally wounded in a lane off the right-hand side, where a plaque on the wall now recalls his gallantry." The dying O'Rahilly wrote his signature on the pavement with his own blood. See "The O'Rahilly."

Orchil. In notes to the 1895 edition of *Poems* (reprinted in Allt and Alspach, 796), Yeats identifies Orchil as "a Formorian sorceress." The Formoroh were a mythological race of "gods of night and death and cold." See "The Madness of King Goll."

Ormondes. The earls of Ormonde were the ancient Butler family, which Joseph Hone in his biography of Yeats, says was "next to the Fitzgeralds the most illustrious of the Anglo-Irish medieval families." Yeats looked back with pride to the Butlers from whom he claimed descent, abetted by the possession in the family of a silver cup bearing the Ormonde crest. Later, George Moore, in his *Hail and Farewell*, twitted Yeats about this claim, perhaps maliciously. Portraits of many of the Ormondes hang in the National Gallery, Dublin. See "Demon and Beast."

O'Roughley, Tom. Tom of Roughley, Roughley being a place name of a village and point of land near the Rosses [q.v.] in county Sligo, and associated in Yeats's mind with fishing. Tom's attitude toward death —"What's dying but a second wind?"—certainly reflects the poet's own. See "Tom O'Roughley."

Oscar. Frequently spelled Osgar and, in Irish legend, the son of Oisin. Among the Fianna, Oscar was known as the best in spear throwing and other physically demanding activities; but he was also known as much for his kindness as for his bravery. It is unlikely that this is the Oscar of "The Statesman's Holiday." There, a more likely association would be to Oscar Wilde, who boasted, as Yeats quotes him in the Yeats *Autobiography*, "He who can dominate a London dinner-table can dominate the world." But the legendary Oscar is found in "The Wanderings of Oisin." With regard to Oscar's "pencilled urn," this is a reference to Oscar's grave marker with its Ogham [q.v.] markings. The reference also appears in an earlier poem by Sir Samuel Ferguson called "Aideen's Grave." Aideen was the wife of Oscar, son of Oisin, son of Finn. She died of grief when Oscar and almost all the Fianna lost their lives at the Battle of Gabhra [q.v.]. Ferguson's poem, in part, reads:

> The great green rath's ten-acred tomb
> Lies heavy on his urn.
> Bold Oscar; mighty heart and limb
> A cup of bodkin-pencilled clay
> One handful now of ashes grey:
> And she has died for him.

See "The Statesman's Holiday" and "The Wanderings of Oisin."

P

Pairc-na-Carraig [park' na kar'ig]. One of the seven woods at Coole [q.v.], the estate of Lady Gregory in county Galway. Pairc-na-Carraig means field of the rock, from pairc, which means a field or enclosure in Irish, and carraig, which signifies a rock, usually one more or less elevated from the surface of the ground. See "I Walked Among the Seven Woods of Coole," the dedicatory poem to *The Shadowy Waters*.

Pairc-na-Lee [park' na Lee']. One of the seven woods at Coole, the estate of Lady Gregory in county Galway. Pairc-na-Lee means field of the calves, from pairc, meaning a field or enclosure, and laogh, which means calf and from which lee is derived. See "In the Seven Woods" and "I Walked Among the Seven Woods of Coole," the dedicatory poem of *The Shadowy Waters*.

Pairc-na-Tarav [park' na tar' ev]. One of the seven woods at Coole, Lady Gregory's estate in county Galway. Pairc-na-Tarav means field of the bulls, from pairc, meaning a field or enclosure, and tarbh, the Irish word for bull. See "I Walked Among the Seven Woods of Coole," the dedicatory poem to *The Shadowy Waters*.

Paistin Finn. From the Irish an Paistin Fionn [en pas' teen fin], meaning fairhaired maid, and the title of a centuries-old song well known in Ireland. Earlier translations of the song from its original Irish were made by John D'Alton and published in *Irish Minstrelsy*, edited by James Hardiman; and, in a famous rendering by Sir Samuel Ferguson [q.v.], called "Pastheen Finn," and found in *Poems of Sir Samuel Ferguson*. As Yeats indicates at the end of poem I of "Two Songs Rewritten for the Tune's Sake," this song is from his play *The Pot of Broth*, much altered from the other versions. See Yeats's play *The Pot of Broth* and poem I of "Two Songs Rewritten for the Tune's Sake."

Palmer, Samuel (1805–81). English landscape painter and etcher. Palmer was a follower of William Blake [q.v.], whom he met in 1824. Among

Palmer's works that Yeats was familiar with were his illustrations of *The Shorter Poems of John Milton,* particularly the etching for "Il Penseroso," called "The Lonely Tower," included in D. J. Gordon's *W. B. Yeats: Images of a Poet.* In "Under Ben Bulben," when Yeats mentions the artists Edward Calvert, Richard Wilson, Blake, and Claude Lorraine, he says they "Prepared a rest for the people of God, / Palmer's phrase." Palmer's phrase that Yeats is recalling is one that Palmer used while discussing Blake's woodcuts for Thornton's *Virgil,* quoted at length in A. H. Palmer's *Life and Letters of Samuel Palmer,* as well as in Gordon, "They are like all that wonderful artist's works the drawing aside of the fleshly curtain, and the glimpse which all the most holy, studious saints and sages have enjoyed that rest which remaineth to the people of God." See "The Phases of the Moon," and "Under Ben Bulben."

Pan. In Greek mythology, the god of flocks and shepherds. Pan was a pastoral fertility god. He dwelt in grottoes and had a terrifying voice, but he is also credited with inventing musical pipes made of reeds. See "News for the Delphic Oracle."

Paragon. Homer's paragon is a reference to Helen of Troy. [*See* Helen and Homer.] See "The Double Vision of Michael Robartes."

Paris. The Trojan prince, son of King Priam and Queen Hecuba of Troy. At his birth, it was predicted that he would cause the downfall of Troy, and so he was sent away to a remote island to live as a shepherd. Later, Zeus randomly chose him to settle the dispute between Athene, Hera, and Aphrodite over which goddess should possess the Apple of Discord, which was inscribed "for the fairest." Paris chose Aphrodite, who had offered him the love of the most beautiful woman in the world. She took him to Sparta, where he saw Helen, wife of Menelaus. Paris persuaded her to elope with him to Troy, thus leading to the Trojan War, so vividly depicted by Homer in the *Iliad.* See "His Wildness," which is poem X from "A Man Young and Old"; and "Lullaby."

Parmenides and **Treatise of Parmenides.** Parmenides of Elea (fl. fifth century B.C.), Greek philosopher. The treatise of Parmenides was a poem entitled "Nature," dealing with his abstract, mystical doctrine of reality. Parmenides is an important figure in several of Plato's dialogues, notably in the dialogue called Parmenides and in the Sophist. Yeats commented on Parmenides in his notes to *The Cat and the Moon and*

Certain Poems (reprinted in Allt and Alspach, 829). See Yeats's poem "The Gift of Harun al-Rashid."

Parnell, Charles Stewart (1846–91). Irish nationalist leader. Though a Protestant, Parnell succeeded in uniting the different and often clashing elements among Irish patriots of whatever religious persuasion. Frequently called the uncrowned king of Ireland, he pursued a policy of obstruction against the English, even when imprisoned for his activities. Forged letters were used in an unsuccessful attempt to defame him; but his career came to an abrupt end in the scandal of the divorce of Captain William O'Shea and his wife, Katherine, with Parnell named as corespondent. Parnell later married Mrs. O'Shea. The affair, however, turned the Catholic clergy against Parnell, and the English capitalized on it to help end his influence. His followers were now divided into Parnellites and anti-Parnellites. Parnell failed in his efforts to reunite the factions, and his health failed as well. Future Irish freedom owed much to the work of Parnell, but he died a broken man. Yeats wrote in his autobiographical writings,

> I had seen Ireland in my own time turn from the bragging rhetoric and gregarious humour of O'Connell's generation and school [*see* Great Comedian], and offer herself to the solitary and proud Parnell as to her anti-self, buskin following hard on sock, and I had begun to hope or to half hope, that we might be the first in Europe to seek unity as deliberately as it had been sought by theologian, poet, sculptor, architect, from the eleventh to the thirteenth century.

In a letter of September 1936, in which he enclosed an earlier version of his poem "Come Gather Round Me, Parnellites" (see Wade; but see also Yeats's essay on Parnell in *Essays and Introductions*), Yeats wrote to Dorothy Wellesley as follows:

> About three weeks or a month ago a man, Harry Harrison, an old decrepit man, came to see me. As a young Oxford undergraduate fifty years ago he had joined Parnell's party and now had written a book to defend Parnell's memory. Mrs. O'Shea was a free woman when she met Parnell, O'Shea had been paid to leave her free, and if O'Shea had been able to

raise £20,000 would have let himself be divorced instead of [naming] Parnell. The Irish Catholic press had ignored his book. It preferred to think that the Protestant had deceived the Catholic husband. He begged me to write something in verse or prose to convince all Parnellites that Parnell had nothing to be ashamed of in her love. The result is the enclosed poem. . . . You will understand the first verse better if you remember that Parnell's most impassioned followers are now very old men.

In addition to being outraged by O'Shea, "the husband what had sold his wife / and after that betrayed," Yeats was appalled by the fact that earlier Irish heroes, such as Emmet, Fitzgerald, and Tone, were "killed" by "strangers," that is, by the English, whereas Parnell was "killed" by the Irish themselves. Standing alone against mob opinion, Parnell reminds Yeats of Jonathan Swift [q.v.], who, as a line in Yeats's play *Words upon the Window Pane* has it: "hated the common run of men." In his earlier poem, "To a Shade," Yeats associated Hugh Lane [q.v.], and his troubles, with Parnell, who is the shade come from Glasnevin cemetery. Glasnevin is the Dublin cemetery where Parnell is buried, as is O'Connell, Yeats's Great Comedian. Also, to Yeats, the leaders that followed Parnell in time, De Valera [q.v.], Cosgrave [q.v.], even the fascist O'Duffy [q.v.], were of the crowd and lacked the bitter wisdom of a Swift or a Parnell. See "Parnell's Funeral," song II of "Three Songs to the Same Tune," "Come Gather Round Me, Parnellites," "Parnell," and song I of "Three Marching Songs."

Parnellites. *See* **Parnell.**

Party, The. Refers to the anti-Parnellites. [*See* Parnell.]

Pater, Walter Horatio (1839–94). English critic and essayist. Pater had an enormous influence on writers at the turn of the century. Yeats acknowledged Pater's influence on his "Rosa Alchemica" and wrote: "If Rossetti was a subconscious influence, and perhaps the most powerful of all, we looked consciously to Pater for our Philosophy. Three or four years ago I re-read Marius the Epicurean, expecting to find I cared for it no longer, but it still seemed to me, as I think it seemed to us all, the only great prose in modern English." The above occurs in the *Autobiography,* as does Yeats's quoting of Oscar Wilde in praise of

Pater. Speaking of Pater's *Studies in the History of the Renaissance,* Wilde says, "It is my golden book; I never travel anywhere without it, but it is the very flower of decadence: the last trumpet should have been sounded the moment it was written." See "The Phases of the Moon."

Patrick or **Saint Patrick** (ca. 389–ca. 461). English missionary to and a bishop in Ireland as well as patron saint of Ireland, Saint Patrick took Christianity to Ireland in the year 432, when he landed at Wicklow. His name is associated with many places in Ireland [*see* Cro-Patrick], and the traditional stories of Ireland are filled with accounts of his miracles and his teachings, among them his driving the snakes out of Ireland and his using the shamrock to explain the Holy Trinity to the heathens. One of the oldest accounts deals with the encounter between Saint Patrick and Oisin [q.v.] when the latter returned to Ireland after countless years in the mythical Country of the Young [q.v.]. Lady Gregory recounts this story in her book *Gods and Fighting Men,* for which Yeats wrote a preface; but Yeats himself had included the encounter in "The Wanderings of Oisin." The assumption that the Patrick of Yeats's poem "Ribh Denounces Patrick" is indeed Saint Patrick seems borne out by the fact that the poem was originally titled "Ribh Prefers an Older Theology." See "Ribh Denounces Patrick," which is poem II of "Supernatural Songs"; and "The Wanderings of Oisin."

Paudeen. An Irish word signifying an uncouth or uncultivated person, often applied to middle-class shopkeepers. During the Lane [q.v.] controversy over the building of a gallery to house Sir Hugh Lane's pictures, in 1913, Yeats fought valiantly to help secure the necessary funds for the new gallery, against the opposition of people who had opposed Parnell as well. Yeats leveled his supreme attack on the "wealthy man" who would not contribute more unless it was proved that "the people" wanted pictures. In his poem, the people are the Paudeens and biddys, not the ones to make such decisions. See "To a Wealthy Man Who Promised a Second Subscription to the Dublin Municipal Gallery if It Were Proved the People Wanted Pictures" and "Paudeen."

Pavlova, Anna Matveyevna (1882–1931). Russian prima ballerina universally acclaimed, particularly for her performances as the dying swan in the ballet "The Death of the Swan," created for her by Michael Fokine. Yeats lists her in his poem among beautiful and much-admired entertainers, descendants of Helen, daughter of Leda. See "His Phoenix."

Pearse, Patrick (or Padraic) Henry (1879–1916). Irish patriot and educator. Pearse was in command of the Irish forces in the Easter Uprising of 1916 and was one of the sixteen men the English executed when the uprising failed. Pearse had "kept a school," the Saint Enda's School for boys in Dublin, which he founded in 1909 as a bilingual school. Active in the Gaelic League, dedicated to reviving the Irish language, Pearse was editor of its journal and was as well a poet, playwright, and story writer. On Easter Monday, 1916, standing before the General Post Office building in Dublin, Pearse read the proclamation of "The Provisional Government of the Irish Republic to the People of Ireland," in which he said,

> In every generation the Irish people have asserted their right to national freedom and sovereignty: six times during the past three hundred years they have asserted it in arms. Standing on that fundamental right and again asserting it in arms in the face of the world, we hereby proclaim the Irish republic as a sovereign independent state, and we pledge our lives and the lives of our comrades in arms to the cause of its freedom, of its welfare, and of its exaltation among the nations.

Full accounts of this proclamation and of the uprising are given in every Irish history book, particularly well done by the Irish writer, poet, and playwright Padraic Colum in his book *Ourselves Alone!* Thereto are the accounts of the leaders of the uprising, their surrender, their condemnation to death without trial because England was at war with Germany at the time, and their deaths, which, indeed, turned the tide of public opinion against the English, making martyrs of Pearse and his comrades in arms. Yeats associates the statue of Cuchulain, the great heroic figure of Irish mythology whose statue is still in the Post Office, with Pearse and Connolly [q.v.] and the others. See "Easter 1916," "Sixteen Dead Men," "The Rose Tree," "The O'Rahilly," song III of "Three Songs to the One Burden," and "The Statues."

Peleus. In Greek mythology, the king of the warlike Myrmidons. Peleus married the sea nymph Thetis and from this union was born Achilles [q.v.]. A famous painting of Peleus and Thetis by the French painter

Nicholas Poussin (1613–75) is in the National Gallery in Dublin, where Yeats would have seen it most of his lifetime. The painting, where "Peleus on Thetis stares," is titled "The Marriage of Thetis and Peleus" (Mariage de Thétis et Pelée). See "News for the Delphic Oracle."

Perseus. In Greek mythology, the youth who was the slayer of Medusa, the most famous of the three Gorgons. Medusa had snakes for hair and a face so hideous that anyone looking on her would turn to stone. To accomplish this feat, Perseus was given a sickle by Hermes, a mirror-like shield by Athene, and a helmet from Hades, given him by nymphs, that made him invisible, along with a bag and winged sandals. With these aids he was able to cut off Medusa's head while he was invisible and was looking in the shield-mirror and not directly at her. See "Her Triumph," which is poem IV of "A Woman Young and Old."

Pestle. The pestle of the moon refers to a belief, cited in the *Dictionary of Mythology, Folklore, and Symbols,* that an inhabitant of the moon pounds out the drug of immortality. See "On Woman."

Peter. In "The Fiddler of Dooney," a reference to Saint Peter, but elsewhere a name for an exuberant. Christ's disciple Saint Peter is frequently represented as the keeper of the gates of heaven to whom all must appeal for entrance. The statement from the Gospels (Matthew 16:18), "Thou art Peter, and upon this rock I will build my church," may be vaguely echoed in "The Friends of His Youth," where Peter "perches on a stone," but his outburst, "I am King of the Peacocks," suggests relationship to Queen Hera, whose sacred bird was the peacock. See "The Fiddler of Dooney"; "The Friends of His Youth," which is poem VII of "A Man Young and Old"; and "Summer and Spring," VIII of the same.

Petronius Arbiter, Caius, or **Titus** (ca. A.D. 37–ca. 68). Roman writer. His best-known work is the fragmentary *Satyricon,* in which he takes delight in describing current vices. But he is also known as Petronius Arbiter or as Arbiter Elegantiarum, judge of elegances, and it is this that brings him to Yeats's mind as he visits the dying lady Mabel Beardsley, sister of Aubrey Beardsley. Petronius is supposed to have committed suicide to escape a death sentence from Nero. See "Her Courtesy," poem I of "Upon a Dying Lady."

Pharaoh. The name given to the ancient kings of Egypt. A number of

well-preserved mummies of pharaohs have been discovered by archae-
ologists. In some of these, kernels of grain have been preserved and are
sometimes called mummy wheat, as Yeats does in his poem "Conjunctions." See poem VIII of "Vacillations."

Phidias. The Greek sculptor of the fifth century B.C., widely held to be
the greatest sculptor of the classical period, if not of all time. Only
fragments of his work remain, but his statue of Zeus was held to be
one of the seven wonders of the world. Phidias generally worked in
bronze or in ivory, the latter frequently adorned with gold in a technique called chryselephantine. He was in charge of the construction of
the Parthenon, a feature of which was the chryselephantine statue of
Athene, which was surrounded by golden grasshoppers and bees. See
"Nineteen Hundred and Nineteen" and "Under Ben Bulben."

Phoenix. The legendary and solitary bird that lived for more than five
hundred years and then burned itself to death on a funeral pyre from
the ashes of which a new phoenix arose. Thus the bird has been
through the ages a symbol of immortality. In his poem called "His
Phoenix," Yeats mentions women, so attractive to him, from Leda
[q.v.], "that sprightly girl trodden by a bird" to famous ladies of the
stage to ordinary women loved by many men, but none to equal the
immortal phoenix of his youth. Many critics immediately suggest Maud
Gonne [q.v.] as his phoenix, but it might have been a childhood love.
See "The Lover Asks Forgiveness Because of His Many Moods" and
"His Phoenix."

Pierced Hands. A reference to the Crucifixion as Conchubar [q.v.] saw it
in a vision, according to Yeats. But in his notes to "The Secret Rose,"
given in *Collected Poems,* Yeats acknowledges that he changed the old
story in which a Druid told Conchubar that the eclipse he saw was
caused by Christ's being crucified. Conchubar, enraged, took his sword
and rushed into a grove of trees, felling them as he would Christ's
enemies. Years earlier, Conchubar had been hit in the head by a ball
thrown from a sling where it remained, as Yeats describes. But now, in
his rage, the ball started out and his brains came with it. Thus, according to this story, Conchubar died. See "The Secret Rose."

Pilot Star. A name for Polaris, the North Star, by which mariners traditionally guided their ships. See "He Thinks of His Past Greatness When
a Part of the Constellations of Heaven."

Plato. Also **Platonic** and **Platonist** (ca. 427–347 B.C.). Greek philosopher, disciple of Socrates and teacher of Aristotle. Plato's influence on Yeats is vast. His name is mentioned many times in the poetry, and many elements are drawn from Plato's dialogues: the Platonic Year, in which the heavenly bodies finally return to their original positions (Yeats writes at length about the Platonic Year in "The Great Year of the Ancients" section of *A Vision*) is from the *Republic,* as is Plato's spindle; Plato's parable of dividing an egg with a hair is from the *Phaedo.* As Yeats indicates in "Mad as the Mist and Snow," Plato's works stood on the study shelf of his tower home, along with works of Horace, Homer, and Cicero. In "Among School Children" Yeats shows particular interest in the way three philosophers look at reality: Plato in the "ghostly images of things"; Aristotle in nature; and Pythagoras in his measurements of art. But in old age this did not satisfy Yeats. In a letter to Olivia Shakespeare in December 1926 (in Wade), he says, "Here is a fragment of my last curse on old age. It means that even the greatest men are owls, scarecrows, by the time their fame has come." He then quotes stanza VI, where the names of the three philosophers occur. See "The Tower," "Nineteen Hundred and Nineteen," Song II of "Two Songs from a Play," "Among School Children," "His Bargain," "Mad as the Mist and Snow," "The Delphic Oracle upon Plotinus," and "What Then?"

Plautus, Titus Maccius (ca. 254–184 B.C.). Roman dramatist, particularly adept in comedy and farce. Plautus had a vast influence on writers of the Renaissance and after, among them Ariosto, Shakespeare, and Molière. Ariosto translated Plautus for the pleasure of his patron, Duke Ercole [q.v.], regardless of the tastes of the onion-sellers. See "To a Wealthy Man Who Promised a Second Subscription to the Dublin Municipal Gallery if It Were Proved the People Wanted Pictures."

Playboy of the Western World, The. Title of the play by John Millington Synge [q.v.], first produced at the Abbey Theatre in Dublin in 1907. The production provoked riots that lasted one week. See "On Those That Hated *The Playboy of the Western World,* 1907."

Plotinus. Plotinus of Alexandria (ca. 205–270), founder of neoplatonism. His idea of emanation is an extension of the Idea of Good in Plato. What is known of Plotinus comes to us from his disciple Porphyry (ca. 233–ca. 304), who edited his teacher's works and wrote of him in

"The Cave of the Nymphs" and in "Life of Plotinus." In a preface to the works, Prophyry claimed that the Delphic Oracle had written a poem about Plotinus. Yeats knew these writings on Plotinus from the English translation by Stephen McKenna, who also translated the Delphic poems. Yeats's poem "The Delphic Oracle upon Plotinus," is a reworking of a Delphic poem depicting Plotinus's struggle in swimming to the Elysian Fields. In the latter poem "News for the Delphic Oracle," Yeats indicates that Plotinus has safely arrived. In the preface to his play *The Words upon the Window-Pane* (reprinted in *Explorations*), Yeats wrote, "Plotinus said that we should not 'baulk at this limitlessness of the intellectual; it is an infinitude having nothing to do with number or part' (Ennead V. 7. I.); yet it seems that it can at will re-enter numbers and part and thereby make itself apparent to our minds. If we accept this idea many strange or beautiful things become credible." See "The Tower," "The Delphic Oracle upon Plotinus," and "News for the Delphic Oracle."

Pollexfen. Yeats's maternal relatives were the Pollexfens of Sligo [*See* Genealogical Information]. His mother was Susan Pollexfen, and it was in nearby Drumcliffe Churchyard that the poet chose to be buried. Among the Pollexfens mentioned in the poems are Alfred, Elizabeth, George, John, and William. [*See* below.]

Pollexfen, Alfred. The youngest of Yeats's maternal uncles, described by Yeats in his *Autobiography* as "stout and humourous." He was a sailor and not much at home, but returned to Sligo in his fiftieth year where he died. Again in his *Autobiography,* Yeats notes the presence of a seabird, and wrote "A sea bird is the omen that announces the death or danger of a Pollexfen." See "In Memory of Alfred Pollexfen."

Pollexfen, Elizabeth. Yeats's maternal grandmother. She had been a Middleton [q.v.] and a cousin of her husband. Hone, in his biography of Yeats, writes, "William Pollexfen's wife was a kind, gentle and patient woman who read the Bible regularly . . . ambitious for her large family of sons and daughters. . . . Husband and wife were devoted; when she sat near him he was at peace." See "In Memory of Alfred Pollexfen."

Pollexfen, George. Yeats's maternal uncle, who was also his closest friend among all his relatives. George Pollexfen was a well-known and skillful horse rider in Sligo and Mayo, the adjoining county. Joseph Hone quotes Yeats's father as writing, "George on a race-course, above all if mounted on a wild and splendid horse, was a transformed being. . . . I never saw any man on horseback to compare with him, horse and man made a unity of grace and strength." In his later years, George Pollexfen became an astrologer and mystic, and it was this mutual interest that brought him close to Yeats, who always stayed with his Uncle George when he visited in Sligo. Uncle and nephew held séances and conducted occult experiments, notable for the psychic reaction of Uncle George's clairvoyant servant, Mary Battle, who influenced the poet's *Celtic Twilight*. Pollexfen was an active mason, as were many of the Pollexfens. [*See* Masons.] See "In Memory of Major Robert Gregory" and "In Memory of Alfred Pollexfen."

Pollexfen, John. Little is known of this maternal uncle, except that he followed the sea, as had both his Pollexfen and Middleton forebears, and was lost at sea or else died in some remote, unknown place. See "In Memory of Alfred Pollexfen."

Pollexfen, William. Yeats's maternal grandfather and an enormous influence on Yeats in his early childhood. In his *Autobiography,* Yeats writes, "I think I confused grandfather with God." He feared and respected him and remembered him as "an old cross Pollexfen." In "Pardon, Old Fathers," he speaks of him as the "silent and fierce old man." Yeats's father, as Hone reports in his biography of the poet, said that "The Yeats's have 'knowledge of the art of life and enjoyment,' but the Pollexfens are full of the materials of poetic thought and feeling." "By marriage with the Pollexfens I have given a tongue to the sea cliffs." Yeats has written that this was the only compliment that ever turned his head. See "In Memory of Major Robert Gregory," "In Memory of Alfred Pollexfen," "Under Saturn," and "Are You Content?"

Pope's Chapel. The Sistine Chapel in the Vatican is the private chapel of the pope. It was built in 1473 by Pope Sixtus IV. Among the great art treasures in the chapel are the famous frescoes painted on the ceiling by Michelangelo, which required his lying flat on his back on scaffolding. The frescoes, begun in 1508 and completed in 1512, are titled "Creation," "Deluge," and "Last Judgment." The heroic figure of Adam is central to the "Creation." See "Long-Legged Fly."

Poseidon. In Greek mythology, Poseidon is the principal god of the sea. He is the brother of Zeus. Beneath the sea, Poseidon maintains a palace where he keeps his brazen war horses. In a contest with Athene to see who could serve man best (in some accounts, the contest is to see who should have the honor of naming the capitol of Attica), Poseidon produced a war horse as a gift to man, but Athene is said to have created the olive and was adjudged the winner. Poseidon's symbol of power was the three-pronged trident, with which he could shake the land and control the sea. See "Colonus' Praise."

Post Office. The General Post Office in Dublin, principal scene of the fighting during the Easter Uprising of 1916. The Post Office is located on the west side of O'Connell Street (once Sackville Street) and was completed in 1818 from designs of Francis Johnston. The building boasts a grand Ionic portico, eighty feet wide, with fluted columns. It was gutted by fire during the uprising and was subsequently restored. In 1934, Oliver Sheppard's statue of Cuchulain [q.v.] was installed in the Post Office. Yeats associates the heroic Cuchulain's presence there with the heroism of Pearse [q.v.] and Connolly [q.v.], the leaders of the Uprising. The statue is suggestive of the death of Cuchulain, and Yeats related directly to it in the song that ends his play *The Death of Cuchulain*.

> What stood in the Post Office
> With Pearse and Connolly?
> What comes out of the mountain
> Where men first shed their blood?
> Who thought Cuchulain till it seemed
> He stood where they stood?
>
> No body like his body
> Has modern woman borne,
> But an old man looking on life
> Imagines it in scorn.
> A statue's there to mark the place,
> By Oliver Sheppard done.
> So ends the tale that the harlot
> Sang to the beggar-man.

See song III of "Three Songs to the One Burden" and "The Statues."

Priam. The king of Troy, father of Paris and Hector. In Homer's *Iliad*, Priam begs Achilles to return the body of his slain son, Hector, for a proper burial. In the accounts of Troy's fall, Priam is murdered in cold blood, an act generally credited to Neoptolemus (also called Pyrrhus), a son of Achilles. See "The Sorrow of Love."

Primum Mobile. In the Ptolemaic system of the universe, the primum mobile, or first mover. Its movements enable all the other spheres down to the sphere of Earth to have movement. Or, as Yeats explains in his essay "Ideas of Good and Evil," reprinted in *Essays and Introductions,* "Dante, like other mediæval mystics, symbolised the highest order of created beings by the fixed stars, and God by the darkness beyond them, the Primum Mobile." See "My Descendants," which is poem IV of "Meditations in Time of Civil War."

Propertius, Sextus (ca. 50–ca. 16 B.C.). A native of Umbria, educated in Rome, Propertius wrote four volumes of elegiac poetry, most of it love poetry inspired by the beautiful "Cynthia." See "A Thought from Propertius."

Proteus. In Greek mythology, an aged deity, subject of Poseidon, the sea god. Proteus was credited with great knowledge and great prophetic powers; but to get his prophecy, one had to steal upon him and keep him from escaping one's grasp, even as Proteus exercised his power to change instantly into any form he wished. Yeats takes this image directly from the sonnet by Pierre de Ronsard [q.v.] that Yeats acknowledges imitating in the epigraph to his poem. See "At the Abbey Theatre."

Pythagoras. Greek philosopher, native of Samos, who lived in the sixth century B.C. He founded a brotherhood dedicated to temperance and purity, and his philosophical system included such doctrines as the mathematical basis to the universe, the transmigration of souls, and musical principles involving intervals between heavenly bodies and its attendant harmony of the spheres. Pythagorean mathematics influenced many artists. Yeats, in his tract "On the Boiler," reprinted in *Explorations,* wrote:

> There are moments when I am certain that art must once again accept those Greek proportions which carry into plastic art the Pythagorean numbers, those faces which are divine because all there is empty and measured. Europe was not born when Greek galleys defeated the Persian hordes at Salamis, but when Doric studios sent out those broad-backed marble statues

against the multiform, vague, expressive Asiatic sea, they gave
to the sexual instinct of Europe its goal, its fixed type.

Pythagoras is the subject of many legends that tell of his manly
beauty; of his knowledge of his previous existences; and in a legend
recounted in Plutarch's life of Numa Pompilius, of Pythagoras's golden
thigh, which he was wont to flash at the Olympic games to the delight
of the multitudes. Dryden translated Plutarch's lines from "Numa
Pompilius," *The Lives of the Noble Grecians and Romans,* later revised
by Arthur Hugh Clough, "For it is said of Pythagoras, that he had
taught an eagle to come at his call, and stoop down to him in his flight;
and that, as he passed among the people assembled at the Olympic
games, he showed them his golden thigh, besides many other strange
and miraculous seeming practices." Of the three great systematizers of
Greek philosophy, Yeats is interested in the way each locates reality:
Plato in the "ghostly images of things"; Aristotle in Nature; and Pythagoras in his measurements of art, Pythagorean numbers. [*See* Plato.]
See "Among School Children," "The Delphic Oracle upon Plotinus,"
"The Statues," and "News for the Delphic Oracle."

Q

Quattrocento. The fifteenth century. Used particularly in relation to the art of that century. See "Among School Children," "Her Vision in the Wood," which is poem VIII of "A Woman Young and Old."

R

Rachlin [rah'lin]. A reference to Rathlin Island, ancient Reachrainn, situated off the north coast of county Antrim in Ulster Province. See "The Wanderings of Oisin."

Raftery, Anthony (1784–1834). Poet, wandering minstrel, and composer of Irish songs. Blind through small pox, Raftery learned to play the violin and became a wandering minstrel-poet, attending fairs and gatherings in the Irish countryside. Raftery was very popular in the Galway area; and in 1903, Yeats wrote in his essay "The Galway Plains" (reprinted in *Essays and Introductions*), "It was here that Raftery, the wandering country poet of ninety years ago, praised and blamed, chanting fine verses, and playing badly on his fiddle." Raftery spent a great deal of time in Coole [q.v.] and Ballylee [q.v.], but he is buried where he was born, near Killeenan in county Mayo, where Lady Gregory [q.v.] erected a tombstone over his grave in 1900. (Lady Gregory's detailed account of Raftery forms chapter 1 of her *Poets and Dreamers*.) Because Raftery was blind, Yeats associated him with Homer, the more so because Raftery commended in song a local Ballylee Helen named Mary Hynes, the peasant girl referred to in Yeats's poem "The Tower." Yeats recounted the stories of Raftery and Mary Hynes in a chapter of *The Celtic Twilight*, (reprinted in *Mythologies*). The chapter is entitled "Dust Hath Closed Helen's Eye" (Yeats took that title from "In Time of Pestilence," by Thomas Nashe, 1567–1601); and there Yeats sets down Raftery's verses about Mary Hynes, saying that they were translated for him by a friend and by country people themselves. Following are some of the verses:

> Going to Mass by the will of God,
> The day came wet and the wind rose;
> I met Mary Hynes at the cross of Kiltartan,
> And I fell in love with her then and there . . .

The table was laid with glasses and a quart measure,
She had fair hair, and she sitting beside me;
And she said, "Drink, Raftery, and a hundred welcomes,
There is a strong cellar in Ballylee."

. . . Her hair was shining, and her brows were shining too;
Her face was like herself, and her mouth pleasant and sweet.
She is the pride, and I give her the branch,
She is the shining flower of Ballylee.

In the same essay, Yeats writes of speaking to a local man about the poem, and particularly about the line "There is a strong cellar in Bal-lylee," "He said the strong cellar was the great hole where the river sank underground, and he brought me to a dark pool, where an otter hurried away under a gray boulder, and told me that many fish came up out of the dark water at early morning 'to taste the fresh water coming down from the hills.' " The imagery is important to Yeats's poem "Coole Park and Ballylee." The river that sank underground is the river at Ballylee that runs beside Yeats's tower home, Thoor Ballylee [q.v.]; the river, running underground for a spell, rises to the surface again at Coole, Lady Gregory's nearby estate. See the poem "Coole Park and Ballylee."

Red Branch. The literal translation of Craobh Ruaoh [krev'roo], the name of the great hall at Emain [q.v.] and the seat of Conchubar and the champions of Ulster. Because of the great hall, the champions became known as the Heroes of the Red Branch, and the ancient stories that make up their saga are known as the Red Branch cycle or the Ulster cycle. The mountain of Crevroe [q.v.], located near the river Callam, near Navan in Ulster, is believed to be the very site of the great hall. See "Fergus and the Druid," "Cuchulain's Fight with the Sea," and "The Wanderings of Oisin."

Rembrandt. John Synge [q.v.] was supposed to have said to Yeats that the portrait of Lady Gregory by Mancini [q.v.] was the greatest portrait he had seen since those of Rembrandt van Rijn (1606–69), the Dutch painter. For Yeats's own musings on Rembrandt, see "Phase Twenty-three" *A Vision.* See "The Municipal Gallery Revisited."

Rhadamanthus. In Greek mythology, the son of Zeus and Europa [q.v.] and the brother of Minos [q.v.]. Rhadamanthus, a law-giver known for his integrity, established Cretan law and, like his brother, was made a judge of the dead in Hades after his own death. See "The Delphic Oracle upon Plotinus."

Ribh [riv]. An imaginary Christian hermit and mystic. Yeats, in notes to *A Full Moon in March* (reprinted in Allt and Alspach, 857), called Ribh "An imaginary critic of St. Patrick. His Christianity, comes perhaps from Egypt like so much early Irish Christianity, echoes pre-Christian thought." In a letter to Olivia Shakespeare dated July 24, [1934] (in Wade), Yeats projects his poem of Ribh and the legendary loves, Baile and Aillinn, "I have another poem in my head where a monk reads his breviary at midnight upon the tomb of the long-dead lovers on the anniversary of their death, for on that night they are united above their tomb, their embrace being not partial but a conflagration of the entire body and so shedding the light he reads by." In *The Identity of Yeats,* Richard Ellmann, points out that "Ribh's peculiar religion is based as much on hatred as on love of God, and concentrates on the sensual rather than the spiritual side of celestial life. Where Crazy Jane [q.v.] usually maintains that there is a spiritual aspect to physical delight, Ribh defends the converse." Yeats, in the notes to *The King of the Great Clock Tower* (reprinted in Allt and Alspach, 837–38), wrote of "that old hermit Ribh," saying "I would consider Ribh, were it not for his ideas about the Trinity, an orthodox man." See "Ribh at the Tomb of Baile and Aillinn," "Ribh Denounces Patrick," "Ribh in Ecstasy," and "Ribh Considers Christian Love Insufficient." These constitute poems I, II, III, and V of "Supernatural Songs."

Rice. *See* **Spring-Rice.**

Robartes, or **Michael Robartes** [the pronunciation is usually given as **ro bar'tees**]. Imaginary character created by Yeats and used in *A Vision* and a number of poems. Robartes is a scholar, visionary, and recluse. Yeats wrote of his use of that name and the name of Owen Aherne [q.v.], in notes to *Collected Poems:*

> I now consider that I used the actual names of two friends, and that one of these friends, Michael Robartes, has but lately returned from Mesopotamia where he has partly found partly thought out philosophy. I consider that Aherne and Robartes, men to whose namesakes I had attributed a turbulent life or

death, have quarrelled with me. They take their place in a phantasmagoria in which I endeavour to explain my philosophy of life and death. To some extent, I wrote these poems as a text for exposition.—1922.

In the original edition of Yeats's 1899 book of poems, *The Wind Among the Reeds,* many of these poems had the names of Aedh [q.v.], Hanrahan [q.v.], and Michael Robartes in the title, where "He," "The Lover," or "The Poet" appears in later editions. In the notes given in the early edition (reprinted in Allt and Alspach 803), Yeats wrote of these three names, "Hanrahan is the simplicity of an imagination too changeable to gather permanent possessions, or the adoration of the shepherds; and Michael Robartes is the pride of the imagination brooding upon the greatness of its possessions, or the adoration of the Magi; while Aedh is the myrrh and frankincense that the imagination offers continually before all that it loves."

Many critics agree that Robartes and Aherne represent aspects of Yeats's personality, and Yeats uses Robartes to develop his own philosophy. In Yeats's "Rosa Alchemica" (reprinted in *Mythologies*), it is Robartes who initiates Yeats into the Order of the Alchemical Rose. In the notes of the early edition of Yeats's collection of poems, *Michael Robartes and the Dancer,* (reprinted in Allt and Alspach, 821–23), Yeats credits Robartes for much of the background for the poem "An Image from a Past Life," but the open book that Robartes left, in "Ego Dominus Tuus," is Yeats's own *A Vision.* See "Ego Dominus Tuus," "The Phases of the Moon," "The Double Vision of Michael Robartes," and "Michael Robartes and the Dancer."

Rocky Voice. Rocky Voice is found in an ancient Irish song called "The Lay of Bin Bolgin," ascribed to Oisin [q.v.] and identifying the Rock's wild son as Echo, in the lines:

> Yes, 'twas delight to hear the cry
> Of hounds along the valleys sweep;
> To hear the rock's wild son reply
> From every cliff and steep.

Yeats's technique of having Echo reply in the last few words spoken by the man is exactly that of another ancient poem/song entitled "Carroll O'Daly and Echo." Both "The Lay of Bin Bolgin" and "Carroll O'Daly and Echo" are found in *Irish Minstrelsy*, edited by James Hardiman, 1831. Bin Bolgin is the same as Ben Bulben [q.v.], the mountain that dominates Sligo. It has a cleft in it known as Alt [q.v.]. A visit to the glen of Alt confirms the echo. See "The Man and the Echo."

Rody. A character who appears in the foxhunter [*see* Foxhunter] incident in Charles J. Kickham's novel *Knocknagow*. See "The Ballad of the Foxhunter."

Ronsard, Pierre de (1524–85). French poet and courtier, noted especially for his poems of love and patriotism. Ronsard was a member of the Pléiade, a group of French poets writing largely in the reign of Henri III (1574–89). The group sought to improve the French language by promoting the literary use of it, especially by enthusiastic imitation of the classics. Yeats recognized in this a parallel to his efforts and those of Lady Gregory and Synge to restore Irish literature written in English to the splendors of Irish mythology and folkways upon which they drew quite as the Pléiade had drawn upon the classics, replacing medieval forms with sonnets, odes, and alexandrines. Of the Pléiade group, one older poet, Pontius de Tyard (1521–1605) had the acclaim of the French people, much as Douglas Hyde [q.v.] had the acclaim of the Irish people, while Yeats, Lady Gregory, and Synge, in their work at the Abbey Theatre, seemed able only to incur the people's criticism and wrath. Thus it is possible to locate the precise poem of Ronsard's that Yeats is imitating in his poem "At the Abbey Theatre." The French of Ronsard is as follows:

> Tyard, on me blasmoit, à mon commencement,
> De quoy j'estois obscur au simple populaire,
> Mais on dit aujourd'huy que je suis au contraire,
> Et que je me démens, parlans trop bassement.
> Toy de qui le labeur enfante doctement
> Des livres immortels, dy-moy, que doy-je faire?
> Dy-moy, car tu sçais tout, comme doy-je complaire
> A de monstre testu, divers en jugement?
> Quand je tonne en mes vers, il a peur de me lire;
> Quand me voix se desenfle, il ne fair qu'en mesdire.
> Dy-moy de quel lien, force, tenaille, ou clous

Tiendray-je-ce Prote qui se change à tous coups?
Tyard, je t'enten bien, il le faut laisser dire,
Et nous rire de luy, comme il se rit de nous.

There is no assurance that Yeats read this in the original French because translations were always available to him, but his indebtedness to Ronsard may be seen more clearly by examining a literal translation of Ronsard's French:

Tyard, I was blamed, at my beginnings,
Because I was obscure to the simple man of the people,
But it is said today that I am to the contrary,
And that I belie myself, speaking too lowly.
You whose labor engenders wisely
Immortal books, tell me, what must I do?
Tell me, for you know all, how may I please
This stubborn monster, diverse in judgment?
When I thunder in my verse, he is afraid to read me;
When my voice deflates, he does but scorn.
Tell me with what tie, force, tentacle, or nail
Shall I hold this Proteus who changes at all blows?
Tyard, I understand you well; one must let him talk,
And laugh at him as he laughs at us.

The above is not the only occasion of Yeats's indebtedness to Ronsard. His poem, "When You Are Old," is clearly adapted from the following poem of Ronsard's:

Quand vous serez bien vieille, au soir à la chandelle,
Assise aupres du feu, devidant et filant,
Direz chantant mes vers, en vous esmerveillant:
'Ronsard me celebrait du temps que j'estois belle.'
Lors vous n'aurez servante ayant telle nouvelle,
Desja sous le labeur à demy sommeillant,
Qui au bruit de mon nom ne s'aille resveillant,
Benissant vostre nom de louange immortelle.
Je seray sous la terre, et fantome sans os
Par les ombres myrteux je prendray mon repos;
Vous serez au fouyer une vieille accroupie,

Regrettant mon amour et vostre fier desdain.
Vivez, si m'en croyez, n'attendez à demain:
Cueilles des aujourdhy les roses de la vie.

But in his version, Yeats moves much further from Ronsard's, as this literal translation indicates:

When you are very old, at evening by the candle,
Seated by the fire, unwinding and spinning,
[You] will say, singing my verses, astonishing yourself,
"Ronsard sang my praises when I was beautiful."
Then you shall have no servant hearing such news,
Already half asleep under her labor
Who at the sound of my name does not reawaken,
Blessing your name with immortal praise.
I shall be underground and [a] phantom without bones
By the myrtle shades I shall take my repose.
You will be at the hearth a hunched old woman,
Regretting my love and your proud disdain.
Live, if you believe me, await not tomorrow:
Gather this very day the roses of life.

Yeats truly makes "When You Are Old" his own poem, but the debt to Ronsard is unmistakable. The literal translations given here were by Professor John B. Rey. In addition to "When You Are Old," see "At The Abbey Theatre."

Rosicross or **Father Rosicross.** A reference to Christian Rosenkreuz or Rosencrux, founder of Rosicrucianism, the mystical belief whose symbols are principally the rose and the cross. Material, garnered from the *Encyclopædia Britannica,* 1960, indicates that old documents called *Fama Fraternitatis* and *Confessio,* published in 1614, tell us that Christian Rosenkreuz was born in 1378 and lived for 120 years, to 1484. His tomb was hidden for 120 years and rediscovered in 1604, at which time the Rosicrucian Order, first founded in the fifteenth century, gained new momentum. Rosenkreuz had traveled far, particularly in the Middle East, and was everywhere well-received and everywhere acquired secret wisdom. On his return to his native Germany, he imparted this wisdom to three others, and thus the order was established. Rosicrucianism, which varies from branch to branch, claims an esoteric wisdom combining the teachings of Egyptian Hermeticism, Christian Gnosticism, Jewish Kabbalism, as well as occult and alchemical doctrines and practices. Yeats himself was a member of an esoteric society called the Order of the Golden Dawn. In his essay called "The Body of the Father Christian Rosencrux," from *Ideas of Good and Evil* (reprinted in *Essays and Introductions*), Yeats wrote, "The followers of the Father Christian Rosencrux, says the old tradition, wrapped his imperishable body in noble raiment and laid it under the house of their order, in a tomb containing the symbols of all things in heaven and earth, and in the waters under the earth, and set about him inextinguishable lamps, which burnt on generation after generation, until other students of the order came upon the tomb by chance."

Yeats also says there that he thinks the history of the imagination is similar to the body of Father Rosencrux—the lamps of wisdom and romance being set over it until its rediscovery. See "The Mountain Tomb."

Rosses, The. The name in Irish signifies points of land or peninsulas. The Rosses at Sligo is about three miles long. Yeats describes this Rosses in his essay "Drumcliffe and Rosses" in *The Celtic Twilight* (reprinted in *Mythologies*), "a little sea-dividing, sandy plain, covered with short grass, like a green table-cloth, and lying in the foam midway between round cairn-headed Knocknarea [q.v.] and Ben Bulben [q.v.]." Yeats also said in his *Fairy and Folk Tales of the Irish Peasantry* (reprinted in Allt and Alspach, 797), "Rosses is a very noted fairy locality. There is here a little point of rocks where, if anyone falls asleep, there is danger of their waking silly, the fairies having carried off their souls." Both of Yeats's maternal families, Pollexfens and Middletons, had summer places at The Rosses, and the young Yeats spent much time there. See "The Stolen Child," "At Algeciras—A Meditation upon Death," and "Alternative Song for the Severed Head in *The King of the Great Clock Tower*.

Roxborough. The name of the ancestral estate of the Persses of Galway, the family into which Lady Gregory [q.v.] was born. One of her ancestors, Dudley Persse, acquired extensive land around Kiltartan [q.v.], during the time of Charles II and James II. On the largest and richest of his properties, he built Roxborough House, which gave its name to the area. During the Irish Civil War, the house was burned down. See "In Memory of Major Robert Gregory."

Rury. Ancestor of Baile [q.v.], Buan's son. See "Baile and Aillinn."

S

Sack. In the British House of Lords, the lord chancellor traditionally sits on a wool-stuffed sack covered with red cloth cover. See "The Statesman's Holiday."

Sailing Seven, The. In Greek mythology, the seven daughters of Atlas and Pleione were transformed into stars, known as the Pleiades. The name is from the Greek word meaning to sail, and the bright stars of the Pleiades were widely used in navigation. However, Yeats may have had in mind simply the seven planets recognized by early astronomers: sun, moon, Mars, Mercury, Jupiter, Saturn, and Venus. In the first version of "A Cradle Song," published in *The Countess Kathleen* and *Various Legends and Lyrics* (reprinted in Allt and Alspach, 118), the line that reads "The Sailing Seven" read "The Old planets seven." See "A Cradle Song."

Saint Augustine. *See* **Augustine.**

St. Denis or **Ruth St. Denis** (1879–1968). American dancer, born Ruth Dennis. Associated with oriental dances, Miss St. Denis had a long association with modern dance as well. Her autobiography is called *An Unfinished Life,* published in 1939. Her luck, over all, was not poor. See "His Phoenix."

Salamis. An island southwest of Athens. Its ancient fame relates to its being the home of Ajax, according to Homer in whose *Iliad* Ajax figures. The island is also important as the site in 480 B.C. where one of the most decisive battles of the Persian Wars (500–449 B.C.) was fought. Xerxes, the Persian leader was defeated there by the Greek fleet under the command of Themistocles, marking the end of the East's domination of the West. But Yeats feels that it was the art of Greece that began the West's ascendancy. In his essay, "On the Boiler" (reprinted in *Explorations*), Yeats says, "Europe was not born when Greek galleys defeated the Persian hordes at Salamis; but when the Doric studios sent

165

out those broad-backed marble statues against the multiform, vague expressive Asiatic sea, they gave to the sexual instinct of Europe its goal, its fixed type." See "The Statues."

Sandymount. A near suburb of Dublin, running along a stretch of Dublin Bay. Sandymount was for many years an important area to the Yeats family. The poet's grandfather, the Reverend William Butler Yeats, retired there from his ministry in county Down. His wife, born Jane Corbet, was from there; and her brother, the poet's Uncle Robert Corbet, owned Sandymount Castle there. The castle was later lost in bankruptcy, but it had been a colorful place with extensive grounds. A notable feature of the castle was a great clock tower. Yeats's father spent much time there while he was an undergraduate in Trinity College; and when he married Susan Pollexfen of Sligo, he brought her there to a nearby rented house called "Georgeville." There, virtually in the shadow of the castle with its clock tower, late at night on June 13, 1865, William Butler Yeats was born. See "Are You Content?"

San Marco. The Convent Church, or Monastery, of San Marco, in Florence, Italy, was reconstructed in 1437 by Michelozzo [q.v.], commissioned by Cosimo [q.v.] de' Medici. The church was remodeled by other hands twice since that time, but the library, designed by Michelozzo in 1441, remains intact in the present structure and houses liturgical manuscripts and fourteenth-century miniatures. See "To a Wealthy Man Who Promised a Second Subscription to the Dublin Municipal Gallery if It Were Proved the People Wanted Pictures."

Sappho. Greek poetess of Lesbos who flourished ca. 600 B.C., and whom Plato called the tenth muse. Sappho ranks among the greatest of lyric poets, especially notable for the passion and simplicity of her love poems. Yeats, in his notes to *The Cat and the Moon and Certain Other Poems* (reprinted in Allt and Alspach, 829), wrote: "I do not think it too great a poetical license to describe Kusta [q.v.] as hesitating between the poems of Sappho and the Treatise of Parmenides [q.v.] as hiding places. Gibbons says the poems of Sappho were extant in the twelfth century, and it does not seem impossible that a great philosophical work of which we possess only fragments, may have found its way into an Arab library of the eighth century." See "The Gift of Harun al-Rashid."

Sato, Junzo. Of whom Yeats wrote in a letter to Edmund Dulac on March 22, 1920 (in Wade):

> A rather wonderful thing happened the day before yesterday. A very distinguished looking Japanese came to see us. He had read my poetry when in Japan and had now just heard me lecture. He had something in his hand wrapped up in embroidered silk. He said it was a present for me. He untied the silk cord that bound it and brought out a sword which had been for 500 years in his family. It had been made 550 years ago and he showed me the maker's name upon the hilt. I was greatly embarrassed at the thought of such a gift and went to fetch George, thinking that we might find some way of refusing it. When she came I said "But surely this ought always to remain in your family?" He answered "My family have many swords." But later he brought back my embarrassment by speaking of having given me "his sword." I had to accept it but I have written him a letter saying that I "put him under vow" to write and tell me when his first child is born—he is not yet married—that I may leave the sword back to his family in my will.

The sword was in Yeats's tower, with which he associates it in the poem "Symbols," where he does not use Sato's name. The name of the maker on the hilt of the sword was Montashigi, possibly an ancestor of Sato. The sword was later returned to Sato's son, in accordance with Yeats's will, but while he owned it, as he says in a letter to Olivia Shakespeare dated October 2, 1927 (in Wade). "I make my Japanese sword and its silk covering my symbol of life." Yeats dedicated his play *Resurrection* (1931) to Junzo Sato. See "My Table," which is poem III of "Meditations in Time of Civil War"; and "A Dialogue of Self and Soul."

Saturn and **Saturnian.** The Roman god of the harvest, identified with the Greek god Cronus. In legend, Saturn was the ruler of the world in its Golden Age of peace and plenty, accounting for the adjective Saturnian, meaning peaceful. Eventually, Saturn was castrated and dethroned by his own son, Jupiter [q.v.]. In astronomy, Saturn is the second largest planet, only Jupiter being larger. Saturnine people, those said to be born under the planet Saturn, are said to be dull, gloomy, taciturn, probably because Saturn typified lead. See "Under Saturn"; "Conjunctions," which is poem X of "Supernatural Songs"; and "On a Picture of a Black Centaur by Edmund Dulac."

Scanavin. A well located near Collooney, very near to Sligo town. Actually called Tubberscanavin, the well of Scanavin, tubber being the Irish word for well. Scanavin, not otherwise identified, could be the name of someone who had lived near the well. See "The Man Who Dreamed of Faeryland."

Sceolan [skyo'len]. One of the two great dogs of Finn [q.v.] and his followers. Sceolan and another whelp called Bran were born to Tuiren, a legendary woman, after a Sidhe [q.v.] had changed her into a hound. The two dogs were famous in the accounts of the Fianna. In early editions of his poem, Yeats spelled the name Sgeolan. See "The Wanderings of Oisin."

Seaghan [shon]. A not uncommon Irish name, but not elsewhere associated with a fool. See "The Shadowy Waters."

Semele. In mythology, a Greek maiden loved by Zeus, who appeared to her in the form of a man. When she continually besought him to appear in his divine form, Zeus finally did so; she was struck with terror and consumed in the blaze of his divine appearance. Zeus, however, rescued their child Dionysus [q.v.]. See "Colonus' Praise."

Sennachie [shan'e he; sometimes shan'e key]. An Irish word, also spelled Shanachie, meaning an ancient storyteller, historian, or learned man. See "The Wanderings of Oisin."

Seven Hazel Trees. Sacred trees beside the well of rivers in Irish legend. In notes to the 1895 edition of his *Poems,* reprinted in Allt and Alspach, 796), Yeats wrote: "There once was a well overshadowed by seven sacred hazel trees, in the midst of Ireland. A certain lady plucked their fruit, and seven rivers arose out of the well and swept her away. In my poems this well is the source of all the waters of the world, which are therefore sevenfold." See "The Wanderings of Oisin."

Seven Lights. The constellation Ursa Major, or the Great Bear, and also called variously the Plough, the Big Dipper, the Wagon, and Charlie's Wain. This constellation, with its seven bright stars, is one of the chief constellations of the Northern Hemisphere. Yeats, in his notes to *The Wind Among the Reeds* (reprinted in Allt and Alspach, 812), wrote that he imagined the rose growing on the Tree of Life, and

I have made the Seven Lights, the Constellation of the Bear, lament for the theft of the Rose, and I have made the Dragon, the constellation Draco, the guardian of the Rose, because these constellations move about the pole of the heavens, the ancient Tree of Life in many countries, and are often associated with the Tree of Life in mythology. It is this Tree of Life that I have put into the "Song of Mongan" [this poem was later retitled "He Thinks of His Past Greatness When a Part of the Constellations of Heaven"] under its common Irish form of a hazel tree; and, because it had sometimes the stars for fruit, I have hung upon it "the Crooked Plough" and the "Pilot" star, as Gaelic-speaking Irishmen sometimes call the Bear and the North Star. I have made it an axle-tree in "Aedh Hears the Cry of the Sedge," for this was another ancient way of representing it.

This poem was later retitled "He Hears the Cry of the Sedge.

Seven Woods. The seven wooded areas of Coole Park, the estate of Lady Gregory in county Galway. The separate names of the seven woods (entries for each of them may be consulted) were Inch Wood, Kyle-Dortha, Kyle-na-no, Pairc-na-Carraig, Pairc-na-Lee, Pairc-na-Tarav, and Shan-Walla. See "In the Seven Woods."

Shade. Yeats's shade is Charles Stewart Parnell [q.v.], whose burial place is in Glasnevin Cemetery in Dublin and whose statue stands in O'Connel Street, Dublin. The man of Parnell's "own passionate serving kind" is Hugh Lane [q.v.] whose efforts to give Dublin a great art collection resulted in an attack on his character not unlike that which destroyed Parnell. See "To A Shade."

Shadowy Horses. The Shadowy Horses and the Horses of Disaster are the same. In a note to his book of poems *The Wind Among the Reeds* (reprinted in Allt and Alspach, 808), Yeats wrote:

November, the old beginning of winter, or of the victory of the Formor, or powers of death, and dismay, and cold, and darkness, is associated by the Irish people with the horse-shaped Pucas, who are now mischievous spirits, but were once Formorian divinities. I think that they may have some connection with the horses of Mannannan, who reigned over the country of the dead, there the Formorian Tethra reigned also;

and the horses of Mannannan, though they could cross the land as easily as the sea, are constantly associated with the waves. . . . I follow much Irish and other mythology, and magical tradition, in associating the North with night and sleep, and the East, the place of sunrise, with hope, and the South, the place of the sun when at its height, with passion and desire, and the West, the place of sunset, with fading and dreaming things.

See "He Bids His Beloved Be at Peace."

Shan-Walla [shan'wol'a]. One of the seven woods at Coole, Lady Gregory's estate in county Galway. Shan-walla is probably from the Irish sean-bhaile, meaning old townland; but it could also be from sean-bhalla, meaning old wall. See "I Walked Among the Seven Woods of Coole," the dedicatory poem to *The Shadowy Waters*.

Shawe-Taylor, John. Nephew of Lady Gregory and first cousin of Hugh Lane [q.v.]. It was Shawe-Taylor who audaciously brought together the conference that led to the peaceful settlement of the Land Question quarrel between landlords and tenants. Yeats devoted an essay to him in *The Cutting of An Agate* (reprinted in *Essays and Introductions*), noting that Shawe-Taylor was an unusually handsome man and a courageous one, the only passenger who dared leap from ship to tender in a great storm: "I do not think I have known another man whose motives were so entirely pure, so entirely unmixed with any personal calculation, whether of ambition, of prudence or of vanity. He caught up into his imagination the public gain as other men their private gain." Lady Gregory, writing of her two nephews (for which see her *Journals*), when Shawe-Taylor and Hugh Lane were both dead at an early age, and having dedicated her play *The Image* to their memory, said, "And so we must say 'God love you' to the Image Makers, for we do not live by the shining of those scattered fragments of their dreams." The ancestral home of the Shawe-Taylors was Castle Taylor, about fifteen miles from Galway town. John Shawe-Taylor's mother was Elizabeth Persse, Lady Gregory's sister. See "Coole Park, 1929."

Sheba. Queen of the wealthy Sba region of South Arabia. The visit of the Arabian queen to Solomon [q.v.] is recounted in 1 Kings, 10:1–13. According to the biblical account, they lavished great wealth and admiration upon each other. In other versions of the story, Sheba becomes

Solomon's wife. For Yeats, the royal pair symbolize Yeats himself and
his wife. Her ability in automatic writing, which she revealed on their
honeymoon, a form of a gift of tongues, utterly bewitched him and led
ultimately to his writing of *A Vision*. See "Solomon to Sheba," "On
Woman," and "Solomon and the Witch."

Shelley, Percy Bysshe (1792–1822). The English poet who was an early
and important influence on Yeats. In his *Autobiography*, Yeats, recalling
his early years, says, "I had begun to write poetry in imitation of Shelley
and of Edmund Spenser." He also says that Shelley's *Prometheus Unbound* was his sacred book. Later, in his poem "Blood and the Moon,"
Yeats has the line "And Shelley had his towers, thought's crowned
powers he called them once." The reference is to Shelley's *Prometheus
Unbound*, act 4, line 103. In *A Vision*, Yeats places Shelley in the same
phase of the moon as himself, Phase 17, along with Dante and Landor.
In this phase, Unity of Being is most possible. The mask of this phase,
Yeats writes there, may "represent intellectual or sexual passion; seem
some Ahasuerus or Athanase." Even earlier, in his *Autobiography*, he
had written of these two creations of Shelley, "In later years my mind
gave itself to the gregarious Shelley's dream of a young man, his hair
blanched with sorrow, studying philosophy in some lonely tower [Atha-
nase], or of his old man, master of all human knowledge, hidden from
human sight in some shell-strewn cavern on the Mediterranean shore
[Ahasuerus]." Yeats follows this with a long quotation about Ahasuerus
from Shelley's *Hellas*, the passage which Yeats says, "above all ran
perpetually in my ears." T. R. Henn, whose study of Yeats is called *The
Lonely Tower*, cites there the passage from Shelley's "Prince Athanase"
that seems to come nearest the mark:

> His soul had wedded Wisdom, and her dower
> Is love and justice, clothed in which he sate
> Apart from men, as in a lonely tower . . .

See "The Phases of the Moon" and "Blood and the Moon."

Sidhe [shee]. The name of the Irish fairy folk. In his notes to the
poem "The Hosting of the Sidhe," given in *Collected Poems*, Yeats
writes:

> The gods of ancient Ireland, the Tuatha de Danaan [*See* Da-
> naan], or, the Tribes of the goddess Dana, or the Sidhe, from

Aes Sidhe [es shee] or Sluagh [sloo] Sidhe, the people of the
Faery Hills, as these words are usually explained, still ride the
country as of old. Sidhe is also Gaelic for wind, and certainly
the Sidhe have much to do with the wind. They journey in
whirling wind, the winds that were called the dance of the
daughters of Herodias in the Middle Ages, Herodias doubtless
taking the place of some old goddess. When old country people see the leaves whirling on the road they bless themselves,
because they believe the Sidhe to be passing by.

Earlier, in his notes to *The Wind Among the Reeds* (reprinted in Allt
and Alspach, 800–801, and 806), Yeats also explained that the great of
old times, such as Caoilte [q.v.] and Niamh [q.v.], and the great Queen
Maeve [q.v.] whose cairn may still be seen on Knocknarea [q.v.] are
among the Tribes of Danu and are kings and queens among them. Irish
tales are filled with accounts of the ability of the Sidhe to change shapes.
See "The Hosting of the Sidhe" and "The Old Age of Queen Maeve."

Sidney. Sir Philip Sidney (1554–1586), soldier, statesman, and author.
Soldier, he was fatally wounded at the Battle of Zutphen; statesman, he
was a chief courtier to Elizabeth I and was frequently involved in diplo-
matic missions and in positions of government and was also the very
ideal of knighthood in his time; author, he wrote the *Arcadia, The
Defense of Poesie,* and the sonnet sequence *Astrophel and Stella,* which
assured wide acceptance of the sonnet form. Edmund Spenser [q.v.],
of whom Sidney was a friend and patron, wrote an elegy, called
"Astrophel," upon the death of Sidney, not to mention many references to Sidney's magnificence, scattered throughout Spenser's works.
Yeats, in his elegy to Lady Gregory's son, has Spenser's tributes to
Sidney in mind. See "In Memory of Major Robert Gregory."

Sinai, Mount. Associated with Moses and the receiving of the Ten Com-
mandments, it is located in the easternmost part of Egypt in the southern part of the Sinai Peninsula. See "The Phases of the Moon."

Sinbad the Sailor. Famous character in the *Arabian Nights,* where his
seven voyages are recounted. The incident of the Loadstone Mountain
[q.v.] occurs in the sixth voyage. Yeats sometimes identifies himself
with Sinbad, or at least he associates Sinbad with the shores near Sligo,
where he had spent so much of his boyhood. "I have walked on Sin-

bad's yellow shore and never shall another's hit my fancy," he wrote in his *Autobiography*. See "A Prayer on Going into My House."

Sistine or **Sistine Chapel.** The Sistine Chapel, or Pope's Chapel, in the Vatican in Rome, private chapel of the Roman Catholic pope. It was built in 1473 by Pope Sixtus IV. Among the great art treasures in the chapel are the famous frescoes painted by Michelangelo [q.v.] on the chapel's ceiling. The frescoes are titled "Creation," "Deluge," and "Last Judgment." In the "Creation," Michelangelo has depicted the muscular and heroic figure of Adam. Two statues by Michelangelo, "Morning" and "Night," are in the Medici Chapel, New Sacristy, in Florence. See "Michael Robartes and the Dancer" and "Under Ben Bulben."

Sleiveens [sliv eens]. In his notes to *Fairy and Folk Tales of the Irish Peasantry* (reprinted in Allt and Alspach, 797–98), Yeats wrote: "Sleiveen, not to be found in the dictionaries, is a comical Irish word (at least in Connaught) for a rogue. It probably came from sliabh [sleev], a mountain, meaning primarily a mountaineer, and in a second- ary sense, on the principal that mountaineers are worse than anybody else, a rogue. I am indebted to Mr. Douglas Hyde [q.v.] for these details, as for many others." Yeats, there, also defines shoneen as "a little gentry John [Sean], and is applied to upstarts and 'big' farmers, who ape the rank of gentlemen." See "The Ballad of Father O'Hart."

Sleuth Wood. A lovely, rising woodland on the south shore of Lough Gill, the lake that counts Innisfree [q.v.] among its many islands. Lo- cated but a few miles from Sligo, Sleuth Wood is near the town of Dromahair [q.v.]. The local people also refer to the area as Slish or Slesh Wood. See "The Stolen Child."

Slievenamon [sleev na mon]. A mountain in county Tipperary on which, according to legend, there was a famous palace of the fairy folk, particu- larly sacred to the women of the De Danaan [*see* Danaan]. Patrick W. Joyce, in his *Irish Names of Places,* says that here the women enchanted Finn [q.v.] and his followers, and the mountain took its name from these women. It is called in Irish, Sliabh-na-mban-fionn, which means the mountain of the fair-haired women. See "The Grey Rock."

Sligo. The name of the town and of the county in western Ireland in Connaught Province. The name was derived from the Irish word for sea shells, sligeach [sly'ga], which abound in the Sligo River that flows out to the sea. The history of Sligo, town and county, goes back beyond recorded history to the legends of ancient races and fairy folk that have come down in song and story. Yeats spent much of his boyhood in Sligo town and its county environs, for both of his parents had roots there. On his mother's side were the Pollexfen and Middleton relatives. Their business offices were on the quay side, from where they supervised their shipping and milling interests. On his father's side, there was Great Aunt Mickey Yeats, daughter of John Yeats, the poet's great-grandfather, the country scholar who was a clergyman at Drumcliff [q.v.]: "He that in Sligo at Drumcliff / Set up the old stone Cross." It is in the churchyard at Drumcliff, next to his great-grandfather's church, that the poet is now buried. It is accurate to say that almost all of the poet's references to Irish places can be located in Sligo or in county Galway, but it is Sligo with Ben Bulben, Knocknarea, Innisfree, Glen Car, Lissadell, Rosses, and Sleuth Wood, to mention but a few, that dominates Yeats's Irish imagery from the beginning of his career to the end. See "The Meditation of the Old Fisherman," "The Fiddler of Dooney," "Under Saturn," and "Are You Content?"

Smaragdine or the **Great Smaragdine Tablet.** Refers to the Tabula Smaragdine (1541) or the Emerald Tablet, a mystical work attributed to Hermes Trismegistus. In *The Literary Symbol*, W. Y. Tindall wrote:

> Hermes Trismegistus is the Egyptian god Thoth, somewhat Hellenized. Associated at first with the moon and the ibis, dog-headed Thoth became secretary to Osiris, in which capacity he invented speech and writing, not to mention the signs of the zodiac and alchemy. Since magic depends upon words, he became magus-in-chief and, under Greek auspices, the Logos or creator of things. This god of words and original secretary was destined to become the patron of Renaissance writers. Reappearing in the romantic period, but separated from the idea of nature it had affirmed, Hermetism once more gave men of letters method. Emerson, Baudelaire, Mallarmé, Yeats, and Joyce himself are among these denatured Hermetics . . . . Tabula Smaragdine (1541) or The Emerald Tablet, another work attributed to Hermes, expressed the essence of Hermetism with unforgettable neatness: "As above, so

below," a phrase that for many in later times became all that
need be known of Hermes and, indeed, all that was known.

In the same work, Tindall also called Yeats "the conspicuous Herme-
tist of our time." In a note to "The Trembling of the Veil" section of
his *Autobiography,* Yeats wrote about the "Hermetic Students," the
group founded by MacGregor [q.v.] Mathers and others to which for
a while Yeats belonged. See "Ribh Denounces Patrick," which is poem
II of "Supernatural Songs."

Solomon. The ancient Hebrew king (ca. 973–933 B.C.), especially noted
for his wisdom, for the loveliness of the Song of Solomon, for his large
harem, and for his association with the Queen of Sheba [q.v.]. Her
splendorous visit to Solomon is recorded in 1 Kings, 10:1–13. In other
versions of the story of Solomon and Sheba, their love endures and she
becomes his wife. Of this Yeats, in his *Autobiography,* wrote: "It seems
to me that true love is a discipline, and it needs so much wisdom that
the love of Solomon and Sheba must have lasted, for all the silence of
the Scriptures. Each divines the secret self of the other, and refusing to
believe in the mere daily self, creates a mirror where the lover or the
beloved sees an image to copy in daily life; for love also creates the
Mask."

For Yeats, Solomon and Sheba became symbols for himself and his
wife, being especially bewitched by her talent for automatic writing
that led to his writing of *A Vision.* See "Solomon to Sheba," "On
Woman," and "Solomon and the Witch."

Spartan. A reference to the Spartan boy mentioned in Plutarch's Life of
Lycurgus. The boy hid a fox beneath his tunic and steadfastly refused
to acknowledge its presence there even as the fox literally ate the boy's
heart out. See "The Curse of Cromwell."

Spenser, Edmund (ca. 1552–99). The English poet whom Yeats, in his
Autobiography, claimed as one of his earliest influences. In 1902, Yeats
wrote a lengthy introduction for *Poems of Spenser:* Selected and with an
Introduction by W. B. Yeats (T. C. and E. C. Jack, Edinburgh, n.d.)
and his essay on Spenser is reprinted in *Essays and Introductions.* Yeats,
in a letter to Lady Gregory, March 19 [1918], (in Wade), acknowledged that he modeled his elegy "In Memory of Major Robert Gregory" "on what Virgil wrote for some friend and on what Spenser wrote

of Sidney [q.v.]." The image out of Spenser that Yeats refers to in "The
Municipal Gallery Revisited" is to be found in Spenser's ode to the
Earl of Leicester, entitled "The Ruins of Time," which is dedicated to
the Countess of Pembroke, sister of Sir Philip Sidney. The pertinent
lines (216–17) from Spenser's ode are: "He now is gone, the whiles
the Foxe is crept / Into the hole, the which the Badger swept." See
"The Municipal Gallery Revisited."

Sphinx. The sphinx of Greek mythology was a winged lion with a woman's head who accosted anyone who came near her dwelling place at
Thebes, destroying anyone who could not answer her riddle, which no
one could until Oedipus answered it. The most famous sphinx, however, is the Great Sphinx of Gizeh in Egypt, carved of rock with paws
of masonry and bearing a man's head, "the lion body and the head of
a man" in Yeats's poem "The Second Coming," where the sphinx
symbolizes the post-Christian cycle of history, the symbol of the next
cycle—the "rough beast." In "The Double Vision of Michael Robartes," the sphinx symbolizes "all things known / In triumph of intellect," as Yeats explains in section XI of "The Completed Symbol," in
A Vision. See both "The Second Coming" and "The Double Vision of
Michael Robartes."

Spiritus Mundi. Literally, the spirit, or breath, of the world. Yeats himself
gives an explanation of Spiritus Mundi in a note to the 1921 edition of
Michael Robartes and the Dancer (reprinted in Allt and Alspach, 822),
where he writes that the images in dreams are never precisely the same
as those of personal concrete memory, and he adds, "Robartes traces
these substitute images to different sources. Those that come in sleep
are (1) from the state immediately preceding our birth; (2) from the
Spiritus Mundi—that is to say, from a general storehouse of images
which have ceased to be a property of any personality or spirit." In
earlier writings, as in his *Autobiography,* Yeats used *Anima Mundi,* soul
of the world, to mean the same as *Spiritus Mundi,* saying:

> Whence came that fine thought of music-making swords, that
> image of the garden, and many like images and thoughts? I
> had as yet no clear answer, but knew myself face to face with
> the *Anima Mundi* described by Platonic philosophers, and
> more especially in modern times by Henry More, which has

a memory independent of embodied individual memories, though they constantly enrich it with their images and their thoughts. (In a footnote to this passage, Yeats adds: "Constantly enrich" must not be taken to mean that you can, as some suggest, separate a soul from its memory like a cockle from its shell. 1926.)

See "The Second Coming."

Spring-Rice, Sir Cecil (1859–1918). British ambassador to the United States (1913–1918), at the time of the Roger Casement [q.v.] trial for treason. Yeats, having read *The Forged Casement Diaries* by Dr. William J. Maloney [q.v.], imputes to Spring-Rice an important connection with the campaign to discredit Casement by circulating certain obscene, personal diaries, supposedly in Casement's handwriting, among influential people who might otherwise have signed a petition for Casement's reprieve. As a result, no protest of Casement's sentence to be hanged was forthcoming. For a very long time the British government permitted no one to see the actual diaries; very few people even now have seen them. See "Roger Casement."

Stella. A reference to Esther Johnson (1681–1728), immortalized as the Stella of *Journal to Stella* by Jonathan Swift. Pupil and friend of Swift, Stella's exact relationship with the famous Dean of Saint Patrick's Cathedral, Dublin, remains somewhat of a mystery. Yeats uses the relationship as part of the plot of his play *The Words upon the Window Pane.* See "The Seven Sages."

Straits. The Straits of Gibraltar. Algeciras [q.v.], about six miles from Gibraltar, lies across the Straits from Morocco. Yeats visited Algeciras in the fall of 1927. See "At Algeciras—A Meditation upon Death."

Strafford, Thomas Wentworth, first earl of Strafford (1593–1641), created lord deputy of Ireland in 1632 and lord lieutenant in 1639. As Edmund Curtis points out in his *History of Ireland,* in Strafford "Ireland found one of its greatest viceroys." His policy was to increase the economic prosperity of the Irish and yet make them dependent upon the Crown. And Curtis continues: "In an account of his office to the King in 1636 he could rightfully boast that he had endowed the Church, wiped out the Irish debt, given the Crown a surplus of £50,000, and raised an army to keep peace between parties." Ultimately, his enemies both in Ireland and in the English Long Parliament, in 1640, ruined Strafford's work and schemes alike and "did much to bring the great viceroy to the scaffold in May 1641." A portrait of Strafford hangs in the National Gallery in Dublin. See "Demon and Beast."

Swift, Jonathan (1667–1745). Dublin-born clergyman, poet, and satirist, famous for his blistering attacks on controversial issues of the day and on stupidity and vice everywhere. Yeats himself, in the Introduction to his play *The Words upon the Window-Pane* (reprinted in *Explorations*), said, "Swift haunts me; he is always just around the next corner." Yeats was particularly fascinated with Swift's epitaph, which Swift wrote five and a half years before his death. Yeats's own epitaph, as given in "Under Ben Bulben," is in part an echo of it. Yeats spent a great deal of time composing translations of the Latin of Swift's epitaph. He included one version in the Introduction mentioned above, which is the version Yeats included in his *Collected Poems*, as "Swift's Epitaph," but two other versions are given in Lady Gregory's *Journals*. She says, in her entry for January 28, 1930, that Yeats had written the two renderings of Swift's epitaph on a half-sheet of paper. Swift's epitaph in Latin, which appears above his tomb in Saint Patrick's Cathedral, Dublin, where Swift was the Dean for many years, reads as follows:

> Hic depositum est corpus
> Jonathan Swift S. T. P.
> Hujus ecclesiae cathedralis Decani
> Ubi saeva indignatio
> Ulterius cor lacerare nequit
> Abi, viator,
> Et imitare, si poteris,
> Strenum pro virili liberatatis vindicem.

John Middleton Murray, in his *Jonathan Swift*, has translated the epitaph into English as follows:

> The body of Jonathan Swift, Doctor of Divinity, Dean of this Cathedra Church, is buried here, where fierce indignation can lacerate his heart no more. Go, traveller, and imitate if you can one who strove his utmost to champion liberty.

Maurice Johnson, in his "Swift and the Greatest Epitaph in History" (*PMLA,* 68 [September, 1953]: 820–21), calls the epitaph a conscious work of art and says:

> Saeva indignatio is reminiscent of the passage most often quoted to characterize Juvenal; Se natura negat, facit indignatio versum (If nature denies the power, indignation would give birth to verses), Satire 1.79. It is usually assumed that Swift had Juvenal in mind when he composed his epitaph . . . .
> [There are also echoes of the Old Testament (Nahum 1:6; Psalms 69:24; and Micah 7:9) where the wrathful anger of God at man's weakness is expressed.]

Johnson also points out that Swift is imitating the Roman custom of addressing passers-by because Roman tombs were along the highways near Rome. Yeats, buried in a roadside cemetery at Drumcliff [q.v.], may have had this in mind in the "Horseman, pass by!" of his own epitaph, although there are Irish legend, biblical reference, and occult elements involved as well. Another bond between Yeats and Swift is made evident in his "On the Boiler" (reprinted in *Explorations*), where Yeats proudly asserts that the Irish have as good blood as there is in Europe. He lists as the true Irish people Berkeley, Swift, Burke, Grattan, Parnell, Augusta Gregory, Synge, and Kevin O'Higgins. And he adds, "If the Catholic names are few history will soon fill the gap. My imagination goes back to those Catholic exiled gentlemen of whom Swift said that their bravery exceeded that of all nations." See "Blood and the Moon," "The Seven Sages," "Swift's Epitaph," and "Parnell's Funeral."

Synge or **John Synge.** John Millington Synge (1871–1909). Dublin-born Irish dramatist of Protestant parentage. Synge met Yeats in Paris, where Synge had come from wandering about Europe playing on his fiddle. Yeats, learning that Synge knew Irish from his study of it at Trinity College, Dublin, persuaded him to go to the Aran Islands, off the west coast of Ireland, to soak up peasant life and atmosphere. In his essay "J. M. Synge and the Ireland of His Time" (reprinted in *Essays and Introductions*), Yeats said that it was on the Irish islands where Synge "Found his genius and his peace. Here were men and women who under the weight of necessity lived, as the artist lives, in the pres-

ence of death and childhood, the great affection and the orgiastic moment when life outleaps its limits, and who, as it is always with those
who have refused or escaped the trivial and the temporary had dignity
and good manners where manners mattered."

In the last six years of his life, Synge created the plays for which he
is famous: *In the Shadow of the Glen, Riders to the Sea, The Well of the
Saints, The Tinker's Wedding, The Playboy of the Western World,* and the
unfinished *Deirdre of the Sorrows.* Synge also wrote poetry and his book
on the Aran Islands, and he was, with Yeats and Lady Gregory, a
director of the Irish National Theatre [*see* Abbey]. In 1907, when *The
Playboy of the Western World* was first presented, it caused riots that
lasted for a week, Yeats finally throwing open the doors of the Abbey
for a public discussion of he play, Yeats's father with him [*see* "Beautiful
Lofty Things"]. In his *Autobiography,* Yeats not only called John Synge
"the greatest dramatic genius of Ireland" but said, in response to criticism of Synge:

> When a country produces a man of genius he never is what
> it wants or believes it wants; he is always unlike its idea of
> itself . . . . Synge was the rushing up of the buried life, an
> explosion of all that had been denied or refused, a furious
> impartiality, an indifferent turbulent sorrow. His work, like
> that of Burns, was to say all the people did not want to have
> said. He was able to do this because Nature had made him
> incapable of a political idea.

In the extracts from his 1909 diary, published later as part of his
Autobiography under the title "The Death of Synge," Yeats reveals his
deep feeling for Synge, his anger and impatience with those who had
opposed Synge, and his admiration for Synge's courage in facing death.
The entry for March 24, 1909: "Synge is dead. In the early morning
he said to the nurse, 'It is no use fighting death any longer,' and he
turned over and died. I called at the hospital this afternoon and asked
the assistant matron if he knew he was dying. She answered, 'He may
have known it for weeks, but he would not have said so to anyone. He
would have no fuss. He was like that.' She added, with emotion in her
voice, 'We were devoted to him.' "

Later, the acting text of *Deirdre of the Sorrows* was assembled from

Synge's manuscripts by Yeats, Lady Gregory, and the actress Molly Allgood, beloved of Synge. But perhaps Yeats's greatest tribute to Synge is expressed in a speech he made while in Sweden to receive the Nobel Prize for literature in 1923 (reproduced in his *Autobiography*):

> When your King gave me medal and diploma, two forms should have stood, one at either side of me, an old woman sinking into the infirmity of age and a young man's ghost. I think when Lady Gregory's name and John Synge's name are spoken by future generations, my name, if remembered, will come up in the talk, and that if my name is spoken first, their names will come in their turn because of the years we worked together. I think that both had been well pleased to have stood beside me at the great reception at your Palace, for their work and mine has delighted in history and tradition.

In his poem "The Municipal Gallery Revisited," Yeats pays further tribute saying, "We three alone in modern times had brought / Everything down to that sole test again, / Dream of the noble and the beggar-man." The oil painting of Synge in the Municipal Gallery in Dublin is by the poet's father, J. B. Yeats. A chalk drawing of Synge by Robert Gregory is in the National Gallery of Ireland, Dublin. See "In Memory of Major Robert Gregory," "Coole Park, 1929," and "The Municipal Gallery Revisited."

T

Talma, François Joseph (1763–1826). French tragedian. Considered one of the greatest tragic actors of his time, Talma left the Comédie Française to found the Théâtre de la République at the time of the French Revolution. He was especially famous for his Shakespearean roles, particularly Othello, Lear, Macbeth, and Hamlet. In "On the Boiler," (reprinted in *Explorations*), Yeats wrote:

> We who are the opposites of our times should for the most part work at our art and for good manners' sake be silent. What matter if our art or science lack hearty acquiescence, seem narrow and traditional? Horne [Herbert P. Horne (1864–1916), architect, poet, and writer on art] built the smallest church in London, went to Italy and became the foremost authority upon Botticelli. Ricketts [Charles Ricketts (1866–1931), painter, sculptor, and stage designer] made pictures that suggest Delacroix [q.v.] by their colour and remind us by their theatrical composition that Talma once invoked the thunderbolt.

In "An Introduction for My Plays" (reprinted in *Essays and Introductions*), Yeats, referring to one of his most valued associates at the Abbey Theatre, Frank Fay, said: "He was openly, dogmatically of that school of Talma which permits an actor, as Gordon Craig [one of the most famous of all stage designers and an associate of Yeats] has said, to throw up an arm calling down the thunderbolts of heaven, instead of seeming to pick up pins from the floor. . . . Synge, Lady Gregory, and I were all instinctively of the school of Talma." See "A Nativity."

Tara. Chief fortress of the ancient Firbolg [q.v.], then of the Danaan [q.v.] folk, and finally the seat of the high kings of Ireland. Patrick Joyce, in his *Irish Names of Places,* explains that teamhair [ta' wer] is a simple word signifying an elevated spot commanding an extensive prospect. Its genitive form was teamhrach [ta' rah]. It is this form that gave its present name to Tara, located in county Meath, the Tara that was the great hill-fortress of legend, later to become the seat, and palace, of Irish kings. See "In Tara's Halls" and "The Two Kings."

Tent-Pole of Eden. A reference to the pole star, Polaris. See "Veronica's Napkin."

Teresa, Saint. Teresa Sanchez, Cepeda Davila y Ahumada (1515–82), founder of the Discalced Order of Carmelite Nuns of the Primitive Rule of Saint Joseph, at Avila in 1562; canonized in 1622. Fragrant odors and oil were said to distil from her tomb, and her flesh was found uncorrupted when her grave was reopened nine months after her death. Her body is still preserved incorrupt at Alba, according to *The Catholic Encyclopedia,* 1913. Saint Teresa, a mystic, is also the author of numerous works, including two mystical treatises, *The Way of Perfection* and *The Castle of the Soul.* See poem VIII of "Vacillations."

Thebiad. The name given to the upper part of the valley of the Nile. Saint Anthony [q.v.] introduced Christian monastic life into the Thebiad. See "Demon and Beast."

Thetis. A nereid or sea nymph desired by both Zeus and Poseidon but given in marriage to a mortal, Peleus [q.v.], because it had been prophesied that her son would be greater than the father. The wedding of Peleus and Thetis, subject of a famous painting by Nicolas Poussin that hangs in the National Gallery in Dublin, was celebrated by all the gods except Eris, goddess of strife and discord, the only divine not invited. Eris, however, came to the wedding and threw into the company's midst the golden apple of discord, designated to be given to the fairest among those present. It was immediately coveted by Aphrodite, Hera, and Athene. Final judgment was left to Paris, prince of Troy. He gave the apple to Aphrodite when she promised him the beautiful Helen. The dissension that followed the elopement of Helen and Paris led to the Trojan War. The child of Thetis and Peleus was Achilles [q.v.], and in the *Iliad* of Homer, Thetis appears on several occasions to comfort her son during the siege of Troy. See "News for the Delphic Oracle."

Thoor Ballylee. *See* **Ballylee.**

Three Rock. Three Rock Mountain, a 1,763-foot promontory south of Dublin. From the summit of Three Rock there are magnificent views of Dublin Bay, the Hill of Howth, and the inland ranges. See "The Peacock."

Timon. Greek misanthrope who lived about 450 B.C. Notorious for his hatred of mankind, Timon chose to live apart from all society. Aristophanes and Lucian have treated Timon in their works, but the most famous treatment is Shakespeare's *Timon of Athens.* See "An Acre of Grass."

Timor. Better known as Tamerlane (ca. 1336–1405), the great Mogul conqueror. Also known as Timur and as Tamberlaine, he was ruthless and unmerciful in his conquest, plunging on zealously and dying even as he prepared to invade China. Christopher Marlowe's *Tamberlaine the Great* is no doubt the most famous treatment of the figure in literature. Yeats places Timor among those who laugh in the face of death. See "Her Courage," poem VI of "Upon a Dying Lady."

Tiraragh [tir a ra]. The name applied to a barony in Sligo. The area received its name from a son of Dathi [q.v.], a king of Ireland. As P. W. Joyce indicates in his *Irish Names of Places,* the son's name was Fiachra [fe'eire], and his land or district was known as Tir-Fhiachrach, and later simply as Tiraragh. See "The Ballad of Father O'Hart."

Tom. As Tom the Lunatic, the masculine counterpart of Crazy Jane [q.v.] John Unterecker in his *Readers' Guide,* says, "for like Crazy Jane, 'Tom the Lunatic,' though momentarily blinded by age, though momentarily accepting the imagery of death . . . , penetrates deceptive flesh to see beyond it in an imperishable reality."

Yeats's source for Tom may be in Paddy Flynn, the storyteller of Sligo whom the children pestered and of whom Yeats wrote in "A Teller of Tales," the first account in *The Celtic Twilight* (reprinted in *Mythologies*), "The first time I saw him he was cooking mushrooms for himself; the next time he was asleep under a hedge, smiling in his sleep."

The Tom of "Roger Casement" is, along with Dick, a substitution by Yeats for the name of the English poet Alfred Noyes, which had appeared in the first version of the poem because Yeats then believed that Noyes had some part in circulating the personal diaries of Roger Casement [q.v.], diaries Yeats believed to be forgeries. When Noyes, in a letter to the Irish newspaper where Yeats's poem was first published, explained his innocence of any attempt to frame Casement, Yeats considered it a noble letter and changed the line in his poem. There is no special significance to the Tom of "Colonel Martin." See "Tom the Lunatic," "Tom at Cruachan," "Old Tom Again," "Roger Casement," and "Colonel Martin."

Tone or Wolfe Tone. Theobald Wolfe Tone (1763–1798), famous Irish revolutionary who sought to unite Catholics and Protestants against English oppression. To this end, he founded the Society of United Irishmen. Expelled from Ireland, he worked for his cause in America and France. He led a number of unsuccessful expeditions to Ireland and on one such, in 1798, he was caught, tried, and sentenced to death. Tone, however, committed suicide before the sentence could be carried out. Both Maud Gonne and Yeats worked to raise the money for a memorial monument to Tone, Yeats actually becoming president of the Wolfe Tone Memorial Association in 1898. As we learn from Yeats's *Autobiography*, the plans were abandoned when it was impossible to bring Irish political factions together. (Today, there is a monument to Tone in Saint Stephen's Green, Dublin.) See "September 1913," "Sixteen Dead Men," and "Parnell's Funeral."

Treatise of Parmenides. The treatise of the fifth century B.C. philosopher, Parmenides [q.v.] was a poem entitled "Nature," dealing with his abstract, mystical doctrine about reality. See "The Gift of Harun al-Rashid."

Tristram. The hero of the famous medieval romance Tristram and Isolde, also called Tristan and Iseult. Tristram is sent to Ireland to bring Isolde to Cornwall for her marriage to his uncle Mark. Unknowingly, Tristram and Isolde swallow a love potion that makes it impossible for them to love anyone but each other. They go through many meetings and separations before dying of their love. In one such meeting, they are discovered asleep by Mark; but there is such an innocence about them (and in some accounts a sword between them) that Mark leaves them undisturbed in their sleep. In his essay "Poetry and Tradition" (reprinted in *Essays and Introductions*), Yeats writes, "it is only . . . before a love like that of Tristan and Iseult, before noble or enobled death, that the free mind permits itself aught but brief sorrow." See "Lullaby."

Troy. The ancient city located near the mouth of the Dardanelles in Asia Minor. Described by Homer in the *Iliad*, Troy was a great city, ruled over by Priam. When Paris, prince of Troy, brought Helen to Troy, the

Trojans elected to keep her and fight rather than return her to the Greeks. Thus began the Trojan War, which ended finally with the defeat of the Trojans and the sacking and burning of Troy, called Ilium in Latin. Hector, Priam's eldest son, was the chief defender of the topless towers of Troy, until his death at the hands of Achilles. See "The Rose of the World"; "No Second Troy"; "When Helen Lived"; Poem I of "Two Songs from a Play"; "His Memories," which is poem VI of "A Man Young and Old"; poem III of "Three Songs to the Same Tune"; "The Gyres"; and poem II of "Three Marching Songs."

Tully. *See* **Cicero.**

U

Uladh [ul' a]. The early name of Ulster Province, which embraces the north of Ireland. The Uladh cycle of mythological stories, also called the Ulster cycle, the Red Branch cycle, or the Cuchulain cycle, includes Cuchulain's life, the famous war between Queen Maeve of Connacht and Ulster, known as the Tain Bo Cuailgne or The Cattle Raid at Cooley; also the touching story of Deirdre, who fled from Ulster to Scotland with her lover Naoise and his brothers to escape the wrath of Conchubar, to whom she had been promised. See "Under the Moon" and "Baile and Aillinn."

Urbino. The Italian commune built on an isolated hill 1,480 feet above sea level. Urbino is east of Florence and southwest of Pesaro. Its center of interest is its great ducal palace, built in 1465–82 for Federigo da Montefeltro, father of Guidobaldo [q.v.]. Under their benevolent patronage, Urbino flourished as a center of art and literature. The ducal palace at Urbino is the setting of Castiglione's *Book of the Courtier,* a book Lady Gregory read to Yeats and one that had a lasting influence upon him. See "To a Wealthy Man Who Promised A Second Subscription to the Dublin Municipal Gallery if It Were Proved the People Wanted Pictures" and "The People."

Usna [oosh' na], from the Irish Uisneach. The three sons of Usna were Naoise [q.v.], Ardan, and Ainnle. Naoise was the lover of Deirdre [q.v.]. Helped by his two brothers, he carried Deirdre off to Alba (Scotland) to escape the wrath of Conchubar [q.v.], to whom Deirdre was promised before she fell in love with Naoise. Conchubar, with offers of forgiveness, tricked them into coming back; but the three children of Usna were taken and beheaded nearly as soon as they returned. Deirdre uttered a beautiful lament over the dead bodies and then killed herself. The story forms one of the famous episodes in the Red Branch [q.v.] saga. In Lady Gregory's account of the story in

Cuchulain of Muirthemne, the children of Usna are described as follows: "The colour of raven is on their hair, their skin is like the swan on the wave, their cheeks like the blood of the speckled red calf, and their swiftness and their leap are like the salmon of the stream and like the deer of the gray mountain; and the head and shoulders of Naoise are above all the other men of Ireland." Yeats was also familiar with the translation of Deirdre's lament made by Sir Samuel Ferguson, praising that translation in his notes to the 1895 edition of *Poems* (reprinted in Allt and Alspach, 799). See "The Rose of the World."

V

Valley of the Black Pig. *See* Black Pig.

Veronese or Paul Veronese. Paolo Veronese (1528–88), Italian painter of the Venetian School. Veronese is noted for the purity of color, fine differentiation of tone, and opulence of decor. *The Rape of Europa* is one of his most famous works, and is of course a theme—mortal woman visited upon by a god (see Yeats's "Leda and the Swan")—that fascinated Yeats. See "Michael Robartes and the Dancer."

Veronica, Saint. Legendary saint of the first century. According to the *Dictionary of Catholic Biography*, she was the woman who wiped the face of Christ when he fell on the way to Calvary, an image of His face becoming imprinted on the cloth. A veil, said to be this relic, has been venerated at Saint Peter's, Rome, since the eighth century; but no marks are now apparent. [There are differing opinions about its authenticity.] Actually, the name of the woman is not known; Veronica may have been developed from the words *vera icon* (true image), but even this is hypothesis. See "Veronica's Napkin."

Vijaya. A Hindu name meaning victory. See "Anashuya and Vijaya."

Von Hugel, Baron Friedrich (1852–1925). Noted theologian and teacher in the Roman Catholic faith. His father had been named a baron of the Holy Roman Empire and thus brought the title into the family. Von Hugel lived most of his life in England. His best known work is *The Mystic Element of Religion* (1908; new and rev. ed., 1923). A principal idea of von Hugel's, according to John Unterecker in his *Reader's Guide*, is that the artist's vision is essentially Christian. Vivienne Koch, in her *W. B. Yeats: The Tragic Phase*, writes:

> In von Hugel, Yeats found an eruditely argued thesis regarding the impact of mystical experience on spiritual life. Von Hugel, as early as 1908, was trying to revive Kierkegaard. Yeats also

found in von Hugel an attractively simple, if naive, scheme to account for the character of Western culture. But it was von Hugel's conclusion that proved most congenial to Yeats, for it squared with his own assessment. Von Hugel wrote that it was "only through self-renunciation and suffering that the soul can win its true self, its abiding joy in union with the source of life . . . and the choice between two things alone: the noble pangs of spiritual childbirth, of painful joyous expansion and growth; and the shameful ache of spiritual death, of dreary contraction and decay."

In *The Unicorn*, Virginia Moore finds the riddle of the lion and honeycomb in Judges 14:8–9. She finds in it the explanation of Yeats's departure from the otherwise congenial von Hugel, the antithetical from the primary. "No, he [Yeats] could not travel all the way with a Catholic theologian who did not believe in reincarnation or karma or gyres or phaseless sphere." See poem VIII of "Vacillations."

W

Wadding, Luke (1588–1657). A Franciscan priest who was born in Waterford, Ireland. He was president of the Irish College at Salamanca in 1617; and in 1618, he founded the College and Monastery of Saint Isadore at Rome for the reception of Irish students. He was so highly regarded in Ireland for his devotion to the Irish cause and his kindness to Irish exiles that a petition asking Pope Urban VIII to make him a cardinal of the church was drawn up by the Irish but was intercepted by Wadding before it reached Rome. Wadding's published works total some thirty-six volumes. He is buried at the college he founded in Rome. The painting of Luke Wadding by José Ribera (Lo Spagnoletto), which hangs in the National Gallery in Dublin, was well known to Yeats. See "Demon and Beast."

Wellesley, Dorothy. Dorothy Ashton, Lady Gerald Wellesley (1889–1956), the duchess of Wellington. Married to Lord Gerald Wellesley, later seventh duke of Wellington, Dorothy Wellesley became one of Yeats's dearest friends in the late years of his life. It was in the spring of 1935 that Yeats came upon the poem "Horses" and arranged shortly thereafter to meet the author of it, Dorothy Wellesley, who invited him to visit her at Penns in the Rocks, her country place in Sussex. Yeats made other visits there, and letters were exchanged regularly, many of them preserved in the volume *Letters on Poetry from W. B. Yeats to Dorothy Wellesley.* As he says in one of those letters, Yeats thought Penns in the Rocks "the perfect country house, lettered peace." He was also pleased to learn that Lady Gerald had purchased the ridge opposite her property in Sussex to prevent a bungalow development from going up there: "(For since the horizon's bought strange dogs are still)." And Lady Gerald was pleased that Yeats had included in his poem to her a reference to Brutus, her Great Dane:

Brutus himself had a great majesty, both of form and conduct, and Yeats had observed it. When he seemed too tired to reach a garden seat, the three of us would walk abreast, Yeats's hand and part of his great weight supported on my right shoulder, while my left hand and shoulder was supported by the great dog. . . . The seat reached, the end achieved, and the tremendous Dane would settle down and turn into a piece of black and white marble until, our conversation ended, he would help us back again to the house.

Lady Gerald occupied a villa in France near to that of Mr. and Mrs. Yeats, and she spent much time with the Yeatses during the poet's last days and was at his funeral. Again, in the letters she wrote: "Yeats murmuring poetry to the last gasp: so die, perhaps should die, the truly great." See "To Dorothy Wellesley."

Whig or **Whiggery.** Originally, a Whig was an adherent of Presbyterianism in Scotland, and then one opposed to Catholic succession to the English throne. Ultimately, the term applied to one of the two great parliamentary parties in England, the other being Tory. The term Conservative has replaced Tory, and Liberal has replaced Whig. Yeats seems to have coined Whiggery to denote liberal factions. See "The Seven Sages."

White-Horned Bull or **White Horn.** The great bull in the service of Ailell, the consort of Queen Maeve [q.v.]. In a contest between Ailell and Maeve to determine which of them had more possessions, Maeve was short by one bull that could match Ailell's great White Horn, named Finbanach [fin van' ah]. Learning that there was a great Brown Bull in Ulster, Maeve attempted to secure it by every means possible, even, finally, war. Cuchulain [q.v.] was the great Ulster hero opposing Maeve. The fight for the Brown Bull constitutes the central epic of the Ulster or Red Branch cycle of Irish mythology. See "The Old Age of Queen Maeve," and "Baile and Aillinn."

Wilson, Richard (1714–82). English landscape painter in the classic tradition of Claude [q.v.] Lorraine. It is Claude's tradition that Wilson carries on, just as it is Blake's tradition that Calvert carries on—the four juxtaposed by Yeats. See "Under Ben Bulben."

Windy Gap. The name often given to high and bleak passes between hills and given in Irish as Bearna-na-gaoithe [bar' ne na ge' he], the gap of the wind. A Windy Gap of special note in the ancient annals is the one located in the parish of Addergoole in county Mayo, not far from Sligo, but there are other Windy Gaps in other parts of Ireland as well. See "Running to Paradise."

Witch of Atlas. A naiad and central figure of the poem of that name by Shelley. What the witch "sees" is, as Helen Vendler has explained, "the Platonic forms of all things." Shelley's poem takes the witch "By Moeris and Mareotid lakes" [stanza 58) where "to her eyes / The naked beauty of the soul lay bare (67)." Yeats, as Jeffares points out in his *Commentary,* writes of the Witch of Atlas in *Essays and Introductions,* "When the witch has passed in her boat from the caverned river, that is doubtless her own destiny, she passes along the Nile 'by Moeris and lakes' and sees all human life shadowed upon its waters in shadows that 'never are erased but tremble ever' " (Shelley, 59). In Yeats's poem, the Witch of Atlas is also an aspect, Platonic and occult, in Yeats's life and philosophy, which along with other aspects reviews Yeats's life and philosophy—a summing up. See "Under Ben Bulben."

Wood-of-Wonders. Not identified but perhaps no more than an imaginative stroke of Yeats's to go with the well-known references in the poem. See "Under the Moon."

Y

Yeats, John. The Yeats of "Under Saturn" was John Yeats, the poet's great-grandfather, who was the rector at the church in Drumcliff in County Sligo. It is in that churchyard that the poet is now buried. See "Under Saturn."

Yeats, Michael. The poet's son, Michael Butler Yeats, born August 22, 1921. Michael, according to Yeats's horoscope for him, was Saturn conjunctive Jupiter. In a letter to Olivia Shakespeare dated August 25, 1934 (in Wade), Yeats wrote, "The Jupiter-Saturn civilization is born free among the most cultivated, out of tradition, out of rule." Yeats used this in his poem "Conjunctions." See "A Prayer for My Son."

Yeats, William Butler. The poet used only William Yeats in the inscription placed at his repaired tower, Thoor Ballylee; he uses his last name only as he contemplated his ultimate burial in Drumcliff churchyard, next to the church of which his great-grandfather John Yeats, the Yeats of "Under Saturn," was rector. In his *Autobiography,* Yeats quotes the lines "There one that ruffled in a manly pose / For all his timid heart," indicating that these lines, which are from his poem "Coole Park, 1929," describe himself. Yeats was proud of his family background, and its relation to and involvement with Ireland. In a footnote in his "Introductions to 'The Words Upon the Window-Pane'" (reprinted in *Explorations*), Yeats wrote defending the Irishness of the Protestant aristocracy, much inter-married with Gaelic Ireland after the Battle of the Boyne, 1690; and he says of his own Yeats ancestry: "The family of Yeats, never more than small gentry, arrived if I can trust the only man among us who may have seen the family tree before it was burnt by Canadian Indians, 'about the time of Henry VII.'" Henry VII reigned from 1485–1509. Yeats then says, "Ireland, divided in religion and politics, is as much one race as any modern country." See "To Be Carved on a Stone at Thoor Ballylee" and "Under Ben Bulben."

Genealogical Information
Books Consulted

Genealogical Information

The following data concerning Yeats's relatives are limited to the more significant members of his ancestry. Some of the information has been drawn from chapter 1 of Joseph Hone's biography, *W. B. Yeats*. Dates are given when available and pertinent.

Paternal Ancestors

Jervis Yeats. The poet's great-great-great-great-grandfather. The "Old Dublin Merchant"[1] was in the wholesale linen business in Dublin but probably went there from Yorkshire. As an Irish merchant, he was exempt from certain levies by the Irish parliament. He died in 1712.

Benjamin Yeats. Son of Jervis and the great-great-great-grandfather of the poet. He was a follower of Swift and Irish Protestant Nationalism; married in 1742.

Benjamin Yeats. Son of the previous Benjamin Yeats and the poet's great-great-grandfather. The second Benjamin Yeats lived in wealthy William Street, Dublin. He died ca. 1795; but in 1773 he had married Mary Butler, daughter of John Butler and great-granddaughter of Edmond Butler, who in 1796 had married Mary Voisin, a woman of French Huguenot stock. It is through the Butler family that Yeats's ancestry may possibly go back to the Butlers who were the earls of Ormonde, one of the most illustrious of Irish medieval families.

John Yeats (1774–1846). The poet's great-grandfather and the son of the second Benjamin Yeats and Mary Butler Yeats, the "Old country scholar"[2] and the rector of Drumcliff church.[3] He married a Jane Taylor and went to county Sligo to assume his living as the rector at

1. "Pardon, Old Fathers."
2. Ibid.
3. "Under Ben Bulben."

Drumcliff, thus establishing the roots of the Yeats family in Sligo. Their children were William Butler Yeats, the poet's grandfather; Thomas Yeats; Mary "Aunt Mickey" Yeats; and Matthew Yeats, who became a land agent and raised a large family.

William Butler Yeats (1806–62). The poet's grandfather, the "red-headed rector in county Down."[4] When this William Butler Yeats retired as rector in Tullyish, county Down, he went to live near his wife's paternal home at Sandymount, county Dublin. His wife was Jane Corbet, sister of Robert Corbet, the owner of Sandymount Castle with its great clock tower, and Patrick Corbet, a governor of Penang (the "Sandymount Corbets"[5]). Their parents were William Corbet (1759–1824), the poet's great-grandfather, and Grace Armstrong Corbet, whose father was a Captain Armstrong who died in 1797 and who was a nephew of Major-General John Armstrong (1674–1742), "an Armstrong what withstood / Beside the brackish waters of the Boyne."[6]

John Butler Yeats (1839–1922). Son of William Butler Yeats and Jane Corbet Yeats and the father of the poet. His wife, who died in 1900, was Susan Mary Pollexfen of Sligo. See "Beautiful Lofty Things."

Maternal Ancestors

Anthony Pollexfen. Great-grandfather of the poet. Hone says that he was a barrack-master of probable Cornish extraction, living in Devonshire, England, and married to an Irish woman named Mary Stephens, from county Wexford; he was probably the brother of the Reverend Charles Pollexfen. Anthony Pollexfen died in 1833.

William Pollexfen. The poet's grandfather. A seafaring man born in 1811 at Berwick, Devonshire, William Pollexfen, the "Old merchant skipper that leaped overboard / After a ragged hat in Biscay Bay,"[7] went to Sligo to offer his services to his cousin Mrs. William Middleton, after her husband died. He married her daughter, his cousin Elizabeth Middleton.

4. "Are You Content?"
5. Ibid.
6. "Pardon, Old Fathers."
7. Ibid.

Elizabeth Middleton Pollexfen. The poet's grandmother. She was a cousin of her husband, William Pollexfen, and was the daughter of William Middleton, a seafarer whom Yeats calls "The smuggler Middleton,"[8] and Elizabeth Pollexfen Middleton, daughter of the Reverend Charles Pollexfen of Jersey. Her brother, also a William Middleton, had numerous children, among them Lucy Middleton, who attended séances at George Pollexfen's, and Henry Middleton, who was but a few years older than the poet and an early playmate. Henry Middleton was the original of the hero of Yeats's novel *John Sherman*.

The children of William and Elizabeth Pollexfen:[9] Susan Pollexfen, the poet's mother; George Pollexfen, astrologer and mystic and Yeat's closest maternal relative; Alfred Pollexfen; John Pollexfen; Isabella; and Agnes Pollexfen. Another Pollexfen uncle, William Middleton Pollexfen, designed the Sligo quays and later died in a madhouse.

Yeats's Immediate Family

His brothers and sisters: Robert (1870–73); John "Jack" Butler (1871–1957), artist and illustrator; Susan Mary, called Lily (1866–1949) known for her embroidery designs; and Elizabeth Corbet, called Lolly (1868–1940), manager of the Cuala Press, first publishers of many of Yeats's writings.

Georgie Hyde-Lees Yeats (1891–1967). Wife of the poet, whom she married in 1917. Mrs. Yeats was always called George by the poet.[10]

Anne Butler Yeats. Daughter of the poet, born in 1919, is an artist living in Dublin. See especially the poem "A Prayer for My Daughter."

Michael Yeats. The poet's son, born in 1921. Michael Yeats took his degree in history at Trinity College, Dublin, and studied for the law at King's Inns, Dublin. Married to Grainne ni Eigeartaigh, they have four children.

8. "Are You Content?"
9. See "In Memory of Alfred Pollexfen."
10. See "To Be Carved on a Stone at Thoor Ballylee."

Books Consulted

Alden, John Eliot. *Bibliographica Hibernica*. Charlottesville: Bibliographical Society of the Univ. of Virginia, 1955.

Allt, Peter, and Russell K. Alspach, eds. *The Variorum Edition of the Poems of W. B. Yeats*. New York: Macmillan, 1957.

Annals of the Kingdom of Ireland, The. By the Four Masters. Translated and edited by John O'Donovan. 3 vols. Dublin: Hodges, Smith, 1856.

Arnold, Matthew. *On the Study of Celtic Literature and on Translating Homer*. New York: Macmillan, 1883.

Artom-Treves, Guiliana. *The Golden Ring*. London: Longmans, Green, 1956.

Beckson, Karl E. "The Rhymers' Club." (Ph.D. diss., Columbia Univ., 1959), abstract in *Dissertation Abstracts International* 20 (Sept. 1959): 1021–22.

Bjersby, Birgit M. H. J. *The Interpretation of the Cuchulain Legend in the Works of W. B. Yeats*. Upsala Irish Studies 1. Upsala: Lundequist, 1950.

Blake, William. *The Poems of William Blake*. Edited and with an introduction by William Butler Yeats. London: Lawrence and Bullen, 1893.

———. *The Works of William Blake: Poetic, Symbolic, and Critical*. 3 vols. Edited by William Butler Yeats and Edwin John Ellis. London: Bernard Quaritch, 1893.

Bridge, Ursula, ed. *W. B. Yeats and T. Sturge Moore*. New York: Oxford Univ. Press, 1953.

Bromage, Mary C. *De Valera and the March of a Nation*. London: Hutchinson, 1956.

Brooks, Cleaneth. *The Well Wrought Urn: Studies in the Structure of Poetry*. New York: Reynal and Hitchcock, 1974.

Brooks, Stopford A., and T. W. Rolleston, eds. *A Treasury of Irish Poetry*. New York: Macmillan, 1910.

Brown, Terence. *Ireland: A Social and Cultural History, 1922–1985*. London: Fontana, 1985.

Browning, Robert. *The Complete Poetical Works of Browning*. Boston: Houghton Mifflin, 1895.

Bryant, Sophie. *Celtic Ireland*. London: Kegan Paul, French, 1889.

Burton, Robert. *The Anatomy of Melancholy.* Edited by Floyd Dell and Paul Jordan-Smith. New York: Turod, 1941.

Cassell's Encyclopedia of Literature, 1953. 1:938–39.

Castiglione, Baldesar. *The Book of the Courtier.* Translated by Charles S. Singleton. Garden City, N.Y.: Doubleday, 1959.

Catholic Encyclopedia, The, 1913. 9:565.

Colum, Padraic. *A Boy in Erinn.* Illustrated by Jack B. Yeats. New York: Dutton, 1913.

———. *Ourselves Alone!* New York: Crown, 1959.

———. *Treasury of Irish Folklore, A.* New York: Crown, 1954.

Cooke, John, ed. *Wademan's Handbook of Irish Antiquities.* 3d ed. Dublin: Hodges, Figgis, 1903.

Coxhead, Elizabeth. *Lady Gregory: A Literary Portrait.* London: Macmillan, 1961.

Croker, Thomas Crofton. *Fairy Legends and Traditions of the South of Ireland.* 2d ed. 3 vols. London: John Murray, 1826–28.

Cross, Tom Peete. *Harper and Bard.* Chicago: Rockwell, 1931.

———, and Clark Harris Stover, eds. *Ancient Irish Tales.* New York: Holt, 1936.

Curtain, Jeremiah. *Hero-Tales of Ireland.* Boston: Little, Brown, 1890.

———. *Myths and Folk-Lore of Ireland.* Boston: Little, Brown, 1890.

Curtis, Edmund. *A History of Ireland.* London: Methuen, 1936.

Deane, Seamus. *Celtic Revivals: Essays in Modern Irish Literature, 1880–1980.* London: Faber, 1987.

Delaney, John J., and James Edward Tobin. *Dictionary of Catholic Biography.* Garden City, N.Y.: Doubleday, 1961.

Dinneen, Rev. Patrick S. *An Irish-English Dictionary.* Dublin: Irish Texts Society, 1927.

Documents Relative to the Sinn Fein Movement. Presented to Parliament by Command of His Majesty. London: His Majesty's Stationery Office, 1921.

Donoghue, Denis, and J. R. Mulryne, eds. *An Honoured Guest: New Essays on W. B. Yeats.* London: Edward Arnold, 1965.

Dowson, John. *A Classical Dictionary of Hindu Mythology and Religion, Geography, History, and Literature.* 8th ed. London: Routledge & Kegan Paul, 1953.

Dunn, Joseph. *The Ancient Irish Epic Tale "Tain Bo Culaigne."* London: David Nutt, 1914.

Egerer, Sister Mary Ann Monica, C. S. C. "The Rogueries of William Butler Yeats." Ph.D. diss., Radcliffe College, 1962.

Ellman, Richard. *Eminent Domain: Yeats Among Wilde, Joyce, Pound, Eliot and Auden.* New York: Oxford Univ. Press, 1967.

———. *The Identity of Yeats.* New York: Macmillan, 1954.

————. *Yeats, the Man and the Masks.* New York: Dutton, 1958.

Encyclopædia Britannica, 1960. 19:558.

Encyclopedia of Islam, The. 2:271–72.

Ferguson, Lady. *The Story of the Irish Before the Conquest.* 3d ed. Dublin: Sealy, Bryers & Walker, 1903.

Ferguson, Samuel. *Lays of the Western Gael.* London: Bell & Daldy, 1865.

————. *Poems.* London: George Bell & Sons, 1880.

————. *Poems of Sir Samuel Ferguson.* Dublin: Talbot, 1916.

Finneran, Richard; George Mills Harper; William M. Murphy, eds. *Letters to W. B. Yeats.* 2 vols. London: Macmillan; New York: Columbia Univ. Press, 1977.

Forster, E. M. *Alexandria: A History and a Guide.* Alexandria: Whitehead, Morris, 1922.

Frazer, Sir James George. *The New Golden Bough.* Abridged and edited by Theodor H. Gaster. New York: Criterion, 1959.

Fuller, Loïe. *Fifteen Years of a Dancer's Life.* Boston: Small, Maynard, 1913.

Gordon, D. J. *W. B. Yeats: Images of a Poet.* Manchester: Manchester Univ. Press, 1961.

Graves, Robert. *The Greek Myths.* 2 vols. Baltimore: Penguin, 1959.

Greene, David H., and Edward M. Stephens. *J. M. Synge.* New York: Macmillan, 1959.

Gregory, Lady. *A Book of Saints and Wonders.* Dundrum: Dun Emer, 1906.

————. *Coole.* Dublin: Cuala, 1931.

————. *Cuchulain of Muirthemne.* Preface by W. B. Yeats. London: John Murray, 1902.

————. *Gods and Fighting Men.* Preface by W. B. Yeats. London: John Murray, 1905.

————. *Hugh Lane's Life and Achievement.* London: John Murray, 1921.

————. *Lady Gregory's Journals.* Edited by Lennox Robinson. New York: Macmillan, 1947.

————. *Our Irish Theatre.* New York: Putnam's, 1913.

————. *The Kiltartan History Book.* Dublin: Maunsel, n. d.

————. *Poets and Dreamers.* Dublin: Hodges, Figgis, 1901.

————. *Visions and Beliefs in the West of Ireland.* 2 vols. New York: Putnam's, 1920.

Gullans, Charles B. *Times Literary Supplement,* Nov. 9, 1962, p. 864.

Gwynn, Stephen. *Henry Grattan and His Times.* Dublin: Browne & Nolan, 1939.

————, ed. *Scattering Branches: Tributes to the Memory of W. B. Yeats.* New York: Macmillan, 1940.

Hall, James, and Martin Steinmann, eds. *The Permanence of Yeats.* New York: Collier, 1961.

Hamilton, Edith. *Mythology.* New York: New American Library, 1953.

Handbook for Travellers in Ireland. 3d ed. London: John Murray, 1871.

Hardiman, James, ed. *Irish Minstrelsy.* 2 vols. London: Joseph Robins, 1831.

Hayward, Richard. *This Is Ireland.* London: Arthur Baker, 1955.

Heaney, Marie. *Over Nine Waves.* London: Faber, 1994.

Henn, T. R. *The Lonely Tower.* New York: Pellagrini & Cudahy, 1952.

Holt, Edgar. *Protest in Arms.* New York: Coward-McCann, 1961.

Hone, Joseph. *Thomas Davis.* London: Duckworth, 1934.

———. *W. B. Yeats.* New York: Macmillan, 1943.

———, ed. *J. B. Yeats—Letters to His Son W. B. Yeats and Others.* New York: Dutton, 1946.

———, and M. M. Rossi. *Bishop Berkeley.* introduction by W. B. Yeats. London: Faber, 1931.

Hull, Eleanor. *The Cuchulain Saga in Irish Literature.* London: David Nutt, 1898.

———. *A Text Book of Irish Literature.* 2 vols. London: M. H. Gill, 1906.

Hyde, Douglas. *Abráin atá leagtá ar an reactúire.* Dublin: M. H. Gill, 1902.

———. *A Literary History of Ireland.* London: T. Fisher Unwin, 1899.

———, ed. *Love Songs of Connacht.* 2 vols. London: T. Fisher Unwin, 1895.

Jeffares, A. Norman. *A New Commentary on the Poems of W. B. Yeats.* London: Macmillan, 1984.

———. *W. B. Yeats: Man and Poet.* New Haven: Yale Univ. Press, 1949.

———, and K. G. W. Cross, eds. *In Excited Reverie: A Centenary Tribute to William Butler Yeats, 1865–1939.* London: Macmillan, 1965.

John, Augustus. *Chiaroscuro.* London: J. Cape, 1952.

Johnson, Maurice. *Modern Language Notes* 64 (Apr. 1949): 273.

———. "Swift and the Greatest Epitaph in History." *PMLA* 68: (Sept. 1953): 820–21.

———. *Sin of Wit, The.* Syracuse: Syracuse Univ. Press, 1950.

Jonson, Ben. *Poems of Ben Johnson.* Edited by George Burke Johnston. Cambridge, Mass.: Harvard Univ. Press, 1955.

Joyce, Patrick W. *Irish Names of Places.* 7th ed. 3 vols. Dublin: Talbot, 1901.

———. *Old Celtic Romances.* London: Kegan Paul, 1879.

Kain, Richard. *Dublin.* Norman: Univ. of Oklahoma Press, 1962.

Keating, Geoffrey. *The History of Ireland from the Earliest Period to the English Invasion.* Translated and annotated by John O'Mahony. New York: P. M. Haverty, 1857.

Kelly, John, and Eric Domville, eds. *The Collected Letters of W. B. Yeats.* Vol. 1, 1865–95. Oxford: Clarendon, 1986.

———, and Ronald Schuchard, eds. *The Collected Letters of W. B. Yeats.* Vol 3, 1901–4. Oxford: Clarendon, 1994.

Kermode, Frank. *Romantic Image*. New York: Macmillan, 1957.

Kickham, Charles J. *Knocknagow or The Homes of Tipperary*. Dublin: James Duffy, n. d.

Kinahan, Frank. *Yeats, Folklore, and Occultism: Contents of the Early Work and Thought*. London: Unwin and Hyman, 1988.

Kinsella, Thomas. *Tain Bo Cualgne*. London: Oxford Univ. Press, 1970.

Kirby, Sheelah. *The Yeats Country*. Dublin: Dolmen, 1962.

Koch, Vivienne. *W. B. Yeats : The Tragic Phase*. London: Routledge & Kegan Paul, 1951.

Landreth, Helen. *The Pursuit of Robert Emmet*. New York: Whittlesey House, 1948.

Leslie, Shane. *Saint Patrick's Purgatory*. London: Burne, Oates & Washbourne, 1932.

Lewis, M. G. *The Life and Correspondence of M. G. Lewis*. London: Henry Colburn, 1839.

Lindsay, A. D., trans. *The Republic of Plato*. New York: Dutton, 1950.

Longley, Edna. *The Loving Stream: Literature and Revisionism in Ireland*. Newcastle: Broadaxe, 1994.

Loomis, Roger Sherman. *Arthurian Tradition and Chretien de Troyes*. New York: Columbia Univ. Press, 1949.

Lover, Samuel. *Legends and Stories of Ireland*. London: H. C. Bohn, 1860.

MacBride, Maud Gonne. *A Servant of the Queen*. Dublin: Golden Eagle, 1936.

MacDonagh, Thomas. *Literature in Ireland*. Dublin: Talbot, 1916.

Mackay, Albert G. *The Symbolism of Freemasonry*. New York: Clark and Maynard, 1869.

MacLeish, Archibald. "Public Speech and Private Speech in Poetry." *Yale Review* (Spring 1938): 545–46.

MacNeice, Louis. *The Poetry of W. B. Yeats*. London: Oxford Univ. Press, 1941.

Madge, Charles. *Times Literary Supplement*, July 20, 1962, p. 532.

Maloney, William J. *The Forged Casement Diaries*. Dublin: Talbot, 1936.

Malory, Sir Thomas. *The Works of Sir Thomas Malory*. Edited by Eugene Vinaver. 2 vols. Oxford: Clarendon, 1947.

Mathers, S. L. McGregor, trans. *Kabbala Denudata: The Kabbalah Unveiled*. London: Kegan Paul, 1887.

McCardle, Dorothy. *The Irish Republic*. Dublin: Irish, 1951.

McHugh, Roger, ed. *W. B. Yeats: Letters to Katherine Tynan*. New York: McMullen, 1953.

Michaud, J. F. *Biographie universelle, ancienne et moderne*. Nouvelle édition, 1870–73, 5:292.

Milton, John. *Paradise Regained, The Minor Poems and Samson Agonistes*. Edited by Merritt Y. Hughes. New York: Odyssey, 1937.

Moore, George. *Hail and Farewell.* 3 vols. London: Heinemann, 1911–14.

Moore, Thomas. *The Memoirs of Lord Edward Fitzgerald.* London: Downey, 1897.

Moore, Virginia. *The Unicorn.* New York: Macmillan, 1954.

Noyes, Alfred. *The Accusing Ghost or Justice for Casement.* London: Victor Gollancz, 1957.

———. *Two Worlds for Memory.* Philadelphia: Lippincott, 1953.

Nutt, Alfred. "Ossian and the Ossianic Literature." *Popular Studies in Mythology, Romance, and Folklore.* No. 3. London: David Nutt, 1899.

———. *Voyage of Bran.* London: David Nutt, 1897.

O'Connor, Frank. *The Backward Look.* London: Macmillan, 1967.

O'Connor, James. *History of Ireland, 1798–1924.* New York: George M. Moran, n. d.

O'Connor, Patrick, ed. *Illustrated Catalogue.* Dublin: Municipal Art Gallery, 1958.

O'Grady, Standish. *History of Ireland.* 2 vols. London: S. Low, 1878–80.

———. *Silva Gadelica.* London: Williams and Norgate, 1892.

O'Hart, John. *Irish Pedigrees: or The Origin and Stem of the Irish Nation.* 2 vols. New York: P. Murphy, 1915.

O'Rorke, T. *History, Antiquities, and Present State of the Parishes of Ballysadare and Kilvarnet in the County of Sligo.* Dublin: James Duffy, n.d.

———. *The History of Sligo: Town and County.* 2 vols. Dublin: James Duffy, 1890.

Oxford Companion to the Theatre, The. 2d ed. 1957.

Palmer, A. H. *The Life and Letters of Samuel Palmer.* London: Sealey, 1892.

Parish, Stephen Maxfield, and James Allan Painter. *A Concordance to the Poems of W. B. Yeats.* Ithaca: Cornell Univ. Press, 1963.

Pater, Walter. *Studies in the History of the Renaissance.* London: Macmillan, 1903.

Pearce, Donald R. ed. *The Senate Speeches of W. B. Yeats.* Bloomington: Indiana Univ. Press, 1960.

Pearse, Mary Brigid, ed. *The Home-Life of Padraic Pearse.* Dublin: Browne Nolan, 1934.

———. *The Irish Theatre.* London: Macmillan, 1939.

Ronsard, Pierre de. *Le Second livre des amours, première partie: Amours de Marie.* 2 vols. Paris: Gallimard, 1950.

Rossetti, D. G. *Poems and Translations.* London: J. M. Dent, 1941.

———. *Rossetti's Poems and Translations.* London: J. M. Dent, 1912.

Ryan, Desmond. *James Connolly.* Dublin: Talbot, 1924.

Saul, G. B. *Prolegomena to the Study of Yeats's Poems.* Philadelphia: Univ. of Pennsylvania Press, 1957.

Seymour, St. John D. *Irish Witchcraft and Demonology.* Baltimore: Norman, Remington, 1913.

Shakespeare, William. *King Lear.* Arden edition. With introduction and annotations by Kenneth Muir. Cambridge, Mass.: Harvard Univ. Press, 1959.

Shelley, Percy Bysshe. *The Poetical Works of Percy Bysshe Shelley.* Edited by Edward Dawson. London: Macmillan, 1907.

Spirit of the Nation or, Ballads and Songs. New edition. Dublin: James Duffy, 1901.

Stock, A. G. *W. B. Yeats: His Poetry and Thought.* Cambridge: Cambridge Univ. Press, 1961.

Stokes, Whitley, ed. *Cormac's Glossary.* Translated and annotated by John O'Donovan. Calcutta: Irish Archaeological and Celtic Society, 1868.

Sykes, Sir Percy, ed. *A History of Persia,* 1930. 1:434.

Symons, Arthur. *Poems by Arthur Symons.* New York: Dutton, 1927.

———. *The Symbolist Movement in Literature.* London: Heinemann, 1899.

Synge, John. *Poems and Translations.* Dublin: Maunsel, 1912.

Thurneysen, Rudolf. *Saren Aus Dem Alten Irland.* Berlin: Verlag Von Wiegandt & Orieben, 1901.

Tindall, William York. *Forces in Modern British Literature.* New York: Vintage, 1956.

———. *The Literary Symbol.* Bloomington: Indiana Univ. Press, 1959.

———. "The Symbolism of W. B. Yeats." *Accent V* (Summer 1945): 203–12.

Torchiana, Donald T. *Yeats and Georgian Ireland.* Oxford: Oxford Univ. Press, 1966.

———, and Glenn O'Malley. "Some New Letters from W. B. Yeats to Lady Gregory." *A Review of English Literature* 4 (July, 1963): 8–47.

Tynan, Katherine. *Ballads and Lyrics.* London: Kegan Paul, 1891.

———. *Irish Love-Songs.* London: T. F. Unwin, 1892.

———. *Shamrocks.* London: Kegan Paul, 1887.

Unterecker, John. *A Reader's Guide to William Butler Yeats.* New York: Noonday, 1959.

———, ed. *Yeats: A Collection of Critical Essays.* Englewood Cliffs, N. J.: Prentice-Hall, 1963.

Ure, Peter. *Towards a Mythology.* London: Hodder & Stoughton, 1946.

Vendler, Helen. *Yeats's Vision and the Later Plays.* Cambridge, Mass.: Harvard Univ. Press, 1963.

Waite, A. E. *The Real History of the Rosicrucians.* London: Geo. Redway, 1887.

Wellesley, Dorothy, ed. *Letters on Poetry from W. B. Yeats to Dorothy Wellesley.* London: Oxford Univ. Press, 1940.

Wents, W. Y. Evans. *The Fairy-Faith in Celtic Countries.* London: Oxford Univ. Press, 1911.

Wilde, Lady, ed. *Ancient Cures, Charms, and Usages of Ireland.* London: Ward & Downey, 1890.

Wilde, Sir William. *Irish Popular Superstitions*. Dublin: J. M. Glasben, 1852.

Wilkins, Ernest Hatch. *A History of Italian Literature*. Cambridge, Mass.: Harvard Univ. Press, 1954.

Wilson, F. A. C. *W. B. Yeats and Tradition*. New York: Macmillan, 1956.

———. *Yeats's Iconography*. New York: Macmillan, 1960.

Yeats, W. B. *Autobiographies*. London: Macmillan, 1955.

———. *Autobiography of William Butler Yeats, The*. New York: Macmillan, 1953.

———. *Cat and the Moon and Certain Poems, The*. Dublin: Cuala, 1924.

———. *Celtic Twilight, The*. Introduction by Walter Starkie. New York: New American Library, 1962.

———. *Collected Plays of W. B. Yeats*. New York: Macmillan, 1953.

———. *Collected Poems of W. B. Yeats*. New York: Macmillan, 1959.

———. *Collected Poems of W. B. Yeats*. Edited by Augustine Martin. London: Vintage, 1992.

———. *Collected Works in Verse and Prose of William Butler Yeats, The*. 8 vols. Stratford-on-Avon: Shakespeare Head, 1908.

———. *Countess Kathleen and Various Legends and Lyrics, The*. London: T. Fisher Unwin, 1892.

———. *Essays*. New York: Macmillan, 1924.

———. *Essays and Introductions*. London: Macmillan, 1961.

———. *Explorations*. London: Macmillan, 1962.

———, ed. *Fairy and Folk Tales of the Irish Peasantry*. London: Scott, 1888.

———. *Full Moon in March, A*. London: Macmillan, 1939.

———. *Hour Glass, The; Cathleen ni-Houlihan; The Pot of Broth*. Vol. 2 of *Plays for an Irish Theatre*. London: A. H. Bullen, 1904.

———. *Ideas of Good and Evil*. London: A. H. Bullen, 1903.

———. *In the Seven Woods*. New York: Macmillan, 1903.

———, ed. *Irish Fairy and Folk Tales*. New York: Modern Library, n. d.

———. pseud., Ganconagh. *John Sherman and Dhoya*. London: T. Fisher Unwin, 1891.

———. *King of the Great Clock Tower, Commentaries and Poems, The*. New York: Macmillan, 1934.

———. *Letters of W. B. Yeats, The*. Edited by Allan Wade. London: Rupert Hart Davis, 1914.

———. *Letters on Poetry from W. B. Yeats to Dorothy Wellesley*. New York: Oxford Univ. Press, 1964.

———. *Letters to the New Island*. Edited and with an introduction by Horace Reynolds. Cambridge, Mass.: Harvard Univ. Press, 1934.

———. *Memoirs*. Edited by Denis Donoghue. London: Macmillan, 1972.

———. *Michael Robartes and the Dancer*. Dundrum: Cuala, 1921.

————. *Mythologies.* London: Macmillan, 1959.

————. *On the Boiler.* Dublin: Cuala, 1939.

————, ed. *Oxford Book of Modern Verse, 1892–1935, The.* Oxford: Clarendon, 1936.

————. *Poems.* London: T. Fisher Unwin, 1895.

————. *Poems, The.* New edition. Edited by Richard Finneran. London: Macmillan, 1984.

————. *Poems, 1899–1905.* London: N.p., 1906.

————. *Responsibilities: Poems and a Play.* Dundrum: Cuala, 1914.

————. *Tribute to Thomas Davis.* Oxford: Blackwell, 1947.

————. *Vision, A.* New York: Macmillan, 1961.

————. *The Wanderings of Oisin and Other Poems.* London, 1889.